ELIE WIESEL

Elie Wiesel

Confronting the Silence

JOSEPH BERGER

Yale

UNIVERSITY

PRESS

New Haven and London

Yale University Press books may be purchased in quantity for educational, business, or promotional use. For information, please e-mail sales.press@yale.edu (U.S. office) or sales@yaleup.co.uk (U.K. office).

Set in Janson Oldstyle type by Integrated Publishing Solutions, Ltd.

Printed in the United States of America.

Library of Congress Control Number: 2022937489
ISBN 978-0-300-22898-4 (hardcover : alk. paper)
ISBN 978-0-300-28183-5 (paperback)
A catalogue record for this book is available from the British Library.

10 9 8 7 6 5 4 3 2 1

Frontispiece: Elie Wiesel with his mother and sister Tzipora, shortly before the German army occupied Hungary in March 1944 (Courtesy of Elisha Wiesel)

Amid all the pain and disappointment of Elie's remarkable life, how is it that the darkness did not envelop him or shield him from the sun?
—Samantha Power, U.S. ambassador to the United Nations, at Elie Wiesel's memorial service, December 1, 2016

CONTENTS

CONTENTS

ELIE WIESEL

Introduction

To HIS ADMIRERS, Elie Wiesel had the aura of a prophet. He spoke with eloquent simplicity about grand moral themes, balancing his paradoxical phrases so that listeners absorbed his message into their marrow. Whether explicitly or by suggestion, he summoned a personal history that had endured human malice in his flesh. As an orphaned survivor and witness to Auschwitz and Buchenwald, he spoke with unusual authority. At times, his strikingly chiseled face had a haunted cast that the French novelist François Mauriac described as "the look of Lazarus," the acolyte whom Jesus was said to have raised from the dead.

And yet those who knew him well remarked how deeply human and unaffected he was. He loved to sing, to join with friends in the Hasidic melodies he had grown up with in Sighet, Romania, where he was born, to join in whirling Hasidic wedding dances. He savored the quirks and flavors of Yiddish, his first language, and loved to laugh at a salty Yiddish joke. Though he walked with kings and queens at the climax of his career, he remained a man of modest tastes. He hated wearing tuxedos, took minimal interest in financial matters, and, as his son Elisha told me, he preferred instant coffee to the brewed variety because that was what he had been accustomed to in Europe. In old age, he told friends he wanted to be remembered not for his prestigious honors or as the author of a landmark book about the Holocaust or as a speaker on the world stage but simply as the teacher he had been for more than forty years.

Wiesel became a revered world figure somewhat late in life. In his early forties, he was a working journalist freelancing for French and Israeli newspapers, hungry for scoops and interviews with the powerful and famous, barely scratching out enough to pay the rent and sometimes relying on friends for a decent meal. Yes, he had already published *Night*, his harrowing account of Auschwitz and Buchenwald that would sell millions of copies worldwide by the time of his death, but in 1960 when it was first published in English it had found little more than a thousand readers. For years after its publication, his talks about the Holocaust drew just a few dozen listeners.

Wiesel was a complex figure. He had a sensitive ego that sometimes made it hard for him to work in groups like the council that built the United States Holocaust Museum in Washington, D.C. Although he inspired the creation of the museum, he could not manage or abide the competitive jousting in the council and ultimately resigned its chairmanship before construction had started. There might also have been more than a smidgen of calculation in some of his nobler actions and speeches that served him and his cause. As the novelist Thane Rosenbaum wrote after his death: "Soft spoken but with the instincts of a Broadway press agent, he knew how to leverage a story and deliver the perfect sound bite."

Yet Elie Wiesel became the torchbearer not just for the

survivors. He was the most admired ambassador of the Jewish faith in the world, as well as a voice of conscience in many of the places where human rights were trampled. He expanded his message to draw attention to other genocides and warn the world that the lessons of the Holocaust had not been learned, that ethnic hatred, persecution of vulnerable minorities, and mass violence persisted in sundering humanity.

"Turning point or watershed, that tremendous catastrophe which has traumatized history has forever changed man's perception of responsibility toward other human beings," he told a special session of the U.N. General Assembly in 2005 that commemorated the sixtieth anniversary of the liberation of the death camps. "Those who survived Auschwitz advocate hope, not despair; generosity, not rancor or bitterness; gratitude, not violence. We must be engaged, we must reject indifference as an option. Indifference always helps the aggressor, never his victims. And what is memory if not a noble and necessary response to and against indifference? But will the world ever learn?"[1]

In 1986, he was awarded the Nobel Prize for Peace for being "a messenger to mankind" conveying lessons of "peace, atonement and human dignity" and "a hard-won belief" that "the forces fighting evil in the world can be victorious." After his death on July 2, 2016, the Holocaust scholar Michael Berenbaum praised him as an "heir of Jeremiah with his message of rebuke but also of Isaiah with his words of consolation."[2]

"He was," as I said in the obituary I wrote for the *New York Times*, "defined not so much by the work he did as by the gaping void he filled. In the aftermath of the Germans' systematic massacre of the Jews of Europe, no voice had emerged to drive home the enormity of what had happened and how it had changed mankind's conception of itself and of God. But by the sheer force of his personality and his gift for the haunting phrase, Mr. Wiesel, who had been liberated from Buchenwald as a sixteen-year-old with the indelible tattoo A-7713 on his arm, gradually exhumed the Holocaust from the burial ground of the history books."[3]

So how did this frail, soft-spoken writer from a village in the Carpathian Mountains become such an influential presence on the world stage? This is the question at the core of this biography.

1

Sighet, My Sighet

JUST AS ONE cannot appreciate William Faulkner without absorbing something of Oxford, Mississippi, or John Updike without savoring his upbringing in Shillington, Pennsylvania, one cannot fully appreciate Eliezer Wiesel without stepping into his hometown, Sighet, where he was born on September 30, 1928.

"Why is it that my town still enchants me so?" he asks in his memoirs. "I left Sighet but it refuses to leave me."[1]

He sometimes talked about Sighet as a shtetl, a Jewish hamlet, tucked into the Carpathian Mountains in what is today northern Romania near the Hungarian and Ukrainian borders, but it was actually a fairly bustling and multifarious town of 25,000. According to the 1941 Hungarian census, 10,144 inhabitants—or forty percent of the population—were Jews. They worked as watchmakers, tailors, cabinetmakers, printers, weavers, lumberyard workers, and merchants. Many were Hasidim, followers of charismatic rebbes like Rabbi Joel Teitelbaum, the Satmar Rebbe, whose court was the not-too-distant Hungarian town of Satu-Mare (Satmar), and Rabbi Israel Hager, the Vizhnitzer Rebbe, whose original court was in Vizhnitz, now in Ukraine. Although Elie's father was not a Hasid, his mother and his maternal grandfather were, so Hasidic styles, flavors, and melodies, along with a philosophy that emphasized fervent, even ecstatic expression of the commandments, seeped into his soul.

Sighet was set among rolling hills and farmland close to the Tisa River and, as Wiesel wrote, "girt with the shimmering crests of soaring mountains."[2] Wiesel might have romanticized Sighet as a cozy, bucolic village, yet it was relatively cosmopolitan even in 1928. It boasted an elegant hotel, several villas, a well-manicured park, a culture hall, a Catholic basilica, a sixteenth-century Protestant church, eight synagogues, and thirteen smaller *shtiblach*, room-sized Jewish prayer houses. (Today, Sighet's only active synagogue is the Vizhnitz Kloyz Synagogue, a Moorish and Baroque prayer house from the late nineteenth century.) Nineteen newspapers and a number of literary reviews were circulated and there was also a Jewish publishing house. There were at least two Jewish bookstores run by rabbis where Elie would spend his meager allowance. (When he was deported to Auschwitz, he "had in my knapsack more books than food.")[3] Because it was in a patch of Transylvania that oscillated between Hungary and Romania, Eliezer grew up speaking and reading four languages, acquiring a linguistic ease that may help explain his later ability to write in French, English, Hebrew, and Yiddish.

"Back then, before the torment, it was a little Jewish city, a typical shtetl, rambunctious and vibrant with beauty and faith, with its yeshivas and its workshops, its madmen and its princes, its silent beggars and noisy big shots," he wrote in a piece for the travel section of the *New York Times* in 1984. "In the Jewish streets, the businessmen argued in the morning and made up by evening; in the *shtiblach*, the Hasidim said their prayers, studied Talmud, told those wonderful stories about their miracle-working rabbis. . . . The city rested on the Sabbath, blossomed on the Day of Atonement, danced on the eve of Simchat Torah."[4]

The Wiesels lived in a four-room cinder-block house on Serpent Street with a pitched, shingled roof and a fenced-in backyard. Across the street lived a judge who sat on the Jewish community's *beth din*—its religious court for resolving business and personal disputes. A few doors down was the home of his paternal grandmother, Nissel, the widow of the pious man for whom Elie was named and a tender woman who indulged her grandson's wishes. Other cousins lived across the Tisa in Solotvyno, then part of Czechoslovakia. The family was comfortable enough to support a gentile maid to help his mother with household chores and to vacation in a mountain village called Fantana. But like most other hardworking Jews in town, they knew they were always one setback away from ruin.

His father, Shlomo, owned a grocery, and Shlomo's wife and three of the children pitched in: Elie's older sisters Hilda and Beatrice (Batya) dealing with the customers, and his little sister, Tzipora, at the cash register. Elie seems to have escaped such duties because like so many of Sighet's Jewish boys, he was the focus of the family's ambition for a *talmid chochem*, a scholar of the sacred texts. When he was but three years old his father draped him in a *tallis* and packed him off to *cheder*, literally the one-room school where students learned the basics of Hebrew and began to read the Torah. Each day Elie headed out to *cheder* before dawn, returned home for breakfast, left again to learn secular subjects in the public elementary school, then returned to *cheder* after lunch.

Dark-eyed, thin, and suffering from migraines and phobias, Elie found his white-bearded *melamed*, or *cheder* teacher, frightening—the antithesis of his mother. Sarah Wiesel, born Sarah Feig, was a nurturing woman whose Hasidic roots were evident in the turban or *tichel* that covered her hair. She lulled him to sleep with Yiddish songs like *Oyfn Pripetshik* and *Rozhinkes mit Mandlen*. A lifetime later, he would put his infant son Elisha to sleep with his mother's lullabies.

But to picture Sarah as a typical *Yiddishe Momme*, loving but unwordly, would diminish her. For a Hasidic woman in a patriarchal culture, she had boundless ambitions for her children. She read magazines from the great cultural centers of Vienna and Paris and longed for her studious boy to acquire a cosmopolitan perspective, to know about movements like Zionism that were agitating the Jewish world at the time, and to imagine him performing feats like playing the violin in a symphony orchestra.[5]

In the memoir he wrote when he was sixty-six years old, Elie confessed that he was not quite as sickly a child as he made himself out to be. He just liked being home with his mother and felt "rejected" and "imperiled" when she was away, clinging to her skirts even when she went to the ritual bath. In *cheder*, when he read Torah stories, he would conjure his mother's face and imagine her as Eve in the Garden of Eden or Moses' sister Miriam.

"Smile all you want, Dr. Freud, but I was attached to my mother, maybe too attached," he wrote. "When she left me to help out at the store, I would tremble under my blanket."[6]

His father, by contrast, was a more remote figure. A burly man with a neatly trimmed goatee, Shlomo Wiesel was a leader of Sighet's Jewish community, sought out by many for his Solomonic judgment. Although observant in the traditional Orthodox mold, he was emancipated enough to encourage his son to study modern Hebrew so that he could read the works of contemporary authors.[7] Yet, Wiesel starts his memoirs with the words: "I never really knew my father. It hurts to admit that but it would hurt him even more if I [were to] delude myself. The truth is I knew little of the man whose merest glance could stir me. What was the secret of his inner life? What was he think-ing as he stared in silence at some far off, invisible point in space? Why did he conceal his cares and disappointments from me? Because I was too young, or because he thought me incapable (or worse) of comprehending them?"[8]

As important in molding the Elie Wiesel the world would come to know was his maternal grandfather, Reb Dovid Feig, an exuberant man with ruddy cheeks and a lush white beard who was an ardent disciple of the Vizhnitzer Hasidic rebbe. Dodye Feig, as he was affectionately called, lived in Bichkev, a farm-ing village near Sighet, and ran a small farm store. "He fed his cows, tilled his land, and climbed the trees to pick plums, ap-ples and apricots."[9] Elie visited him during vacations, reveling in his independence among the fruit trees and the wide river. On occasion Reb Dovid would show up at the Wiesels' home for the Sabbath, dressed in a silk caftan and round fur *shtreimel* atop his head and with a song cheerfully welcoming the angels who protect children, doing so in a resonant voice and "so much love and so much conviction that I would hear a rustling of wings above my head."[10]

"People also loved him for his kindness," Wiesel wrote in a portrait of his grandfather. "He gave freely of himself. No one ever left him empty-handed. If he was short of money, he would offer a cigarette or a pinch of snuff or at least a story, a good word."[11] It was an ethic Wiesel never forgot and tried to live up to as an adult.

Reb Dovid loved to sing the Hasidic melodies of the Vizh-nitz court as well as more secular songs of Romanian shepherds that were adapted by Hasidim for their liturgical music, and that love of singing was passed on to Elie. So were the stories Reb Dovid told about the great Hasidic masters like Rabbi Nach-man of Bratslav and the Rebbe of Kotzk, tales that were woven into books like *Souls on Fire* and *Four Hasidic Masters* that Wie-sel crafted between the writing of his many novels. "I owe him my love of tradition, my passion for the Jewish people and its unfortunate children," Wiesel wrote.[12]

As in the surrounding *shtetlech* and ghettoes, the week revolved around the Sabbath. "You went out into the street on Saturday and felt *Shabbat* in the air. Stores were closed, business centers at a standstill, municipal offices deserted. For the Jews as well as their Christian neighbors, it was a day of total rest. The old men gathered in synagogues and houses of study to listen to itinerant preachers, the young went strolling in the park, through the woods, along the riverbank. Your concerns, anxieties and troubles could wait: Shabbat was your refuge."[13]

After closing up their shops or finishing their work on Friday afternoons, Jewish men would bathe in the *mikveh* to ritually purify themselves for the Sabbath and attend evening prayers—in Elie's father's case, in the Great Synagogue, a grand two-story building with a frieze emblazoned with the Ten Commandments. Then they would head home for the week's one sumptuous meal. On a table covered with a white cloth and glowing with a freshly baked challah, the women dished out plates of gefilte fish, boiled chicken, and potato kugel. In every household, the same Sabbath songs could be heard and the same blessings over the wine and challah.

The next morning was spent at prayer followed by a lunch of *cholent*—a stew cooked overnight on a steady flame so as not to violate the Sabbath injunction against lighting a fire. The meal was by custom followed by a nap. In his most devout days, Elie practiced silence on the Sabbath—*ta'anit dibbur*—so that not one profane word would violate the day's sanctity. This part of his youthful attraction to Judaism's mystical side endured in his lifelong passion for silence.[14]

When Elie was eight, the Vizhnitzer Rebbe, Israel Hager, visited Sighet, and Sarah brought Elie along when she went to seek the tzaddik's counsel. After a discussion of various family matters, he sat Elie on his lap and asked his mother for a few minutes alone with the boy. When the session was over, his mother emerged with tears in her eyes. Years later Wiesel found out from a cousin that the Rebbe had told her that her son "will become a *gadol b'Israel,* a great man in Israel, but neither you nor I will live to see the day."[15]

At the yeshiva, Elie, already growing the *payess*—sidecurls—typical of Hasidic Jewish boys, spent most of his day burrowing ever deeper into the Torah and its commentaries. As he got older, he took up the Talmud with deep earnestness—the Mishnah (the collection of oral laws offering detailed rabbinic instructions for carrying out the often generalized commandments of the Torah, compiled around 200 C.E.) and the Gemara (the extensive commentaries and debated explications of the Mishnah first published around 500 C.E.). At his bar mitzvah in October 1941, he, like other observant boys reaching that milestone, was called to the Torah to chant a blessing and asked to read the *haftorah*, a chapter from the Prophets. Afterward, there was a simple kiddush of sacramental wine and refreshments laid out for the worshipers. As their gift, his parents gave him a gold watch, one that would figure in a poignant incident a few years later. Of course, in preparation for the bar mitzvah, Elie was taught how to strap the two leather boxes of *tefillin*—phylacteries—onto his forehead and left biceps, an act aimed at directing the attention of the head and heart during prayer that he would continue to do daily, with few interruptions, for the rest of his life.

In this period, he became obsessed with conceptions of God. "I sought Him everywhere, the better to love Him, to enjoy His gifts, to share His suffering in our exile: in the chapels of tailors and shoemakers, in the great synagogue of the rich, and in the House of Study where the poor gathered."[16] As a grown man, Wiesel looked back with bemusement at his absorption in "not-of-this-world" Jewish texts, about matters like the duties of the High Priest in the Holy Temple, while the world of that time was full of concrete dangers. "There was no high priest, no Temple," he told Israel Shenker in an interview in 1979. "Jews were being killed outside the door and we studied Talmud."[17]

In his early childhood, he was a diffident boy, eager to win the affection of his classmates, sometimes bribing them with gifts from the lunch his mother would pack (usually buttered bread and a piece of fruit) and more than once, money taken from the till at his father's grocery. "I feared exclusion and isolation, but as much as I yearned to be part of the group, to be like the others and with the others, I always remained apart," he wrote.[18] Although he made friends as he approached his teenage years, that feeling of detachment persisted even after he became a world-famous champion of Holocaust survivors and human rights.

Among the Jews of Sighet—the children as well as the adults—there was always an undercurrent of fear in the air. Part of that feeling derived from a taboo against associating with anything Christian despite Christianity's ubiquitous iconography and institutions. Elie, like other Sighet boys, would cross to an opposite sidewalk rather than pass in front of a church. But mostly the fear was based on a realistic awareness of a deep, sometimes violent strain of anti-Semitism among the Hungarians, Romanians, and Ukrainians in the community. A letter from a Jewish National Fund official who visited the surrounding county in 1920 made clear that there had been a recent spate of pogroms and that Jews were suffering.[19] Wiesel remembered that hooligans went out to beat Jews twice a year—on Easter and Christmas. "There were the louts and cowards, steeped in some ancestral hereditary hatred, who would attack us and beat us; like Dracula, they apparently needed to draw some blood—Jewish blood—to feel proud of themselves," he recalled.[20]

Although the yeshiva day was long, there was time for play, for games. Elie spurned soccer and skiing and he never learned to swim, but he liked to play chess and cards. There were also public entertainments: a Yiddish theater troupe came to Sighet, as did an acrobat on stilts. An occasional movie with a shapely actress stirred Elie's adolescent imagination as did a judge's daughter whose silky blond hair he long remembered. He tried to squelch his lust with prayer and immersions in the *mikveh*.

"Despite (or because of) the prohibitions, there were times when my glance roamed where it shouldn't have, in the direction of a young female neighbor or a beautiful stranger passing through the neighborhood. This troubled me, and I punished myself. Satan was leading me astray, casting a spell over me. He wanted to make me his slave, his prey; he was trying to capture my soul and poison it."[21]

Around this time, his father bought him a second-hand violin and found a local police captain to instruct him. Many Jewish boys studied this instrument, but in Elie's case the aspiration was unconventional: to have him play regularly for a Hasidic rebbe after *shabbos* services were over. Wiesel recalled his lessons with a laugh: the police captain could squeeze enchanting folk melodies out of the violin, but he also appreciated the bottle of *tuika* that Elie's father had passed along, and drank the strong plum liquor while Elie played. "Had he been as good a teacher as he was a drinker I would perhaps be more than the amateur violinist I am today," Wiesel wrote in *One Generation After*, his volume of essays, tales, and dialogues.[22] He also recalled that when he arrived at Auschwitz and heard an orchestra playing, his father admonished him that had he not given up on the violin he could have secured the safety of a seat in the camp orchestra. Wiesel notes that, actually, none of the players of the Auschwitz orchestra survived the war.

Music nevertheless remained essential to him all his life. Young Elie joined the choir of Sighet's Great Synagogue, and the skills he learned helped him earn a bit of money as a choir leader in postwar France. Many years later, he would compose a cantata that was performed in Carnegie Hall.

As a teenager he was enthralled by the study of *kabbalah*, with a "master" he identified only as Kalman. He found the occult mesmerizing. He once buried coins in the ground and murmured incantations in the belief that the stash would grow, though when he checked back a few days later, the money was gone. Along with two friends, he concocted and tasted an occult elixir to hasten the coming of the Messiah in order to defeat Hitler. When the two boys fell ill, his father angrily ordered him to stop the nonsense and give up *kabbalah* for the practical knowledge of modern Hebrew. But mysticism never lost its allure for Elie.

2

Deportation

Remote as Sighet was from the heart of Europe, news fil-
tered in: The astonishing ascension of Hitler to the helm of
enlightened Germany. The Spanish Civil War. The Munich ap-
peasement that doomed Czechoslovakia. Kristallnacht. Disil-
lusioned refugees—soldiers and civilians—from Czechoslovakia
passed through town. Then, after Germany invaded Poland on
September 1, 1939, Polish refugees streamed in. They carried
tales of rabbis having their beards clipped off or being forced
to scrub sidewalks, of Jews conscripted as forced laborers, of
random killings and beatings. The men whispered about these
atrocities in synagogue as they prayed on Rosh Hashanah and
Yom Kippur, but the consensus was that, as in World War I, the
persecutions would only go so far. This was Germany, after all,
the world's most civilized nation, the land of Goethe and Heine,
of Bach and Beethoven. There was even a moment of optimism
in 1940 when the Germans and Soviets redrew the map of Po-

land, Hungary, and Romania, and Sighet became part of Hungary again just as it had been when Elie's mother was a child.

Then, in the summer of 1941, an order came down demanding the deportation of all Jews in Hungary who could not document their Hungarian citizenship. In *Night*, Wiesel describes how those so identified were crammed into cattle cars and shipped off, their destination undisclosed. One of the deportees was Moshe the Beadle—the synagogue's caretaker. It was he who had introduced Elie—at just thirteen years of age—to the *Zohar*, the principal book of *kabbalah*. Elie had been convinced that his studies with Moshe would draw him closer to a time when questions and answers would become one.

Months later, Elie was stunned to see Moshe sitting on a bench in Sighet. Miraculously, he was back, and Elie listened intently to his story. Moshe's train had crossed into Polish territory, and in eastern Galicia the Jews were transferred to trucks that took them to a clearing in a forest. They were forced to dig mass graves and then the Germans shot them with machine guns and rifles. Somehow Moshe survived by pretending to be one of the corpses and made his way back to Sighet.

"People not only refused to believe his tales, they refused to listen," Wiesel wrote in *Night*. "Some even insinuated that he only wanted their pity, that he was imagining things. Others flatly said that he had gone mad."[1]

The Moshe the Beadle episode in *Night* evokes the well-documented transport of the twenty thousand Jews who could not prove their Hungarian citizenship to the city of Kamenets-Podolsk in German-occupied western Ukraine. On two days in late August 1941, the vast majority of these deportees were shot by the mobile killing units known as *Einsatzgruppen*, the first large-scale massacres of the Final Solution. About two thousand people managed to escape the slaughter and, like Moshe, return to their towns.[2] Decades later, the literary critic Alfred Kazin accused Wiesel of embellishing his memoir *Night* for effect, citing in particular the Moshe the Beadle story. Indeed, it is hard to believe that Moshe, described as a man with an intellect sharp enough to penetrate the *Zohar*, would have his eyewitness account shrugged off by his fellow citizens in the town where he lived. Yet disbelief that a civilized people would commit such atrocities was common across Europe. Moreover, in the realm of memoir, many will argue that an author deserves artistic license to heighten an effect in the pursuit of evoking an essential truth. And in the case of *Night*, which has been translated into scores of languages, that larger truth is clearly portrayed.

The years 1942 and 1943 seemed to pass Hungary's Jews by. Sighet took hope from the promising news of the Soviet army's defeat of the Germans at Stalingrad, the first Allied bombardment of Germany, and the preparations for a second European front. In the face of relentless pressure from Hitler and his lieutenants, Hungary's prime minister, Miklós Kállay, wagering that the Allies would defeat the Germans, refused to deport the country's Jews, although he did agree to a number of anti-Semitic laws and the drafting of forced labor battalions. Elie Wiesel dreamed of escaping to Palestine with his family and conveyed this wish to his father, but Shlomo vacillated. Almost fifty, he felt he was too old to start a new life and preferred to think that the war would soon be over. As more and more Polish Jews who had found their way to Hungary showed up in town, more than a few found themselves at the Wiesels' door, where Elie's father arranged to get them false papers and some cash, and bribed the local police with a few bottles of palinka, a fruit brandy, to let them remain. His gift of foreign currency to one refugee led to Shlomo's arrest and transfer to Budapest for questioning, although after several weeks he was released.

"When he saw us waiting at the station, a sad, disenchanted smile I had never seen before flickered across his face," Wiesel wrote years later. "Had he been beaten? Tortured? What had they done to him to give his face that grayish color, those lines of exhaustion and resignation? I didn't dare ask, yet I yearned to know."[3]

On March 19, 1944, German forces occupied Hungary and a new prime minister, General Döme Sztójay, agreed to begin deportations. Reports reached Sighet of beatings, public humiliations, and the vandalizing of shops and synagogues in other Hungarian towns by collaborating fascists. Elie's family again mulled some options but seemed paralyzed, comforting themselves with the knowledge that previous bad omens had not turned out so badly and that ultimately God would provide. Within days German soldiers, in tanks, jeeps, and motorcycles, entered Sighet and billeted themselves in local homes, including a house across the street from the Wiesels. The German army officers brought the ladies of that neighboring house a box of chocolates.

During a Sabbath visit, Elie heard his father and grandfather lamenting the takeover of Budapest by the Hungarian fascists and the recent promulgation there of anti-Jewish laws similar to the Nuremberg Laws enacted by the Nazis in 1935, which forbade Jews from owning businesses, practicing law or teaching, and marrying non-Jews. His father wondered, "Will God simply stand by?" But his grandfather responded: "God is God, and His ways are sometimes incomprehensible—and so they must be. If you could always understand what He is doing, He would not be what He is, you would not be what you are."[4] That sense of an inscrutable, mysterious God would haunt Elie for the rest of his life as he grappled with the seeming absence of God as the six million were slaughtered. As Dodye Feig climbed into his horse-drawn cart to leave, he whispered some parting words to his grandson that would be seared into his psyche: "You are Jewish, your task is to remain Jewish. The rest is up to God."[5] It was the last time he saw his grandfather.

On the eve of Passover 1944, the Germans ordered Sighet's synagogues shuttered. With Moshe the Beadle at their table, the family conducted its last seder and recited the story of the exodus from Egypt "with bowed heads and heavy hearts," not daring to "ask ourselves if, once again, God would intervene to save us."[6] Moshe tried to warn the family about what was in store, but Elie's father told him that sadness was forbidden on Passover. When the door was opened for the Prophet Elijah, Moshe disappeared.[7]

Wiesel admits in a literary aside that he deployed Moshe as a character in many novels—as a madman or drunkard—to underscore this resistance; he considered him the first survivor, a messenger of the dead who "shouted his testimony from the rooftops and delivered it in silence, but either way no one would listen." Clearly, the grown Elie Wiesel identified strongly with Moshe as a messenger warning the world to remember the Holocaust and man's capacity to commit the unspeakable. Indeed, the Norwegian Nobel Committee chose its words carefully when it extolled him as a "messenger to mankind."

On the seventh day of Passover, the Germans arrested the leaders of Sighet's Jewish community and ordered Jews to turn over any gold, silver, or jewelry they possessed. Hungarian police invaded homes, rifling through drawers and closets. Three days later, every Jew had to wear a yellow star, though Elie said this decree bound him intimately to the Jews of the Middle Ages who wore the wheel-like rouelle in the ghettoes of Italy and in France. "I felt I was living—not learning but living—an incandescent chapter of history, one that later generations would study."[8]

Further decrees followed, banning Jews from railways, buses, parks, movie theaters, and restaurants and setting a 6 P.M. curfew. By mid-April, two ghettoes were demarcated within Sighet and Jews had to resettle there. Elie's home was already in the larger of the ghettoes so the family did not have to move, but they had to take in relatives forced out of their own homes. Living conditions were excruciatingly cramped. Nevertheless, the self-deception carried on, with Jews telling themselves that the ghettoes were the limit of what the Germans would do, that soon the Red Army, so close Sighet residents could hear the thunder of Soviet artillery, would take over and things would be better. Only a few tried to slip out of town, to nearby hiding places or to other countries.

The optimism of those who remained was shattered when a delegation headed by Adolf Eichmann visited Sighet to plan the next steps of the Final Solution. Elie's father was summoned to an urgent meeting of the Jewish council that was theoretically running the ghetto. He came back pale and shaken.

"The news is terrible," he announced, his voice breaking. "Transports!"⁹

Jews in the ghetto were to start leaving street by street the following day—May 18—and make their way to the train station for shipment to a destination that remained secret. Rumor had it that they were headed for a group of brick factories in Hungary. No one except the council president knew for sure, and on pain of death he was not permitted to reveal the location.

Women boiled eggs and roasted meat so their families might have something to eat along the journey. Parents packed one bundle or suitcase for each family member—all they were permitted to carry with them. Families congregated on the streets until they joined the exodus. Along the way, Hungarian police struck stragglers with truncheons and rifle butts. Under a blazing sun Elie and his little sister Tzipora wove through the crowd quietly offering water to the thirsty. Elie noticed that even the rabbi, now shorn of his long beard, was bent over by a bundle of his possessions.

"They passed me by, one after the other, my teachers, my friends, the others, some of whom I had once feared, some of whom I had found ridiculous, all those lives I had shared for years," Wiesel recalled in *Night*. "There they went, defeated, their bundles, their lives in tow, having left behind their homes, their childhood. They passed me by, like beaten dogs, with never a glance in my direction. They must have envied me."[10]

Once the smaller ghetto was emptied, residents of the larger ghetto were ordered to move to the vacant homes there. "All Jews outside!" club-wielding Hungarian police shouted as they herded residents toward the smaller ghetto, screaming at them to hurry up and move. *All Rivers Run to the Sea*, the first volume of Wiesel's later memoirs, takes note of the callous impassiveness of his gentile neighbors as they peeked out from their windows.

"My father was crying. It was the first time I saw him cry. I had never thought it possible. As for my mother, she was walking, her face a mask, without a word, deep in thought. I looked at my little sister, Tzipora, her blond hair neatly combed, her red coat over her arm: a little girl of seven. On her back a bag too heavy for her. She was clenching her teeth; she already knew it was useless to complain."[11]

Although the deterioration and death of his father are at the center of *Night*, the sudden loss of his youngest sister seemed even more shattering, and his memories of her in her last days are harrowing to read. Wiesel even admits in his memoir that he has never spoken to his wife Marion or their son Elisha about her because "it mortifies me to talk of her in the past tense, for she is present."

"I see my little sister, I see her with her rucksack, so cumbersome, so heavy. I see her and an immense tenderness sweeps over me," he wrote in *All Rivers Run to the Sea*. "Never will her innocent smile fade from my soul. Never will her glance cease to sear me. I tried to help her, she protested. Never will the sound of her voice leave my heart. She was thirsty, my little sister was thirsty. Her lips were parched. Pearls of sweat formed on her clear forehead. I gave her a little water. 'I can wait,' she said, smiling. My little sister wanted to be brave. And I wanted to die in her place."[12]

In their rooms in the smaller ghetto, religious books were

scattered about and dinner plates were caked with uneaten food, evidence of a hurried departure by the previous inhabitants. But the Wiesels tried to keep up their spirits, deluding themselves that the smaller ghetto might be their final destination. Even if they were deported, they speculated blindly, they might escape the fighting between the advancing Allies and the Germans. Their old housekeeper, Maria, begged them to come to her hamlet in the mountains where there were no Germans and she could offer them refuge in a cabin that could comfortably accommodate the family and Grandma Nissel as well, but his father refused. He didn't yet know what was in store, so why consign his family to the misery of hiding. He also refused to abandon the community. Wiesel's memoir repeatedly emphasizes the naïveté and self-deception of his father and other Sighet Jews.

Around 2012, an unfinished and never published 150-page manuscript of *Night* was located among Wiesel's papers by Dr. Joel Rappel, then archivist of the Elie Wiesel Collection at Boston University, that was far more critical of the communal delusion.[13] That manuscript, written in Hebrew and bearing the title *And the World Was Silent*—the same as in the original Yiddish version of *Night*—was shelved without having been completed for unknown reasons.

"It would not be an exaggeration on my part if I were to say that they greatly helped the genocidal nation prepare the psychological background for the disaster," Wiesel said in the Hebrew manuscript, speaking of innocents like his relatives and some community leaders. "In fact the professional optimists meant to make the present easier, but in doing so they buried the future. It is almost certain that if we had only a little of the truth—dozens of Jews or more would have fled."[14]

Wiesel also blamed leaders of the Allies for concealing the horrors of the death camps, thereby fostering the willful blindness in places like Sighet. In one of the first interviews he gave as a promising young novelist and also in his memoirs, Wiesel condemned leaders like Roosevelt, Churchill, and Pope Pius XII, and even the Haganah, the Jewish paramilitary army in Mandatory Palestine, for knowing what fate awaited the Hungarian Jews and not warning them to flee. "Why was there no mention in the broadcasts we got from the BBC?" he asked Joseph Wershba in a 1961 profile in the *New York Post*. "The camps were not only an indictment of our present world. They remain an indictment of two-thousand years of Christian civilization."[15]

In the unpublished Hebrew manuscript the indictment is blunter, more impassioned. "The world was silent and the Jewish world was silent," he wrote. "Why did they not find it vital to inform us of what was going on in Germany? Why did they not warn us? Why?"[16]

With great tenderness, Wiesel remembered his family's final Friday night meal, a chance for them to gather one last time over challah and wine, before they were to leave the small ghetto. The next day Sighet's remaining Jews were crammed into the synagogue and forced to wait. Twenty-four hours passed, so almost everyone had to relieve themselves in the sanctuary's corners. In the morning, the Jews were marched to the station and, with Hungarian police pressing them, jammed into boxcars used to transport cattle, eighty people to a car, their sole source of sustenance a few loaves of bread and buckets of water. Finally, the last of the four convoys left the station. "A prolonged whistle pierced the air. Wheels began to grind. We were on our way."[17] It was May 21, 1944, and Sighet had been, to use the German term, cleansed of its Jews. "In the space of six weeks, a vibrant and creative community had been condemned first to solitude, then to misery, and at last to deportation and death," Wiesel wrote forty years later.[18]

The train rattled on for three days, with hunger and thirst setting in, and the heat and deepening stench making it difficult to breathe. Again, in *Night*, there is a heart-rending incident that evokes Wiesel's fascination with the prophetic potentialities of madness. In his boxcar, a Mrs. Schachter, whose husband and two of their three sons had been deported on an earlier train, kept crying out in extreme distress. "I see a fire! I see a fire! . . . Jews listen to me. I see a fire! I see flames, huge flames!" Her ten-year-old son tried to console her, but other passengers concluded "she is mad, poor woman," and eventually bound and gagged her.[19] As with the Moshe the Beadle story, this vignette of clairvoyance has such literary thrust that some critics concluded it had to be an exaggeration or embellishment. But as Ruth Franklin argued in an essay in the *New Republic* in 2006, such incidents "are not problems of fact" but "instances of artistic license." The memoirist, she wrote, "must have the liberty to shape his raw materials into a work of art."[20]

Wiesel, in both the French and English versions, actually withheld certain scenes that he had witnessed for fear of diluting the sympathy he wanted readers to feel for the victims. Several of those scenes were included in the unpublished Hebrew manuscript.

"Under the cover of night, there were some young boys and girls who had sexual intercourse," that manuscript says. "The tension of the final days sparked the desires that now sought release. And the heart also added its own touch, so that the sexual scenes did not provoke protest in the carriage. Eat, drink and be merry, for tomorrow we die."[21]

By the third day of travel, the train pulled to a stop and someone near a window read out the station name: Auschwitz.

3

Camps of Death

THE TRAIN and its human freight did not remain long at Auschwitz but rumbled on for another fifteen minutes to Birkenau, the affiliated camp where arrivals were separated between those destined for immediate death in its gas chambers and those sent to work as slave laborers. Now the passengers could actually see the flames that Mrs. Schachter had been shrieking about pouring out of a tall chimney into the black sky, and an "abominable" odor overwhelmed them. Men in striped pajamas, brandishing truncheons, boarded the cars and rushed the frightened Jews out. On the ground, SS men trained their tommy guns on the dismounting swarm.

"Men to the left. Women to the right," one of them shouted.

Elie glimpsed his mother and Tzipora, in her red coat, one hand joined to her mother's, move off to the right. His mother stroked his sister's blond hair before they vanished in the distance.

"I didn't know that this was the moment in time and the

place where I was leaving my mother and Tzipora forever," he wrote in *Night*.[1] He elaborated in an essay he wrote thirty-five years later: "I will see them that way, walking away, to the end of life."[2] Even in old age, he lamented that he had never said goodbye.

Mixed in among the men awaiting the selection were several seasoned inmates. One of them advised the newcomers to lie about their ages. Elie was told to say he was eighteen, not fifteen. His father should say he was forty, not fifty. Younger arrivals urged others to rise up and fight since they had nothing to lose. But older men talked them out of it, telling them that the sages taught that one should never lose faith. One SS officer, Wiesel learned, was the infamous Dr. Josef Mengele, who ordered him to state his age and occupation. Elie said he was an eighteen-year-old farmer and Mengele told him to go left, to a work detail. Had he been told to go right, it would have meant death.

Wiesel described a ditch from which enormous flames were rising, then seeing a truck pull up and disgorge a load of infants and small children who were hurled into the fire. Grown men watched in horror. Some wept. Many recited *Kaddish*. Although some critics questioned whether there ever was such a flaming ditch—mass murder at Auschwitz-Birkenau, they contended, was more efficient than that—Wiesel wrote in his memoirs that he had checked with others who arrived that same night and also consulted documents left by Sonderkommandos—Jews and other prisoners tasked with disposing of the dead—and that "yes, a thousand times yes," live Jewish children were thrown into a fiery pit. The Germans had not been able to funnel so many Hungarian Jews into the existing "showers" and crematoria so they rigged up special "furnaces" for small children. Testimonies from other survivors have supported Wiesel's account, and an exhibition on Auschwitz at the Museum of Jewish Heritage in Lower Manhattan in 2019 documented the existence of the fiery pits, corroborating him as well.

Witnessing such wanton cruelty, Elie felt the first stirrings of rebellion against a God who was a silent bystander.

"Never shall I forget that night, the first night in camp, that turned my life into one long night seven times sealed," he wrote in the book's most quoted passage, one that is etched into the wall of the U.S. Holocaust Memorial Museum. "Never shall I forget that smoke. Never shall I forget the small faces of the children whose bodies I saw transformed into smoke under a silent sky. Never shall I forget those flames that consumed my faith forever. Never shall I forget the nocturnal silence that deprived me for all eternity of the desire to live. Never shall I forget those moments that murdered my God and my soul and turned my dreams to ashes. Never shall I forget those things, even were I condemned to live as long as God Himself. Never."[3]

On the strength of this passage alone, *Night* becomes something singular, transcendent.

The procession of newcomers ended up in a barracks where club-wielding *kapos*—tough, often thuggish deportees who had been selected by the SS to supervise the functioning of fellow prisoners and enforce camp discipline, and rewarded with extra food or cigarettes—instructed Elie and his father to strip off their clothes and have their heads shaved. They were disinfected with a petroleum-based liquid, given quick, hot showers and told to pick out prison uniforms from piles of them set on tables. At dawn, an SS officer warned them: "Here you must work. If you don't you will go straight to the chimney, to the crematorium." In another barracks, his father asked a *kapo* if he could go to the toilet. The *kapo* struck him so hard he fell to the floor and had to crawl back to his spot. Elie looked on, paralyzed, wondering why he had not pounced on the man.

"The instincts of self-preservation, of self-defense, of pride had all deserted us," he wrote, depicting the depersonalization brought on by hunger, cold, and hammer-blows. "I too had become a different person. The student of Talmud, the child I was had been consumed by the flames. All that was left was a shape that resembled me."[4]

Elie's group was instructed to march, leaving Birkenau and trudging for a half hour until they saw the words "Arbeit Macht Frei" ("Work Sets You Free") atop the tall wrought iron gates of Auschwitz. Here, the barracks seemed more solid, cement and brick, rather than wood. As dusk fell on their first day, a Polish *kapo* addressed them and was almost humane in his concern that they not give into despair because "hell does not last forever."

They slept a long time and in the morning were given bowls of soup and submitted to the tattooing of numbers on their left arms. Elie was branded A-7713, an indelible identification seared into his skin that reminded him for the rest of his life of the dehumanization he had endured, of being turned from a vibrant human being with a name into a number.

Auschwitz, the largest of the German camps in the Polish city of Oświęcim (Auschwitz in German), is so notorious that it has become a synonym for the Holocaust itself. That is largely because an astonishing 1.1 million people were killed or died in the Auschwitz-Birkenau complex, one million of them Jews, mostly from inhaling Zyklon B in the four gas-chambers disguised as showers, or through typhus, starvation, medical experiments, or the exhaustion of forced labor. But Auschwitz was not exclusively an extermination camp like Treblinka, Belzec, and Sobibor. It was also a sorting center for work assignments at forty-five nearby satellite camps or at more distant camps. As a result, 200,000 of the prisoners who passed through the gates of Auschwitz actually survived.

Elie and his father's time in Auschwitz itself—not its satellite labor camps—lasted three weeks, during which they were never called to work. Instead, they idled the days away, in his case in Block 17, sleeping on bunk beds, subsisting on soup, black coffee, and stale crusts of bread. At night, he joined in the whispered singing of Hasidic melodies. He no longer prayed. "I concurred with Job! I was not denying His existence, but I doubted His absolute justice."[5]

At the end of those three weeks of idleness, their group was marched for four hours through the countryside, under the watch of ten SS men, to an industrial subcamp of Auschwitz called Buna. Ten thousand slave laborers, most of them Jewish, were confined there in 1944. Buna could be endured, he heard from other laborers, as long as one had the strength to work and could avoid the most grueling assignments.

Elie and his father were dispatched to what seemed to be an electrical products warehouse. They were assigned to count light bulbs, bolts, and other small parts and could do so while sitting on the ground, no small mercy given how weakened they were. Elie even joined in singing Zionist songs with two Czech brothers, Yossi and Tibi, whom he befriended. The vignette is one of many in *Night* that underscore the contrast between random cruelty and the mundane, commonplace diversions that marked the experience of many at Auschwitz.

One day, Elie was summoned to the hospital block. A dentist, a Jew, had been under orders to extract the gold crowns of all inmates for the enrichment of the Germans, and now it was Elie's turn. Elie twice persuaded him he was sick and managed to save the tooth. But he felt himself growing weaker, ravenous for an adequate meal, and spent his days obsessively thinking about the next ration of soup and stale bread.

The routines at Buna were often broken by sudden violence. One time, Idek, the *kapo* in charge of his unit, leaped onto him for no apparent reason and viciously beat him until he was covered with blood. A French girl, a Jew with false Aryan papers, who had been assigned to the warehouse, wiped the blood off his forehead, slipped him some bread, and urged him to wait to exact his revenge. Another time, he and his father were loading diesel engines onto trains under German supervision when Idek lashed out again, this time at his father, hitting him repeatedly with an iron bar until "he seemed to break in two like an old tree struck by lightning." Rather than reaching out to help, Elie found himself angry at his father for failing to avoid Idek's attack. "That was what life in a concentration camp had made of me," Wiesel wrote.[6]

Perhaps the most disturbing element of *Night* is the reversal of roles between father and son. At one point, the father was forced by a Polish foreman, Franek, to march in step like a soldier, which he had never been. When he blundered, Franek's blows rained down on him. Elie had to teach him to march—right, left, right, left—while other inmates shouted: "Look at the little officer teaching the old man to march!"

On a Sunday morning, a day the Buna inmates were spared from work, Elie glimpsed Idek copulating with a half-naked young Polish girl in a barracks whose inmates he had cleared out for that purpose. When Elie chuckled at what he was seeing, Idek whipped him twenty-one times in front of the other inmates.

On another barbarous day, Elie witnessed the hanging of three Jews at once, one of them a *pipel*—a *kapo*'s assistant—who refused to reveal how a cache of weapons ended up in his block. Wiesel described him as a child, "a sad-eyed angel." The inmates were ordered to march past the dangling bodies and Wiesel noticed that although the other two men were clearly dead, with their tongues hanging out, swollen and bluish, the youngest, who was actually a teenager, was still moving; he was too light to have his neck snapped by the hanging. He continued writhing for a half hour until he expired. *Night* powerfully evokes the conversation between Elie and other onlookers.

"For God's sake, where is God?" one inmate asked.

"And from within me, I heard a voice answer, 'Where He is? This is where—hanging here from this gallows.'"[7]

Some fellow Auschwitz survivors said there was no boy—all three were grown men. But this is a small point. There were other documented hangings, including one depicted in *Night* of a teenage boy accused of stealing, and it's entirely possible that Wiesel, writing ten to fifteen years after his ordeal, might have inadvertently conflated the hangings. Boy or man, Wiesel's grievance against God is scarcely diminished.

As summer wound down, Elie endured other tests of his faith. On Rosh Hashanah, ten thousand men gathered in a large open-air plaza to pray, Jewish *kapos* and block leaders among them. By this time Elie's cynicism was reaching a peak. "Why, but why would I bless Him?" he wrote. "Every fiber in me rebelled. Because He caused thousands of children to burn in His mass graves? Because He kept six crematoria working day and night, including Sabbath and the Holy Days? . . . How could I say to Him: Blessed be Thou, Almighty, Master of the Universe, who chose us among all nations to be tortured day and night, to watch as our fathers, our mothers, our brothers end up in the furnaces?"[8] By Yom Kippur, while other slave laborers fasted, Wiesel swallowed his ration of soup and nibbled his crust of bread, turning those acts "into a symbol of rebellion, of protest against Him," and feeling deep inside "a great void opening."[9]

Wiesel expressed even deeper anger in the unpublished Hebrew manuscript of *Night*. "There is no longer a God in the heavens, he whispered with every step he put in the ground." In a subsequent passage, he wrote: "I stopped praying and didn't speak about God. I was angry at Him. I told myself 'He does not deserve us praying to Him.' And really does He hear [our] prayers? Why sanctify Him? For what? For the suffering He rains on our heads? For Auschwitz and Birkenau? This time we will not stand as the accused in court before the divine judge. This time we are the judges and He the accused."[10]

Despite this "agonizing outcry," as Wiesel described it later in life, he and his father got up early one morning and joined a line of Jewish prisoners waiting to strap on an illicitly secured pair of *tefillin*—the two leather boxes containing Torah passages that Orthodox men don during weekday morning prayers, one box strapped on the left arm and one on the forehead. The *tefillin* had been smuggled into the camp by a gentile *kapo* who had been bribed with rations of bread that some prisoners had saved up.[11] In his memoir *All Rivers Run to the Sea*, Wiesel contrasted his clinging to belief with the skepticism of a fellow inmate, the writer Primo Levi, who believed that if God existed He was guilty of letting the murderers do as they pleased, or if His power was too feeble to stop them He was not God. Wiesel insisted that despite his blasphemous response to the hangings at Auschwitz, "I have never renounced my faith in God. I have risen against His justice, protested His silence, and sometimes His absence, but my anger rises up within faith and not outside it." Yet, he added, even if he comes to understand man's role at Auschwitz, he will never understand God's role there or in the deaths of the six million.[12]

Nevertheless, his observance of Jewish ritual—from eating only kosher food and refraining from work on the Sabbath—flagged for many years thereafter. Slowly, though, he found himself returning, like Job, never quite abandoning his quarrel with God, but becoming a synagogue worshiper and Sabbath observer once more, and putting on *tefillin* daily, according to his son, Elisha.[13]

"If I have problems with God, why should I take it out on the Sabbath?" he often said.[14]

Robert McAfee Brown, a Christian theologian who examined Wiesel's religious themes in *Elie Wiesel: Messenger to All Humanity* (University of Notre Dame Press, 1983), suggested that Wiesel came round to the view that God was "the author of the puzzle" of existence, which "makes the stakes more significant and more troubling and (only later) more full of a stubborn hope born out of a willingness to combat evil wherever it appears, on behalf of a God who needs our help."[15]

Wiesel's disillusion with fellow Jews was almost as great as his anger at God. In *All Rivers Run to the Sea*, he talks about his shock at the cruelty of Jewish men who were "attracted by the killer's power," such as the Auschwitz *kapo* who was the son of a Polish Zionist leader and who beat and humiliated not just the religious inmates but also the Zionists. By contrast, the Greek supervisor in his block, Jacob Fardo, never struck a prisoner. Wiesel found consolation in the Jews who shared their meager rations of bread, who reminded fellow Jews that it was the Sabbath, who volunteered for beatings so a father or son would not have to endure one. The range of his experience of human behavior taught the young Wiesel to make fine discriminations among people, to avoid generalizations.[16]

His disappointment extended to those countries fighting the Nazis. As much as he treasured what the United States and its allies had done for him as a refugee, Wiesel's fury over their unwillingness to block the German carnage never diminished. "That not a single Allied military aircraft ever tried to destroy the rail lines converging on Auschwitz remains an outrageous enigma to me," he wrote in *All Rivers Run to the Sea*. "Birkenau was 'processing' ten thousand Jews a day. Stopping a single convoy for a single night—or even for just a few hours—would have prolonged so many lives. . . . But the free world didn't care whether Jews lived or died, whether they were annihilated one day or the next."[17]

What sustained Wiesel through Auschwitz, Buna, and Buchenwald was his closeness to his father, whom he had to himself for the first time in his life. Some of *Night*'s most moving passages revolve around whether his father would be selected for death by Mengele and how he and his father made sure to check up on each other during a death march out of Buna. He felt he needed to stay whole in order to bolster his father's spirits; and he guessed that his father's need to protect his son also kept him from succumbing to despair and exhaustion. "We depended on each other," he wrote. "Because of him, I had to live; because of me he tried not to die." And yet, there were moments when Elie realized what anguish his father suffered looking at his emaciated, withered child, knowing that he might not be able to rescue him from the next selection, one that might prove to be the son's breaking point. "There is no sharper pain, no more shattering grief, than seeing one's father shed tears of impotence," he wrote decades later, as a father himself.[18]

In his last weeks at Buna, Elie hauled heavy stones or pushed wheelbarrows of sand twelve hours a day. His father could not quite keep up with the crushing work. Laborers were desperate, aware that if they grew weak they too would be selected for the gas chambers. "Save us!" some shouted. "You promised . . . We are strong enough to work. We are good workers." Some were never seen again, and other inmates said *Kaddish* for them, but Elie's father survived to work another day.

The weather turned much colder, and even though the workers were given thicker uniforms, these were still too thin to ward off the intense chill of that particular European winter—one of the coldest in decades—and the frigid stone on bare hands became particularly painful. Elie's right foot swelled—in his memoirs he said it was his knee that was infected—and he underwent a short operation to remove fluid, surgery that was performed by a Jewish doctor in the infirmary. Then came the news that with Allied armies approaching, Buna was to be evacuated. Elie wondered if he should remain in the infirmary. He and his father instead decided to join the exodus, especially since those in the infirmary might be killed for being too feeble to work. Years later, Wiesel learned that those in the infirmary were liberated by the Russians. Father and son had made the wrong choice, one that proved fatal for the father.

In *All Rivers Run to the Sea*, Wiesel looked back on his time as a slave laborer and wondered how he had been able to endure. "Was it the will to testify—and therefore the need to survive—that helped me pull through? Did I survive in order to combat forgetting? I must confess that at the time such questions did not occur to me. I did not feel invested with any mission. On the contrary, I was convinced that my turn would come and that my memories would die with me."[19]

As he prepared to join the march out of Buna, Elie's foot was bleeding, still swollen, and excruciatingly painful since it had not had time to heal. But he covered himself in layers of clothing that he was able to snatch from the prison stocks and joined the thousands of prisoners as they left Buna's gates, watched over by squads of SS men armed with machine guns and police dogs. The workers trudged or shuffled for two days from Buna to a camp called Gleiwitz, tramping in darkness, through thick snow and icy wind and over corpses of stragglers, facing the constant threat of being shot if they did not keep up. Elie once more felt his father as a burden. When another inmate lamented having gotten separated from his son during the march, "a terrible thought crossed my mind: What if he [the son] had wanted to be rid of his father?"[20]

One vignette on the death march has seemed "surrealistic" to some readers—including the Holocaust historian Raul Hilberg—who have wondered about its veracity.[21] It was the story of Juliek, a violinist in the Buna orchestra, who clung to his violin throughout the death march and, in a barn piled with the dead and those barely clinging to life, played an exquisite section of a Beethoven concerto.

"I don't know how long he played," Wiesel wrote. "I was overcome by sleep. When I awoke at daybreak, I saw Juliek facing me, hunched over, dead. Next to him lay his violin, trampled, an eerily poignant little corpse."[22]

Georges Borchardt, Wiesel's longtime agent and a man

whose mother was murdered in the Holocaust, makes several points about such disputed scenes in *Night*. First, he said, as in the classic film *Rashomon*, people see the same thing and can give totally different accounts. Second, even if there was not absolute verisimilitude, "you have to organize memory so that it makes sense to the person hearing or reading." Moreover, Wiesel didn't invent the fact that he was in a concentration camp. He didn't invent his father's death. And he certainly didn't invent that he wanted his father to die.[23]

Wiesel himself was quite insistent about the truthfulness of *Night*—his "deposition" as he called it. "Did I serve memory well?" he asked rhetorically. "In fact, if I had to do it over again, I would change nothing in my deposition."[24] What is indisputable is that *Night* stands out among the myriad Holocaust memoirs because of its understated narration, its profound insight into human responses to evil, and its transcendent reckoning with the role of God. It is no surprise that it is often regarded as the greatest single work to emerge from the Holocaust and, along with *The Diary of Anne Frank*, the most popular.

After three days at Gleiwitz, where they survived yet another selection and quenched their thirst with spoonfuls of snow, Elie and his father were crammed into roofless cattle cars with the other prisoners and taken toward Buchenwald, in east central Germany, about five miles from the city of Weimar. Snow fell and the wind howled almost constantly during the seven-hundred-mile journey. On the first morning, the train paused and SS men ordered the living to throw the corpses out of the wagon. Twenty corpses were hurled from Elie's wagon alone, with his father barely alive enough to remain. As the train rolled off, it left behind "in a snowy field in Poland, hundreds of naked orphans without a tomb."[25]

At another stop, passing railroad workmen, stunned by the appearance of the emaciated prisoners, threw pieces of bread into the train, and the prisoners mauled and trampled each other to retrieve them. One son tried to devour his dying father's bread, while other prisoners tried to capture the bread for themselves. In the mayhem, the son was badly injured and soon died.

When after four days the train arrived at Buchenwald on January 26, only a dozen of the hundred or so prisoners in Elie's train car were still alive. One of these was his father, but Shlomo had no strength left to take the shower required upon entering the camp. He pleaded with Elie to let him rest on a mound of snow and Elie pleaded with him in turn to get up and persevere. Although they lost each other for a night, Elie found his father the next morning suffering from a high fever. Shlomo begged Elie to bring him coffee. Elie did so but remarked that his father showed "the gratitude of a wounded animal."

"With these mouthfuls of hot water, I had probably given him more satisfaction than during my entire childhood," Elie observed.[26]

His father, gasping for breath, was suffering from dysentery and barely had the strength to eat. He lay on a cot reserved for the very sick, mumbling incoherently, though at one point he managed to tell Elie where in the basement he had buried the family's few jewels and silver. When a doctor decided there was nothing to be done for the elder Wiesel, he was sent back to his tiered bunk. There the prisoners wanted nothing to do with him. Not only was he delirious but he did not even have the strength to leave the bed to relieve himself. When he began to moan, asking for water, an SS man commanded him to be silent, and when the father persisted, the German gave him a blow to his head. Elie woke on the morning of January 29, 1945, to find another sick inmate in his father's place. What precisely happened to his father? Elie never found out, but surmised that he had died overnight and his body had been carted to a crematorium.

"No prayers were said over his tomb. No candles lit in his memory. His last word had been my name. He had called out to me and I had not answered. I did not weep and it pained me that I could not weep. But I was out of tears. And deep inside me, if I could have searched the recesses of my feeble conscience, I might have found something like: Free at last!"[27] After his father's death, nothing seemed to matter anymore, Wiesel wrote.

Wiesel does not mention this in *Night* or in his subsequent memoirs, but he may have been saved from death by his assignment to Buchenwald's Block 66, a cavernous barrack that at its peak held more than nine hundred boys, 90 percent of them Jewish teenagers but some as young as four years old. Studies of Buchenwald by Kenneth Waltzer, a professor of history at James Madison College and head of the Jewish studies program at Michigan State, found that with manpower short, the SS had turned over day-to-day management of the camp to German and Czech prisoners who were Communists. These Communists wanted to keep the boys alive as "the raw materials with which to make new societies after the war." With their administrative powers, they listed the boys in official documents as unfit for work or transport and thus saved them from being taken to satellite labor camps where the exertion, cold, and extreme hunger might have killed them.

Because Block 66 was at the bottom of a steep hill, the SS preferred not to come down from their offices near the main gate to inspect conditions in the barrack. The SS were also scared off by signs warning of typhus carriers. They did not even require the Block 66 boys to come up for daily roll call, which saved the boys exposure to the bitter cold. They apparently never found out that the Communist overseers had set up a makeshift school inside the barracks where they taught Jewish literature and history, even geometry. It was run by Motele Strigler, who went on to become one of the last editors at the Yiddish *Forward* in New York. After Wiesel won the Nobel Prize, he made an effort with the help of President Vaclav Havel to locate and honor the block elder, a Czech Communist named Antonin Kalina. He found out that Kalina had died.[28]

On April 4, the loudspeakers began blaring orders for everyone to gather in the *appelplatz*, the assembly grounds for roll call, before another evacuation. The Communist overseers gave the Block 66 boys new badges with their Jewish IDs removed and told them not to show up. The SS—aware that Allied troops were closing in—did not immediately force the issue. But on April 10, brandishing guns and guiding police dogs, the SS rounded up the Block 66 boys and ordered them to assemble at the *appelplatz*. Elie waited there expecting to be sent to Weimar and put on a transport, but the SS officers glimpsed Allied planes overhead and fled into the forest, their flight hastened by bursts of gunfire and grenade explosions from prisoners who had secreted weapons smuggled to them by underground groups. By nighttime, American tanks from General George Patton's Third Army drove up to the gates of the camp. The soldiers, their faces ashen, stared in horror at the skeletal prisoners.

"I shall never forget their eyes, your eyes," Wiesel told a Washington gathering of camp liberators in 1981. "You looked and looked, you could not move your gaze away from us; it was as though you sought to alter reality with your eyes. They reflected astonishment, bewilderment, endless pain, and anger—yes, anger above all. . . . Then you broke down. You wept. You wept and wept uncontrollably."[29]

In the famous photograph taken at Buchenwald's liberation, Elie's gaunt face peeks out from the ranks of cadaverous men lying in a four-tiered bunk and staring helplessly at the photographer. Elie had not eaten for six days, and he devoured the first can of food a soldier threw at him, which was lard. Other prisoners barely greeted their liberators before they pounced on the pieces of bread and other morsels they were given. Somehow, the observant prisoners found the strength to organize a ten-man *minyan* and murmur *Kaddish* for the dead. Wiesel noted later that it was both an expression of gratitude to God but also a cry of protest: "Why did you not spare so many others?"

Elie, nearly unconscious, spent two weeks in a hospital that had been used by the camp's SS, hovering, he said, between life and death. When he finally summoned the energy to rise out of bed, he looked in the mirror for the first time since Sighet.

"From the depths of the mirror, a corpse was contemplating me," he wrote, in the concluding passage of *Night*. "The look in his eyes as he gazed at me has never left me."[30]

4

❖❖❖

Recovering

WHEN THE GERMANS rolled into Sighet, Elie Wiesel was a carefree boy of fifteen devoted to his yeshiva studies, to his family, to the embrace of Hasidism and other aspects of observant Jewish culture. Although news of the persecution of Jews in Poland and the Soviet Union had drifted to Sighet, Elie still retained a benevolent sense of the universe and of the God who ruled it. When he emerged from Buchenwald a year later, he was an orphan shorn of his family (he was not yet aware that two of his sisters had survived), his community, and his core beliefs. He challenged and even outright denied the existence of a God who could allow the barbarism he had witnessed.

He had lived through the most horrific event in human history, and the universe had become a very different place, one that could turn overnight into a madhouse of brutal tormentors and humans reduced to desperate, debased creatures bearing numbers not names. It was as if he had awoken on a different galaxy. And he was now just sixteen years old.

In the confusion of a liberated Buchenwald taken over by American G.I.'s, he scoured the lists of survivors that the Red Cross and other organizations were compiling. Although the names of some cousins were there, those of his two older sisters were not. Meanwhile, the American military authorities gathered up all the youngsters who appeared to have been orphaned—there were more than a thousand of them—and found make-shift clothes for them, often a cleaner set of the striped camp pajamas or uniforms intended for Hitler Youth.

When they asked the orphans where they would like to settle, some asked to be sent to Palestine, but the British man-date authorities there would not allow them to immigrate. Oth-ers wanted to return to their Hungarian, Polish, or Ukrainian hometowns, though those were now occupied by the Soviets. When Elie was urged by his American liberators to return to Sighet, he objected. "I did not like the idea of living alone in an abandoned place," he wrote in a magazine article in 1965. "The town they were talking about no longer existed. It had followed the Jews into deportation."[1]

The fate of many of the youngsters was resolved when an offer to take them in was made by France, by General Charles de Gaulle himself. So on June 2, 1945, 426 orphans, ages seven to seventeen, escorted by two Jewish-American chaplains, left Buchenwald for the Norman town of Écouis, arriving four days later. Elie's name appears on the convoy manifest as Lazar Wiezen of Sighet, Orphan #405, with an incorrect birth date of Octo-ber 4, 1928.[2] In Écouis, the Oeuvre de Secours aux Enfants (OSE, known in English as the Children's Aid Society), a Jew-ish organization formed in 1912 that hid hundreds of children from the Nazis, had set up a home for the surviving youth in an abandoned sanatorium. The home received funding from the

American Jewish Joint Distribution Committee, the international relief organization headquartered in New York.

Not surprisingly, social workers encountering the Écouis children found them to be traumatized. Some children could not even remember their own names, so accustomed were they to identifying themselves by their numbers in Auschwitz and Buchenwald. Judith Hemmendinger, a social worker whose father was killed in Auschwitz and who in 2000 published a memoir, *Children of Buchenwald* (with a foreword by Wiesel), described the boys as feral.

"They looked like bandits, suspicious and mute," according to Hemmendinger's account. "Their heads were shorn; all dressed the same, with faces still swollen from hunger and not a smile to be seen. Their eyes bespoke sadness and suspicion. They were apathetic towards the outside world. They likened the supervisors to guards and were terror-stricken at the sight of doctors, who reminded them of Mengele, the man who upon their arrival in Auschwitz had sent the weak ones to gas chambers, the able-bodied to slave labor."[3]

To the adult Wiesel, reflecting on the experience decades later, their behavior was entirely logical. These youngsters, having witnessed the depths of human depravity, were not going to show deference to the innocents who were their teachers.

The staff gave them beds, clothing, medical checkups, and what Wiesel described as lavish meals. They were assigned a room in which to say their daily prayers, and together at one of these services they said *Kaddish* for their slain parents and siblings, underscoring their shared identity as orphans. Elie and Menashe Klein, the twenty-year-old son of a prominent Hungarian Hasidic rabbi who later became the leader of a sect with branches in Brooklyn and Israel and an esteemed arbiter of Jewish law, requested volumes of Torah and Talmud, and these were obtained. Dissecting and pondering together, the pair of young scholars delved into the rabbinical dialectic of the Talmud with a striking ferocity.

"I recovered my religious fervor, perhaps as a way of closing the parentheses on my recent past," Wiesel wrote in *All Rivers Run to the Sea*. "Most of all I needed to find my way again, guided by one certainty. However much the world had changed, the Talmudic universe was still the same. No enemy could silence the disputes between Shammai and Hillel, Abayye and Rava."[4]

Besides studying Talmud, Elie passed the first weeks playing chess and was photographed doing so. Many youngsters still clung to strategies of survival they had developed in the camps, squirreling away crusts of bread under their pillows in case the home ran out or sneaking off to neighboring farms to trade pots, blankets, or other pilfered goods for desired food. When the boys were visited by rabbis, journalists, and government officials, most of them could not or would not speak of their ordeal.

One day a chaplain of the American army came to Écouis. Rabbi Robert Marcus had met the boys before in Buchenwald, so they felt comfortable gathering around him on the lawn. But when he tried to speak he was unable to utter a word. Overcome by his emotions, tears streamed down his cheeks. It had been a long time since the children had seen an adult cry. Something in them thawed, and a few of them also began to cry. One later said, "The chaplain returned us to our souls. He reawakened the feelings we had buried within us." Memories of family and hometown friends that had been "deeply buried in the camps" began to break through the fog of pain and shock.[5]

A few days later the home director called him over and told him he had received a call. It was, he said, from Elie's sister. Stunned, Elie asked which sister and how could he reach her. The director knew only that the sister would meet him at Gare Saint-Lazare in Paris the next day. Anxious and uncertain of how he would make his way around a city, Elie took the train to

Paris, and when he arrived, he promptly saw Hilda, his oldest sister, in the crowd; she "fell into my arms."[6]

How had she found him? She had seen a story about the orphans in a French Jewish newspaper that featured a photograph of Elie with other boys. She told him that after internment in Auschwitz for several months, she and their sister Beatrice had been transferred to Kaufering IV, a subcamp of Dachau near Munich. Hundreds of slave laborers, many infected with typhus and infested with fleas, had been building a giant concrete bunker that would shield German Messerschmitt planes from Allied bombing raids, but she and Beatrice, fortunate to remain together, were assigned lighter jobs; Hilda peeled potatoes in the camp kitchen while Beatrice worked in an office. The sisters were not there long. By April 1945, with American troops approaching, the camp was evacuated and the frail inmates were marched at gunpoint to the Bavarian town of Wolfratshausen, where the sisters were liberated around May 1. Beatrice had contracted tuberculosis and spent time in a sanitorium. When she was healthy enough to leave, she made her way to Sighet, where she learned that an aunt had also returned to the town. But she knew of no other relatives who had survived.[7]

Accompanying Hilda in Paris was an Algerian Jew, Freddo Kudler, a portrait painter, another survivor of the camps who had been liberated from Dachau. He was now her fiancé. Elie and his sister spoke for hours, but they avoided mention of what had happened to their parents and Tzipora. "We felt a need to censor ourselves for we were both afraid of being unable to control our emotions," Elie remembered.

Hilda told him that Beatrice was planning to emigrate to Canada and was biding her time in a displaced persons camp in Kassel, Germany. The three siblings did manage to reunite briefly in Antwerp before Beatrice left for Canada.

On the night of his reunion with Hilda in Paris, Hilda's fiancé urged him to join them at a showing of Charlie Chaplin's

The Great Dictator and, as he relates in *All Rivers Run to the Sea*, there he felt the first sexual stirrings since the war. Aroused by a couple kissing in seats in front of him, he found his hand guiltily defying all his Torah teachings and sliding toward the young woman on his left. He finally took her hand and she did not protest. Clearly, Wiesel was using his memoir to puncture the saintly, chaste aura that surrounded him. "I am a human being too," he seemed to insist.

Back in Écouis, Elie learned he was moving. He and other boys of Orthodox background had requested kosher meals, so the rescue society decided it would be more efficient to house them in a separate home where only kosher meals would be served. Those boys, numbering about one hundred, were sent off to a château-like residence in Ambloy, a village in central France encircled by forests. A photograph of Elie, seated with four other boys in front of the château and smiling under a beret, shows that he had gained a bit of weight.

Slowly, Hemmendinger, who became Ambloy's director, won the orphans' trust. She learned to speak Yiddish while other officials spoke French or German, languages Hungarian and Polish boys did not know. She permitted boys to go to the kitchen at night so they would stop hoarding food. She encouraged religious studies and practices. "Locked into the solitude of a mutilated, violated childhood," Wiesel wrote in a foreword to Hemmendinger's book, "we longed to be left alone. When a representative of the outside world attempted to reach us, we withdrew further. We refused to cooperate with you. We did not want your help, your understanding, your psychosocial investigations, or your charity. You entered our lives too soon; we were still in mourning."[8]

In time the boys formed a fraternity of the damned. They came together over campfires, French lessons, political debates, like one in which they argued whether the bombing of the King David Hotel in Jerusalem, which housed the British civil and military headquarters for Mandatory Palestine, was justified. They also shared a lustful infatuation—mixed with more than a little apprehension—for a beautiful counselor named Niny. Elie and his Orthodox roommate were so besotted they wrote poems about her. "What is sensuality, we reasoned, if not an invitation to physical pleasure? And what is physical pleasure if not the road to the forbidden and to eventual punishment?" he wrote, in a candid analysis of his own yeshiva boy's dilemma.[9]

On Yom Kippur, Hemmendinger recalled, a dispute broke out over *Yizkor*, a memorial service for dead parents, spouses, and siblings. One faction argued that every boy needed to participate. Another faction argued that that would be sacrilege since most boys had no proof their relatives were indeed dead. Eventually, most boys recited the *Yizkor* prayers, including *Kaddish*, while some left the room. For Elie and the other boys, it was a chance to open the floodgates, to weep with "remorse, incomprehension and despair" at all they had lost.

Hemmendinger noted that two boys were so depressed that one was reassigned to a lower floor, for fear he would jump from a window. But other boys had serious plans for the future. One was Kalman Kalikstein, who became a notable nuclear scientist and a professor at Hunter College in Manhattan; the other was his roommate Elie Wiesel. Hemmendinger remembered that Elie was already making notes for what eventually became *Night*.

Toward the end of 1946, the boys were asked to grapple with the prospect of leading more independent lives. More than a few wanted to remain in France. They would study French and learn a trade like watchmaker, furrier, or tailor. Elie was among those who chose France, and he and his group were transferred to a converted château in the village of Taverny, close to the colleges and trade schools of Paris.

Elie was assigned a private French tutor and took lessons in the apartment of the tutor's mother. He was fortunate to have been paired with an erudite, intuitively skillful teacher, François Wahl, who worked with Elie not just on language drills but introduced him to the poetry of Racine and the thought of Pascal and took him to plays at the Comédie-Française. (Wahl became a prominent book editor.) Hemmendinger, who often visited Taverny, was struck by Elie's "insatiable curiosity" and remarked how quickly he absorbed French, mastering the language in a year.[10]

Hemmendinger made sure the boys were exposed to culture as well, inviting a tenant at Taverny—an Israeli piano student who was studying at the Paris Conservatory—to give recitals of music by Mozart, Bach, and Beethoven. She got the boys seats in the front row of the balcony for a performance of *The Magic Flute*. On his own, Elie read Hegel and Spinoza, Kant and Marx, Camus and François Mauriac, sometimes becoming, as he himself admitted, insufferable in his intellectual posturing. The yeshiva boy was immersing himself in literary and philosophical works that mirrored the Talmud in their nuance, complexity, and capacity for intellectual provocation yet took Elie into a deeply secular world. He began to weigh ideas, religious precepts, and ethics from angles that he—and the Jewish texts he had studied as a boy—had barely considered, sometimes heretical thoughts that would give his writings and speeches a more worldly flavor. French soon became Elie's preferred tongue, and when he began writing seriously French was his language of choice. He wrote in French for the rest of his life.

Around this time, Elie encountered a mystic who went by the name of Shushani. His formal name was believed by some to have been Mordechai Rosenbaum, and Hillel Perlman by others. He was a disheveled vagabond of mysterious origins. The adult Wiesel found out much later that he had been born in Lithuania in the mid-1890s and died in Montevideo, Uruguay, in the mid-1960s. Elie's son, Elisha, told me that he learned at his father's *shiva* that Shushani had been excommunicated from a Hasidic sect for arguing that the world does not deserve Jewish children and therefore there was no great impetus to marry and procreate, advice that Wiesel seems to have taken to heart for many years. Yet Shushani was also a brilliant, magnetic scholar of Jewish texts. According to Wiesel, Shushani knew the entire Talmud and several of its commentaries by heart. He also knew the Greek and Latin classics and spoke a Babel of languages, including Hungarian and Sanskrit, the primary liturgical language of Hinduism. He sometimes lectured at Taverny. He spoke on Isaiah and on Job, and probed obscure but challenging questions: What is the difference between prophecy and vision? Does a prophet have a right to reject his ordained mission? What does Job reveal about the Jewish attitude toward suffering and injustice?

For almost three years, while other orphans like Menashe Klein—a Hasidic grand rabbi in the making—were frightened, distrustful, or kept their distance, Elie latched on to him. In Taverny, at another orphans' home in Versailles, and at Elie's first apartment in Paris, they explored intricate questions posed by the Torah and the Talmud. "It is to him I owe my constant drive to question, my pursuit of the mystery that lies within knowledge and of the darkness hidden within light," Wiesel wrote.[11]

The orphans at Taverny were gradually dispersed, and by 1947 the home closed down. A dozen of them made the risky journey to Palestine, where the British were barring entry of Jewish refugees like those marooned for weeks on the renamed freighter *Exodus 1947*. The remaining Buchenwald orphans were either sent off to uncles, aunts, and cousins in the United States, Australia, Canada, or other countries that were taking in refugees, or transferred, as Elie was, to yet another OSE home, this one on Avenue de Paris in Versailles. It already accommodated orphans, both boys and girls, who had been hidden during the war or survived with false papers.

Although a handful of the orphans succumbed to despair or depression, most in time started families and became productive citizens—rabbis, scientists, artists, scholars, and businessmen. To many observers, they are a testament to the human capacity for resilience. Survivors, Wiesel said in *All Rivers Run to the Sea*, are often asked how they managed to readjust, to live, love, and feel joy. "The truth is, it was not that difficult—less difficult than adjusting to death." Death in Auschwitz and Buchenwald became such a daily presence that "when we stumbled over a corpse, we walked on without so much as a second look," Wiesel wrote.[12]

Elie was having breakfast at the Versailles home when a visitor, Ted Comet, a twenty-one-year-old volunteer counselor from Cleveland, approached him. He was trying to find an Eliezer Wiesel, a cousin of his friend Irving Wiesel, a student at Yeshiva University. Comet was startled when the gaunt, doleful seventeen-year-old replied, "C'est moi." Decades after that teenager became the epochal messenger to humanity, Comet took that response as almost prophetic, likening the words to the biblical "Here I am" of Abraham as he expressed his willingness to do God's bidding by agreeing to sacrifice his son Isaac.

"I was very impressed with him," recalled Comet, who was ninety-two years old when I interviewed him in 2017. "There was a quality there of depth, of intelligence and of sadness." He remembered Elie as being the intellectual leader of a *chavrusa*, or study group, of four orphans, one of whom became an expert in astrophysics, another who founded a yeshiva, and a third who became an authority on Occitan, the language of Provence.[13]

Elie used Versailles as a springboard for study, for a short time at the Lycée Maimonides—a Jewish high school—and then, after he was admitted, for classes at the Sorbonne. As often as possible he also visited his sister Hilda and Freddo, now her husband, in their cramped apartment on the Rue Dussoubs.

(At the time, his other sister Bea was still in a displaced persons camp in Germany.) Drawing on his musical experiences in Sighet, he assembled a choir, both at Versailles and at a summer camp in the Pyrenees run by the Joint Distribution Committee. "His singing was extraordinary," Comet told me.

Wiesel tells us in his memoirs that in this period he continued to find himself consumed with beautiful girls, not surprising for someone his age and even more understandable for someone who had been starved for affection for so long. He writes of his unrequited crushes and random encounters, such as when he and a tall woman of about thirty sat across from each other on a train from Paris to Versailles. They allowed their knees to touch and Elie thought he would "faint from happiness." But when the woman asked him why he was smiling and was he in love, instead of conveying his attraction to her, he replied— "stupidly," he wrote—that he was in love with God.

His romantic clumsiness was evident in his work as a choirmaster. "If one of the female singers cast a knowing glance in my direction, I lost my composure," he wrote. "If she smiled at me, my heart would pound as if in anticipation of committing a sin."

Often as the choirmaster, he reacted to these stirrings by intentionally becoming more strict or working to impress the girls with his philosophical erudition. One girl called Hanna tussled with him repeatedly over his management of the choir, and he became obsessed with her. "The truth is I loved her self-assured walk and the way she ran her fingers through her dark hair," he wrote. "I loved her for herself, and to convince myself that I was capable of loving, of yearning, of living, of existing for somebody else. I loved her because she was my first love."[14]

That relationship foundered for six years, until the spring of 1954, when Elie, by then a freelance journalist for the Israeli newspaper *Yedioth Ahronoth*, ran into her on the Paris Metro.

Although she made it clear she was interested in dating him, Elie found himself putting her off, even when she asked if he would consider marrying her. About to leave for an assignment in Brazil, he implored her to keep the question open for a while.

Two or three times, he visited Bea in a displaced persons camp in Kassel, about a hundred miles northeast of Frankfurt, where she worked as an assistant at the office of the U.N. Relief and Works Agency, which was responsible for helping refugees. Although Bea was popular among the D.P. camp supervisors and residents for her genial efficiency, the Americans had rejected her application for a visa because of a lung condition she had picked up in the German labor camps. The Canadians, however, were willing to take her in.

She and Elie talked about her visit to Sighet and their home there, which was now occupied by strangers. All of the Jewish homes had been looted, she told him. Even the jewelry and silverware the Wiesels had buried in the backyard had been taken. Bea gave her brother the dreaded news that, but for Hilda and a few cousins, no one from the entire Wiesel and Feig families had survived.

Elie came away from the D.P. camp visit stunned and disheartened. He also could not shake off his distress at seeing the miserable, unsanitary conditions the Jewish refugees were living in more than a year after the end of the war. Although they now had freedom to move around and enough food to keep from starving, they were languishing for months in barracks that in some cases were in the same barbed-wire concentration camps they had been imprisoned in during the war. Meals were unwholesome and the toilets foul. Refugees were sometimes clothed in uniforms that had been worn by the German SS or in prison garb. Moreover, the United States and most Western countries were not inclined to take in refugees. Congressional debates over bills to expand the annual immigration quotas were tainted by anti-Semitism and xenophobia. A displaced-persons bill in 1948 was written in such a way that it kept out tens of thousands of Polish Jews who had fled to Russia when the Nazis invaded yet gave priority to Christian refugees from Lithuania, Estonia, Latvia, and Ukraine, many of whom had collaborated with the Nazis and even joined Hitler's SS. Although there were some exceptions—five thousand orphaned children were admitted under a special American quota in 1946—the doors did not fully open to the Jewish refugees until 1950, five years after the war's end.[15] In *All Rivers Run to the Sea*, Wiesel reflected that he might someday forgive the Western nations for not doing more to save the Jews of Europe during the war, "but they will never be forgiven for their treatment of the victims" once it had ended.[16]

Naturally, the refugees were eager to resume their lives. They opened schools and synagogues, published newspapers, and entertained themselves with theatrical performances and athletic clubs. They married and gave birth to children who would replace their murdered families. Given all they had endured, it would be understandable if they had decided not to bring children into the world, if they had chosen to succumb to the devastation they had suffered. Yet most survivors were hungry to get back to work or school, to make friends and find lovers, to experience joy after all the bleak years.

On one visit to Germany, Elie ended up staying at the home of an elderly gentile couple whose blond daughter, a war widow, tried to seduce him in the hope that he would pay her for his initiation. But he resisted the temptation, realizing that he would never forgive himself if his first sexual experience was with a German woman.[17]

By mid-1947, the managers of the Versailles home were encouraging the older teenagers to think about venturing out and making plans for a self-reliant future. Wiesel's best friend, Kalman, decided to make his way to Palestine aboard the *Exodus*, which soon became the center of a notorious international incident. Authorities in the British mandate of Palestine refused to let the 4,515 passengers—almost all Jewish survivors—disembark and forced them back to refugee camps in Germany. Elie agonized over whether or not to go to Palestine. Instead he chose to stay close to his sisters, his French teacher, and Shushani, and pursue his studies.

With the help of officials of the OSE, Elie, now nineteen, and three other boys took tiny rooms with shared toilets in a building on the western edge of Paris. They spent weekdays in the city, then came "home" to Versailles for *shabbos*. At the Sorbonne, Elie was soon reading Plato and Freud in French, attending lectures by Sartre and Martin Buber, and immersing himself in the café life of the Latin Quarter. He began to write about the deportations and his experiences at Auschwitz and Buchenwald, but he soon stopped, feeling words were inadequate to capture what he had lived through. He was too young, too raw. He vowed to himself that he would wait ten years before tackling the subject again.

No matter what pleasure he took in study or work, he found the day-to-day struggle to get by dispiriting. The monthly OSE subsidy of eight thousand francs was less than fifty dollars in today's currency; and French government ration cards did not add much. At one point, he took a job tutoring a doctor's son for his bar mitzvah. Later, as a middle-aged writer, Wiesel demonstrated his ability to laugh at himself by relating how he could not simply teach the boy the words and melodies needed for reading his portion of the Hebrew Torah and *haftarah*, but thought he should show him how to plumb each verse's metaphysical mysteries. But the father grew impatient. He viewed the readings as a mere rite of passage and fired Elie, telling him to come back after the boy was married.[18]

Beyond the challenges of scraping by, a despondency had taken hold of Elie, and in his memoirs he revealed that during this period he contemplated throwing himself into the Seine or in front of a Metro train. It was not the dead that drew him, he argued; he lived with them constantly. It was more a feeling of disconnection from his essential self, of not recognizing the person he was becoming and of feeling disengaged from the life he was leading.[19] Clearly, Wiesel had spent his formative years in convulsive transition—from coddled yeshiva boy raised with an ironclad code of conduct to teenager brutalized by a demonic reign of terror to young man wading into a cosmopolitan world where the choices seemed boundless. It would be surprising if, under the circumstances, he was not confused about who he was becoming. Psychologists might argue that Elie had not fully reckoned with his traumatic losses—of his home, his community, his culture and language, as well as his parents, grandparents, and adored little sister. Yet one could surmise that his bewildered, unanchored feeling gave us the Elie Wiesel who eloquently grappled with questions of God and existence for the rest of his life.

5

Cub Reporter

WHILE SHARING an apartment in Paris, Elie was riveted by events in Palestine. Rival Jewish factions had been trying to force the British to yield the former Ottoman territory that the League of Nations in 1922 had proclaimed as a mandate under Britain's control. Some of the Jewish militias resorted to killings and bombings. During 1947 the fledgling United Nations debated a partition plan to divide the territory between Jews and Arabs, and finally passed it on November 29, enraging Palestinian Arabs and neighboring Arab countries. David Ben-Gurion issued a declaration establishing a new state of Israel on May 14, 1948; the following morning, troops from Jordan, Iraq, Syria, and Egypt crossed Israel's borders and full-scale war broke out.

Elie found that he could not stay on the sidelines. In February 1948, he and his roommate and Sorbonne classmate Moshe Lazar had shown up at the Paris offices of the Jewish Agency for Palestine, which was coordinating settlement in Palestine. (Known today as the Jewish Agency for Israel, it leads immigration and absorption efforts.) They asked an official how they might be drafted into the Haganah, the Jewish paramilitary force that soon became the backbone of the Israeli army. The official laughed, telling the scrawny Wiesel he was "not well enough" and shut the door in his face. Lazar, however, was recruited and went on to fight in three Israeli wars (and to become a prominent professor of comparative literature). But at the Jewish Agency, Elie came across a Yiddish weekly published by the Irgun, the more militant Zionist paramilitary faction and the political base of a future right-wing Israeli prime minister, Menachem Begin. He located its not-very-clandestine Paris office and made the same pitch, volunteering to serve in a militia, but the editors, learning of his language skills, made a counteroffer, inviting him to translate Hebrew articles into Yiddish.

And that is how Elie Wiesel became a journalist.

The offer from the Irgun newspaper, *Zion in Kampf* (Zion in Struggle), was quite attractive. The salary was quadruple what he had been living on, and he could now afford to move to a room on Rue de Rivoli that was close to the office and the city center and even boasted the luxury of a sink. The editor became his mentor in the rules of Yiddish—like many Jews, Elie did not quite believe Yiddish was a formal language with an actual grammar—as well as in the conventions of writing for a newspaper.

"If you want to hold the reader's attention," the editor told Wiesel, "your sentence must be clear enough to be understood and enigmatic enough to pique curiosity."[1]

Soon he was choosing the stories to translate, suggesting headlines, composing the front-page layout. He felt useful, a lexical soldier in the fight for the Jewish nation. He met important Irgun personalities there. He might even have encountered the beautiful teenage girl who would eventually become his wife. Marion Erster, a Jewish refugee from Vienna, was hiding guns the Irgun had purchased and intended to smuggle into Palestine. When I interviewed her, Mrs. Wiesel confirmed that at age fifteen or sixteen she was indeed in Paris working for a Zionist youth movement that was absorbed into the Irgun.

"We were taking things from one country to another," she said with a slight laugh. "I did hide guns headed for Israel."[2]

Elie tried again to enlist in the Haganah, but the examining doctor concluded once again that he was too frail for combat. Perhaps his misgivings about military life betrayed him; he was not the kind of person who could allow his individual identity to dissolve into a mass formation, he confessed, and the routines of training and submission to haranguing sergeants were not for him.[3] So he watched from the sidelines in Paris as Israel declared its independence, and its ragtag forces beat back attacks by the armies of Egypt, Syria, Jordan, and Iraq as well as local Palestinian militias. When armistice agreements were signed the following year, Israel ended up retaining the partition plan's Jewish area as well as 60 percent of the territory designated for Arabs. Whatever elation Wiesel felt at the victory was tempered by his disappointment over not having been part of the stunning military triumph. But the conflict did form the basis of his first published piece.

It was a short story derived from the controversial events surrounding the shelling of the *Altalena*, a cargo ship commissioned to deliver weapons and fighters to the Irgun. Prime Minister Ben-Gurion was convinced that the mission violated the plan to merge all of the disparate fighting forces into one army— the Israeli Defense Forces—and ordered an attack on the ship. Sixteen Irgun fighters and three IDF soldiers were killed in the skirmish and the ship was sunk off a Tel Aviv beach. For an issue of *Zion in Kampf* highlighting the event, Elie wrote under the pseudonym Ben Shlomo about two brothers, one fighting for the Irgun, the other for Ben-Gurion's elite Palmach force. The Irgun brother is slain by the Palmach brother in a Cain-

and-Abel, Jacob-and-Esau theme he would return to again and again. Wiesel does not say why he chose fiction rather than journalism to tell the *Altalena* story. Perhaps it was because literature was what he was reading at the Sorbonne. Whatever the reason, this piece was a harbinger of Wiesel's long career as a novelist.

Stung by Ben-Gurion's act, one he considered treasonous, he wrote another piece, this time a journalistic one, questioning the value of victory if it pitted Jew against Jew. Other articles followed—often philosophical in content—and having nothing to do with the propaganda that a publication like *Zion in Kampf* preferred. But Elie's career at the Irgun paper did not last long. The Irgun was absorbed into Begin's Herut political party, which became a right-wing opposition party in the new parliament. In January 1949, it shut down its European offices, casting Elie out of a job.

He responded by plunging deeper into his studies at the Sorbonne. He read more Sartre, Camus, and other existentialists. He began a dissertation on asceticism, a philosophy of self-denial that he had absorbed from his dialogues with Shushani, and he wrote nearly six hundred pages about the Jewish, Christian, and Buddhist interpretations of that perspective on existence. But he never finished his dissertation. He needed to support himself, and doctoral studies did not put food on the table.

In fact, he was often hungry, relying on friends or his sisters for dinner or traveling back to Versailles for a *shabbos* meal. But soon Hilda left for Israel, and Bea for Canada. What saved Elie at this juncture was another stroke of good fortune. The brother of Hilda's husband was an executive in the Amaury press group, which published a newspaper for French Jewish readers, *L'Arche*. The newspaper did not have a correspondent in Israel, and Wiesel volunteered for the job. It would give him a chance to savor the "Promised Land" that had long beckoned.

The trip lasted less than six months, until January 1950,

and it turned out to be deeply disappointing. Like many Jews taking in a land for the first time that is charged with ancestral and spiritual meaning, he wept upon arriving. He was enchanted by the sight of Mount Carmel, "looming high" and inviting "the faithful to approach," and by the mystical beauty of the Galilee, Safed, Tiberias, the Negev, and of course Jerusalem.[4] But seeing the wreck of the *Altalena* off a Tel Aviv beach and a Jerusalem stripped of its emblematic Old City underlined the divisions within Jewish life.[5] Wiesel felt the Haganah in 1948 had left the defense of Jerusalem up to a "tiny group of poorly armed Jews." And nothing emphasized the disunity more than the disdain he sensed among Israelis for the survivors of the Nazi terror. They were scorned as cowards, seen as having gone to the concentration camps too docilely, or even despised as schemers and collaborators—how else could they have eluded the gas chambers? Schoolchildren maliciously called their immigrant classmates *sabonim*, the Hebrew for "little soap cakes." Only *aliyah*, immigrating "up" to Israel as a fulfillment of Zionism, was seen as honorable. After all, the diaspora's rose-colored delusions of assimilation and tolerance had led to Auschwitz, in the opinion of the *sabras* who had been born in Palestine. It was better to forget the past, to bury what was becoming known as the Holocaust or the Shoah (an old Hebrew term for "catastrophe" or "utter destruction").

"They were given housing and commiseration, but little respect," he wrote. "They were made to feel that they themselves were to blame for their suffering. They should have left Europe earlier, as they had been advised to do, or risen up against the Germans. In other words, the immigrants were seen as what young Jews in Palestine refused to be: victims."[6]

Yossi Ciechanover, among Wiesel's closest lifelong friends and a prominent businessman who advised several Israeli prime ministers on foreign affairs, told me that what I called Wiesel's complicated relationship with Israel derived from this period. "It's not so complicated," he said with characteristic Israeli directness. "Elie felt that when the survivors arrived in Israel they were received by the Israelis in a not dignified manner. Israelis blamed them for not trying to save themselves and walking like sheep to the slaughterhouse. He felt that they didn't understand that there had been no choice."[7]

As Wiesel wrote, this attitude "tarnished my joy at breathing the air of Jerusalem." One might speculate that the Elie Wiesel the world came to know, the champion of the survivors, the orator and writer who explained their story to the world in ways that honored, not deprecated their wartime ordeals, was born on that trip. It is also clear that Wiesel's ambivalence toward the state—his love and support for Israel tempered by a feeling that it often falls short of its ideals—may have been shaped on that trip as well. He reconciled his conflicted feelings through a decision to avoid publicly criticizing the Israeli government. Choosing the United States as his home certainly strengthened his resolve to keep his misgivings about Israel to himself.

"He said over and over again that without the state of Israel there is no Jewish people and without the Jewish people there is no Israel," Ciechanover said. "And that's why we must defend her in every situation, during war and peace."[8]

Yet anyone parsing his writing can see that he was not comfortable with the belligerence and ethical lapses of some Israeli leaders. In an essay from 1978 collected in *A Jew Today* that is written in the form of a letter, "To a Brother in Israel," Wiesel said he wants not just to love Israel as his ancestral homeland but to admire it, to "hold it up as an example, find there what cannot be found elsewhere: a certain sense of justice, a certain sense of dignity. I want to find there a society ruled by a vision of probity, justice and compassion." Wiesel's views underwent

nuanced shifts in later years, but at that time he was especially
concerned with compassion for the Palestinians. "Are we wrong
to ask you to adopt a more Jewish attitude toward Palestinian
Arabs, and, particularly, toward Israeli Arabs?" he wrote.[9]

After a few months in Israel, he decided to return to Paris.

6

❖❖❖❖

A Hungarian in Paris

ELIE LOVED PARIS, his future wife Marion later recalled. Indeed, on their first date they spoke about their passion for the city they had individually spent time in as young strivers.[1] For a yeshiva boy from a small Hungarian town, Paris was transformative.

After returning from Israel, Elie moved back into the Hôtel de France, a cheap five-story residence near the Gare du Nord. He had a sunless room overlooking the courtyard, barely large enough for a bed, a dresser, and a sink. The shared bathroom was in the public corridor. "More than once I wondered whether the hotel rented rooms by the hour," he wrote. "I kept running into new customers on the stairway."[2] During the day, he would sit for hours at a sidewalk café with his notebook and write. At the Café de Flore, he would sometimes encounter the philosopher Jean-Paul Sartre.

"I was in the second circle around Sartre," Wiesel later told Joel Rappel, the archivist organizing his papers at Boston

University. "I listened to him and from time to time he said, 'What does the young Jew think about that?'"[3]

He dropped in at the jazz cellars of Saint-Germain-des-Prés and took in classic movies like *Children of Paradise*. He haunted the Latin Quarter's bookstores, voraciously reading Franz Kafka, Ignazio Silone, Miguel de Unamuno, and William Faulkner. Wiesel sketched this period in *The Town Beyond the Wall*, describing how the protagonist Michael, as an impoverished young immigrant in Paris, enters into "the depths of his own solitude" while wrestling with God's and man's culpability for the Holocaust.[4] Embedded in a full-page statement he ran in the *New York Times* in 1977, in which he criticized French president Valéry Giscard d'Estaing for his opposition to Israeli government policies, is a sense of the debt he felt toward France: "I owe France my secular education, my language and my career as a writer. Liberated from Buchenwald, it was in France that I found compassion and humanity. It was in France that I found generosity and friendship. It was in France that I discovered the other side, the brighter side of mankind."[5] And although he did not say so explicitly, it was also in France that this grandson of a devoted Hasid started to become something of a man of the world, reading widely and adventurously, sampling avant-garde philosophies and lifestyles, using his home base to explore new lands and cultures.

By this time Wiesel possessed a potent credential, a press card from the then-struggling tabloid *Yedioth Ahronoth* that he had gotten while in Israel. He was now a freelance foreign correspondent for an actual newspaper. His first article was an interview with Emile Najar, a minister in the Israeli embassy who gave him an overview of the relations between Israel and France. Articles followed about the beginnings of the French war in Indochina, the deaths of the writer André Gide and of Léon Blum, a Jew who was three times elected prime minister of France, and the debate over how to treat those who collaborated with the Nazis.

There was an interview with a poet who turned out to be a former lover of the Greek novelist Nikos Kazantzakis. And there was a feature about an Israeli Mossad agent in Morocco who was told to keep an eye on Elie as a traveler clueless about local mores. The agent pretended to be his guide and got his ribs broken after Wiesel flirted with the wrong girl. For a time, Wiesel even wrote a gossip column about Paris personalities called "Sparks from the City of Light."

His press card was a ticket to travel, and he ventured out to Barcelona, Madrid, Toledo, Tangier, and Casablanca. Each city seemed to produce an epiphany or a situation fraught with ambiguities, puzzling overtones, or mystical coincidences. In a Madrid cellar, he prayed in a Sephardic synagogue where the worshipers were mostly Yiddish-speaking refugees like himself and learned that Francisco Franco, ruthless dictator that he was, was nevertheless hospitable to Jews who had fled the Nazis. In the cathedral in Saragossa, a city associated with the thirteenth-century mystic Rabbi Abraham Abulafia, he was approached by a thin man with "deep-set, somber eyes" who didn't seem to know that Jews still existed. The man showed him a timeworn piece of parchment in Hebrew in which the writer, a Marrano, or secret Jew, named Moshe ben Abraham, urged his descendants not to forget their origins. It had been handed down through the generations in the Saragossa man's family. Later, when Wiesel met the Saragossa man by chance in Jerusalem, the man confided that his name too was Moshe ben Abraham, just like the great rabbi.[6] The anecdote seems another example of Wiesel's fascination with spiritual forces beyond our comprehension.

So does still another curious vignette in the memoir. Wiesel was walking on a deserted street in Barcelona when he encountered a young beggar. "Señor, I'm hungry," the boy pleaded, holding out his palm. Wiesel describes reaching into his pocket for coins and feeling his fingers freezing inside his pocket, unable to hand anything to the boy. The boy's palm, he writes, accused him "of all the sins committed since the first man turned his back on his brother, not far from Paradise." In a trance, Wiesel watched the boy disappear down the street. "I never saw him again. But no—he has a hundred faces and as many names, and he is always hungry."[7]

What is a reader to make of this enigmatic scene? Clearly, it speaks to a lifelong penchant to view the universe in transcendent terms, to allow for the possibility of the mystical and surreal, to see himself as something of a mystic. Not surprisingly, more than a few people saw in Wiesel an otherworldly aspect, like that of a biblical prophet.

Yet his journalism at the time also displays a hard-nosed grip on life's granular realities. In early 1952, Wiesel was working as a French-Yiddish translator during the preliminary talks in Geneva over what reparations Germany would pay to individual Holocaust victims and to the state of Israel as the emblem of the Jewish people. The lead negotiator was Nahum Goldmann, president of the World Jewish Congress. During a closed-door session for the Jewish representatives, some delegates insisted upon closing the talks with the recitation of *Kaddish*. Goldmann was unconvinced and urged his colleagues to worry less about such symbolic gestures and more about obtaining maximum funds for Israel. "Which will profit Israel more," Goldmann asked angry dissenters, "the Kaddish or German financial compensation?" The reporter in Wiesel sensed that he had a scoop about Goldmann's insensitive faux pas, but as a paid translator he knew he could not disclose what he had been privy to. So he resigned his position as translator and wired a story to *Yedioth Ahronoth* that ended up on its front page and caused a worldwide stir in Jewish circles. In response, Goldmann held a press conference in which he blasted the story as a fiction.

Years later, when Wiesel was well known as a writer and speaker, he once again crossed paths with Goldmann. The former World Jewish Congress president admitted that Wiesel's story had been accurate and implied that for organizational reasons—and to maintain his own good name—he had had to call it fabricated. "I'm a politician and you're not," he added. "Write your novels, tell your Hasidic tales, but don't ever get involved in politics. It's not for you."[8]

But as politically naïve as Wiesel could sometimes be, it was those occasions when he abandoned his instinctive caution and confronted American presidents and European anti-Semites that sealed his reputation as a humanist on the world stage.

Later that year, Wiesel went on to cover the formal reparation negotiations between Germany and the World Jewish Congress, meetings that were assailed by Menachem Begin and many Israeli and American survivors as signaling a willingness to accept "blood money" that would allow Germany to offset its guilt for the systematic murder of the six million. Practical considerations notwithstanding, Wiesel was opposed to such payments, fearing they "would inevitably lead to betrayal of the memory of the dead."[9]

Around this time, he began reading the ancient *Upanishads*—containing the fundamentals of Hindu philosophy—and the 700-verse *Bhagavad Gita*. With money from the publication of a cluster of Yiddish articles and his winnings from the first lottery ticket he had ever bought, he flew to India. There he met with a yogi who thirty years earlier had taken an oath not to move from his seated position. "What drives me endlessly from one place to the other, from one country to the other?" Wiesel asked, acknowledging his own restlessness.

He spent "an unforgettable evening" in an ashram, "listening" to stars, contemplating divinity. Yet he was disturbed dur-

ing the trip by more tangible scenes that revealed the wretch-
edness of India's poor, particularly the many orphaned, homeless
beggars he saw on the streets consumed by leprosy or missing
limbs. He wondered why the government would tolerate such
misery. And he was put off by the rigidity of the ancient caste
system. Although Hinduism's answers to the riddles of existence and of God stimulated him, he returned to Paris "more
Jewish than before."[10]

Still, as Frederick L. Downing wrote in a "religious biography" of Elie Wiesel, his perplexity about the persistence of
evil and suffering only increased after his trip to India. Downing speculates that Wiesel concluded that he needed to find the
answers he sought within Judaism and within his own experience as he started to write down in Yiddish his testimony of
Auschwitz and Buchenwald.[11]

7

Night *and Fog*

Wiesel began to write the manuscript that would eventually become his slim masterpiece, *Night*, on a voyage to Brazil in the spring of 1954. He was on assignment from Dov Judkowski, the nephew of *Yedioth*'s owner, and also a survivor. Judkowski, who went on to become the newspaper's esteemed editor-in-chief, had alerted him to suspicious Catholic missionaries working in Israel who were promising survivors free trips to Brazil along with entrance visas and gifts of two hundred dollars if they would convert to Catholicism. Apparently, there were quite a few Jews who were unhappy enough with the struggles of life in Israel to take the missionaries up on their offer, and Judkowski felt their story had the makings of a good exclusive.

Wiesel also needed the six-week ocean voyage to wrestle with that personal matter tearing at his conscience—whether to wed Hanna, the beautiful daughter of a children's home administrator in Versailles with whom he had a contentious relationship but who nevertheless had proposed that they consider marrying. Elie, his memoir suggests, was clearly not ready to contemplate marriage. "When we see each other again, you'll ask the same question and I'll say yes, and it will be a yes without reservations," he told Hanna. "But you'll have to ask it again. Okay?"[1] Those were not the words of a man who knew he wanted to marry.

Wiesel claimed that he actually spent most of the voyage from Marseilles to São Paulo aboard the *Provence* writing down his account of life in the Sighet ghetto, and of his time in Auschwitz and Buchenwald. He wrote feverishly in Yiddish, he said, without stopping to catch his breath.

"I wrote to testify, to stop the dead from dying, to justify my own survival," he said in the memoir. "I wrote to speak to those who were gone. As long as I spoke to them, they would live on, at least in my memory."[2]

Wiesel would say on various occasions that he had taken a vow after Buchenwald not to speak or write about his experience for ten years. Yet in the Yiddish version of *Night*, he states that he started writing an outline within weeks of liberation while in the Buchenwald hospital recovering from food poisoning. And although he claims he wrote the entire draft during the crossing to Brazil, pounding away on a portable typewriter, it is difficult to believe that he could have completed 862 pages in just a few weeks. Moreover, Joel Rappel, the founder of the Wiesel archive at Boston University, came across letters and other evidence suggesting that an embryonic version of *Night* may have been written at the orphanage in Ambloy and that Wiesel boarded the ship in Marseilles with a manuscript that only required editing, which was done by a companion during the crossing. Indeed Wiesel wrote another friend in Palestine saying that he spent much of the voyage sunning himself on deck, a picture at odds with one of Wiesel closeted in his cabin writing furiously.[3] Ultimately, the discrepancies may be much ado about very little, perhaps opening Wiesel to a minor charge of overdramatizing. A writer's mind is always writing, and whether pieces of *Night* were formulated long before the ten years of the pledge expired, the Yiddish manuscript that was Wiesel's first complete draft of *Night* was brought forth on that voyage.

In a piece he wrote for the Yiddish *Forverts* that was translated only recently, Wiesel also told of conducting a Passover seder for fifty of the ship's passengers, thirty of whom were "apostates" who had been enticed by the missionaries. "They sheepishly entered the dining hall and silently sat down at the table, where matzos and kosher wine symbolized their connection to the old traditions of the Jewish people," Wiesel wrote. "At that moment, I remembered our Sages. Even at the gates of Hell, they said, a wicked person can repent. And they were correct, our Sages. It is enough that he witness an old-time Passover seder for even the worst apostate to free himself of his shackles."[4]

As the ship's passengers were getting ready to disembark in São Paulo, Wiesel learned that the gaggle of Hebrew-speaking refugees—there were forty in all—had already made half-hearted conversions, so eager were they to escape the miseries of a struggling new nation. But both he and the group were denied entry to Brazil, so the ship wound its way to Montevideo and then Buenos Aires.

In Buenos Aires, Elie had another lucky break. One of those who came aboard to try to learn about the Israeli group was Mark Turkov, a Jewish publisher who was producing a series of Yiddish memoirs for the Central Union of Polish Jews in Argentina. Turkov noticed the manuscript the young man was clutching, and asked if he could read it.

"I was convinced Turkov wouldn't publish it," Wiesel wrote. "I couldn't see why any editor would be interested in the sad memoirs of a stranger he happened to meet on a ship, surrounded by refugees nobody wanted."[5]

Eventually, that manuscript—which has not been recovered—was whittled down to 245 pages. Years later, Wiesel said he himself did the whittling. In 1956, the book that became the first version of *Night* was published in Argentina under the title *Un di Velt Hot Geshvign* ("And the World Was Silent").

When he got back to Paris, he discovered that Hanna, disappointed that he had not written to her in eight weeks, had left for Palestine ten days before. "I realize what that means," her note said of his silence. "I'm not angry at you." In *All Rivers Run to the Sea* he said, "I was both sad and relieved."[6]

In Paris, Wiesel resumed his footloose life in the Latin Quarter, scribbling away in cafés, hanging out with "starving artists on leave from their garrets," running into an assortment of strange characters—currency smugglers, religious poseurs, vagabonds, impoverished princes—that he said provided fodder for his later novels. In the Pigalle and Les Halles districts, he met the famous streetwalkers of Paris. In *One Generation After*, a volume of memoirs, musings, and fictional dialogues published in 1970, there is a curious story about meeting a prostitute on a summer night near Les Halles, and choosing to hear her views of men over an offer of free sex.

"Do you enjoy making love?" she asks him.

"That depends," he replies.

Later he blames his reluctance to patronize her on the summer heat. But when she cradles his hand he relents. "I had just rediscovered my body," he writes. She tries to kiss him and he pushes away. "Come make love," she says. "It's still the best remedy against feeling lonely, believe me, I know." He refuses and they go their separate ways. Still, he finds himself haunted by her and goes looking for her.[7] Is the story fiction? Clearly, much of the dialogue is his invention. Yet the story offers an insight into the battle raging within the yeshiva boy between carnal temptation and the fear of committing a sin.

Elie finally did have an intimate relationship with a young

American woman "whose beauty left me breathless." Her name was Kathleen and she was introduced to him at the ballet by Shlomo Shragai, a Knesset member from the National Religious Party. Since Elie spoke no English and Kathleen no French, Shragai was a necessary intermediary during intermission. Remarkably, as they talked, Kathleen volunteered to give Wiesel English lessons and, after hesitating, he agreed. Although he discovers that she is a gentile midwesterner engaged to be married, he nevertheless visits her apartment. The scene at her home the next evening is comical. Wiesel takes Kathleen's hand and kisses her, but when she suggests they make love and guides him to her bed, he decides she is a virgin and realizes he does not wish to violate her. Instead he lectures her about the resemblance between the Hebrew words for holiness and prostitute and then, resorting to his immersion in Hinduism, explains the belief that every union is a reunion. By three in the morning she is exhausted and Wiesel goes home. But they see each other every evening for the next few weeks, and although Wiesel never says so explicitly, it is clear that he had gotten over his inhibitions.[8] "As always when I transgressed the rules of my own making, a shiver ran through me: what if my father saw me now, what if my grandfather knew."[9]

The relationship continued for a few months until 1955, but it could not last. There was the matter of the fiancé, a Greek. In fact, she ended up marrying a Jewish industrialist from the Midwest, but his memoir suggests she had one last tryst with Wiesel in New York.

By his mid-twenties, Wiesel was already becoming a respected journalist. He was securing important assignments and occasional scoops and writing lively interviews and evocative features, all of which he would send by telex to Israel from the offices of Radio France. He even snagged an interview with France's Jewish premier, Pierre Mendès-France, though it took several attempts till a meeting occurred. After Wiesel's death,

Shlomo Nakdimon, an Israeli political commentator, perused back issues of *Yedioth Ahronoth* and concluded "his stories enriched it with hundreds of lead headlines and numberless revelations."[10]

Elie was about to become a respected memoirist as well.

In 1954, he had been invited to an Israeli Independence Day celebration at the Israeli embassy in Paris. Among those in attendance was François Mauriac, who had won the Nobel Prize for Literature three years before. Wiesel buttonholed Mauriac at the event. He hoped that by interviewing Mauriac he might secure his help in arranging a meeting with Mendès-France, a friend of Mauriac's. When Mauriac agreed to an interview, Wiesel read and re-read Mauriac's novels, which were full of Catholic themes of sin, forbidden love, and grace.

Their meeting took place at Mauriac's elegant apartment in the posh 16th arrondissement of Paris, though Wiesel was immediately impressed by the novelist's "simplicity and warmth." They talked politics, with Mauriac going off on a lengthy monologue about the extremist parties in France. It's not clear if it was then or later that Mauriac revealed that he had at first supported Marshal Philippe Pétain's regime that collaborated with the Nazi occupiers, because he believed Pétain had "the interest of France at heart." They talked about Israel and the Jews, whom Mauriac described as "a chosen people in more ways than one, a people of witnesses, a people of martyrs."[11] But then Mauriac swerved to his favorite topic—the life and death of Jesus—and Wiesel confronted him:

> When he said Jesus again I couldn't take it, and for the only time in my life I was discourteous, which I regret to this day. I said, "Mr. Mauriac,"—we called him Maître—"ten years or so ago, I have seen children, hundreds of Jewish children, who suffered more than Jesus did on his cross and we do not speak about it." I felt all of a sudden so embarrassed. I closed my notebook and went to the elevator. He

ran after me. He pulled me back; he sat down in his chair, and I in mine, and he began weeping . . . And then, at the end, without saying anything, he simply said, "You know, maybe you should talk about it"—

"It" being Wiesel's ordeal in Auschwitz and Buchenwald. In an essay in *A Jew Today*, he also remembered Mauriac as expressing the view that he, Wiesel, "stands on the border" between the Jewish and Christian testaments, like John the Baptist. The implication was that Wiesel was drawn to the notion of the divinity of Jesus, which the young man gently corrected.[12] Although the encounter was tense, Wiesel called it one of the most important of his life.

"I had no right to hurt him," reflected Wiesel, "especially since he never sought to use his faith as a sword against mine. On the contrary it was because he loved Jesus that he defended Jews, because he suffered at Jesus' suffering that he strove to assuage ours."[13]

Mauriac again wondered why Wiesel had never written about his experience in the concentration camps. "I think that you are wrong not to speak. . . . Listen to the old man that I am: one must speak out—one must *also* speak out."

Wiesel finally disclosed that in fact he had written—in Yiddish—a memoir of his camp experiences. Mauriac urged him to translate that manuscript into French. A year later, when Wiesel had penned a French version, Mauriac was the first person to read it. He was so impressed and overcome that he promptly took it to his publisher, Flammarion. The editor there turned it down, saying, "No one is interested in the death camps anymore." It was a mere nine years after the liberation. Fortunately, Mauriac did not give up and made a subsequent submission to Jérôme Lindon at Les Éditions de Minuit, Samuel Beckett's publisher, which accepted the manuscript for publication. Lindon was pleased when Wiesel came up with a new title, *La Nuit*, and pared the translated Yiddish work down to 178 pages. (It is not clear what cuts he or Wiesel made at his or Mauriac's prodding, although scholars continue to research the steps in that process.) Shrewdly, Lindon commissioned a foreword by the esteemed Mauriac. It was the French version published in 1958 that became the basis of the English translations, which have sold more than fourteen million copies to date.

Ruth Wisse, a professor of Yiddish literature and comparative literature at Harvard, believes the new title turned the book's thrust from a polemic about the world's silence to a more resonant metaphor about "the spiritual darkness of the world." In shaping the translation from Yiddish into French, she wrote, "Wiesel improved the book artistically and also neutered it culturally."[14] Thus, she told me in an interview, he made the book more "understandable and salable" to a new French audience."[15] Writing about the translation issue in the *New Republic*, Ruth Franklin, an award-winning biographer, said in crafting the French version "Wiesel was re-imagining his book not for his shrinking Yiddish readership, but for the global audience that it would eventually attain."[16]

A more critical view was expressed by Naomi Seidman, a professor of Jewish culture at the Graduate Theological Union in Berkeley who now teaches at the University of Toronto. She suggested that Wiesel, in his youthful awe of the famous novelist, reworked the Yiddish version into French in ways that sought to win Mauriac's favor and, therefore, his sponsorship for publication. In aiming the manuscript at a more cosmopolitan audience, she said, Wiesel softened the tone of anger and even vengeance laced through the Yiddish version, which had been written with only a Jewish audience in mind. She also noted that Mauriac, in his foreword, emphasized the Catholic view of suffering, drawn from the life of Jesus. Thus the Holocaust placed Jews on the cross of the concentration camps, but symbolically resurrected them in the creation of the state of Israel. Lost in the fog of that metaphorical transition, she argued, was "the historical animosity of Christian against Jew" and the culpability of not just German Christian perpetrators but of Christian bystanders throughout Europe like the Mauriacs. His own wife, Mauriac acknowledged in the foreword, had looked on in horror at cattle cars of Jewish children at Austerlitz station, many torn from their mothers' arms.

The Yiddish title, Seidman continued, indicts the silent world; the French title indicts no one. The Yiddish dedication to Wiesel's dead parents and sister blames "German murderers"; the French version names no one. The Yiddish version mentions young Jewish survivors running off to steal clothing and potatoes "and to rape German girls"; in the French, the Jewish boys steal provisions and just want to have sex but the girls are no longer explicitly German. In the Yiddish version, Wiesel, after Buchenwald is liberated, stares at his skeletal image in a mirror and smashes the glass with his fist; in the French version he merely stares in the mirror. The Yiddish version also includes this fury-filled passage, which is excised in the French: "Now, ten years after Buchenwald, I see that the world is forgetting. Germany is a sovereign state, the German army has been reborn. The bestial sadist of Buchenwald, Ilsa Koch, is happily raising her children. War criminals stroll in the streets of Hamburg and Munich. The past has been erased, forgotten." What cannot be spoken in French, Seidman concluded, is "the scandal of Jewish rage and unwillingness to embody suffering and victimization."[17]

Rabbi Irving (Yitz) Greenberg, a friend of Wiesel's whose organization, CLAL (the National Jewish Center for Learning and Leadership), engaged in outreach to other faiths, believes that by the time Wiesel was working on the French version he, like most writers, was trying to reach a broader audience and tailored his work accordingly. Moreover, Greenberg suggests, he was writing at a time when people were not yet grappling with the moral implications of the Holocaust, and Wiesel had an "intuitive" sense that a broad audience for *Night* could help correct that silence and "get the message across to the world." As Greenberg points out, in later years especially, Wiesel was far from sheepish about confronting Christian audiences directly about the role that a history of hatred of Jews had played in preparing the soil for a campaign of annihilation. At a symposium on the Holocaust at Manhattan's Cathedral of St. John the Divine in 1974, he lamented the willful skepticism still heard outside the Jewish world about what was done to the Jews, citing a professor of humanities at the Sorbonne who a few weeks earlier had asked Yad Vashem whether the gas chambers were myth or reality. "Thus, one generation after the event," Wiesel told the crowd in the symposium's opening address, "there is a professor of humanities who does not know . . . who asks for proof that Auschwitz indeed existed and that the Final Solution was not a madman's dream but official policy enacted and implemented by hundreds of thousands of men and women."[18]

Wisse, who affectionately recalls several meetings in Boston where she and Wiesel enjoyed conversing in Yiddish, remembers that Wiesel was pained by Seidman's attack. "You have to adapt what you're saying to the people you're speaking to," she told me. "Wiesel was a bright guy, he had *sechel* [common sense] as well. He didn't survive for nothing. He knew that when you were writing for a French audience, you write differently, so of course it reads differently. He wasn't going to say at the end to a French audience that 'the world was silent.'"[19]

Had Wiesel written a polemical indictment of Christians, *Night* would not have achieved universal stature, and it would not have become required reading in schools throughout the world. In a conversation with Michael Berenbaum, John Roth, a Protestant scholar of the Holocaust, said that had Wiesel written his books and speeches only for Jews, Christians like him would never have been exposed to Wiesel's thinking. Berenbaum added that with *Night*, Wiesel had "found a new way to position himself within Jewish tradition, yet still find a Jewish language in which to speak to the modern, post-Holocaust non-Jewish world. He became the symbol of the survivor who emerged from the flames burning with the need to tell the story and engage the world; to warn, chasten and speak out."[20]

Ruth Franklin, writing in the *New Republic*, argues that it is the very spareness of the prose, unembellished by interpretation, or polemic, that gives the memoir its devastating power. "By refusing to add the rationality of explanation or the cynicism of hindsight," she writes, "*Night* takes us back to its terrible story with something resembling innocence, the innocence of a young boy who, like the rest of the Jews of Europe, had no idea what was coming. To read it is to lose one's own innocence about the Holocaust all over again."[21]

8

Coming to America

On a ship to Israel to meet with his editors, Wiesel once again found himself contemplating suicide. As he gazed at the ocean, he wondered what it would be like to merge with the waves, and whether or not he would at last find peace. Fortunately, those thoughts were transient.

Once in Israel he was greeted with an offer from *Yedioth Ahronoth* that lifted his spirits: would he become the paper's New York correspondent? The pay of $160 a month was paltry even by the standards of the time. But Judkowski, the editor, now a good friend, persuaded him that he could supplement his income with speaking engagements, a suggestion that turned out to have enormous impact once Wiesel began accepting such offers. He took the correspondent's job with the fatalism that had been steering him since the war. So in 1956, armed with a journalist's visa, he arrived in New York City.

New York in the mid-1950s was emerging from the shadow

of the postwar period. Crime was low, a subway ride cost fifteen cents, and the recent wave of immigrants displaced by the war lent the city a cultivated European air. After a period of housing shortages resulting from the flood of returning war veterans, more apartments became available as landlords cut up brownstones into rooming houses and sprawling flats into studios and one-bedrooms. An entire family could scrape by on fifty dollars a week, a little more than what Wiesel, a single man, was earning.

After arriving that winter on an El Al flight, he spent a few days at the Alamac Hotel on West Seventy-first Street and Broadway, then camped out in Upper Manhattan with an uncle, Samuel Wiesel, who worked in a necktie factory. During his short stay, he learned something about his father that both touched him and left him angry and perplexed. A few years before the deportations of Hungarian Jews, his uncle had entered the United States on a visa originally approved for Shlomo Wiesel and his family. Shlomo had given the visa to Samuel because he did not feel he, Shlomo, could successfully support his family as an immigrant to the United States. What nagged at Wiesel was the thought that had his father used the visa, his immediate family would have been spared.

Wiesel soon found a room at the Masters residential hotel on 103rd Street and Riverside Drive. It was narrow and cramped, but had a head-on view of the Hudson and the Palisades. This was where he would live—with his many books—until he married in 1969.

In those days especially, the Upper West Side abounded with Jewish refugees. Some had immigrated before the war from Germany, Belgium, and Holland, and had been thriving long enough to afford the large family apartments on West End Avenue and Riverside Drive. Others had survived the death camps or found a measure of safety in the Soviet Union, then spent years confined in D.P. camps run by the Allies. They were trying to rebuild their lives in New York, but for most it was a grinding struggle of working in factories or operating candy stores, work that did not require fluency in English. Most lived in the tenements and shabby brownstone rooming houses closer to Central Park.

The refugees mingled in cafeterias, delicatessens, and dairy restaurants along Broadway like Éclair, Famous Dairy, or Gitlitz, where the air was often electric with big cultural ideas and political reflections. Those humble eateries drew writers and editors like Isaac Bashevis Singer, Irving Howe, Hannah Arendt, and Norman Podhoretz. The ideas they talked about must have seemed congenial to a young man who had spent the past decade in Paris.

With the guidance of other Israeli correspondents, Wiesel acquired a desk in the United Nations press room and made a point of showing up nightly at the old *New York Times* offices on West Forty-third Street to learn the next morning's top stories and telegraph the news to *Yedioth*'s editors in Israel. He got to know Abba Eban, Israel's eloquent delegate to the United Nations, who proved to be an important news source. He learned how to work the crowded circuit of diplomatic cocktail parties and receptions not just to scavenge tidbits of news but to save on lunch and dinner expenses. Without leaving New York, he told his readers in Hebrew about the civil rights struggle in America: the violent, fleeting integration of the University of Alabama by Autherine Lucy in 1956, and Martin Luther King's jailing for organizing the Montgomery bus boycott. In another register, he told Israelis about Arthur Miller's improbable marriage to Marilyn Monroe and Broadway's intoxication with *My Fair Lady*.

To supplement his *Yedioth* income, Wiesel found freelance work with Yiddish newspapers. He took on assignments with the legendary *Forverts (Jewish Daily Forward)*, the country's most circulated Yiddish paper. But it was an assignment with a more obscure Yiddish paper, *Der Amerikaner,* that got Wiesel to carve out a new path as a writer. The editor, David Mekler, was an avid reader of fiction and told Wiesel he had a budget for a novel that could be serialized as a regular feature. Wiesel turned out *Silent Heroes,* a romantic spy escapade, and Mekler ran it. Although Wiesel cared so little about the project he did not bother to read the serial once it was printed, it launched his career as a novelist. He was also delighted to be working in his cradle tongue, which, he felt, best conveyed the pathos and humor of the Jewish experience.

"I need Yiddish to laugh and cry, to celebrate and express regret, to delve into my memories anew," he wrote. "Is there a better language for evoking the past with all its horror? Without Yiddish the literature of the Holocaust would have no soul. I know that had I not written my first account in Yiddish, I would have written no others."[1]

Although new to America, he was no longer new to the adventures of dating. One of the young women he asked out was Irena—Wiesel calls her Aviva in his memoir—the tall blond secretary to *Yedioth*'s owner. She was vacationing in New York and after several walks in Central Park and visits to museums, she accompanied him on a hot, muggy night in July 1956 on his usual excursion to the *Times* office to scan the next day's headlines. After sending his cable to *Yedioth,* he and Irena headed to Times Square to see a movie. (In his memoir, Wiesel recalls the film as *The Brothers Karamazov,* whose existential motifs and debates about a God that permits suffering dovetailed neatly with his own metaphysical views and with what was about to happen. But that film was not released until February 1958.)[2]

As they crossed the frenzied square at Forty-fifth Street and Seventh Avenue, seemingly out of nowhere a taxi plowed into him, its screeching brakes the last sound he heard before losing consciousness. (In his fictional account of the accident he suggests that the taxi drove through a red light and that he

never saw it coming.) The taxi hurled him in the air, as he recalled, "like a figure in a Chagall painting, all the way to 44th
Street."[3] He was left lying on the asphalt unconscious, his body
mangled, his mouth filled with blood. An ambulance took him
to a hospital he does not name that turned him down as an
uninsured indigent, and he ended up at New York Hospital on
Manhattan's Upper East Side. There doctors discovered that
both his legs were broken and his hip, ribs, ankle, and other
bones on his left side had been shattered, a total of forty-seven
fractures along with several ruptured blood vessels besides.
The initial repairs required a ten-hour operation. Afterward,
he was placed in a body cast, with only his head, arms, and toes
exposed. He remained comatose for almost a week and was
hospitalized for months thereafter. Of course, the irony of a
survivor of the death camps who is nearly killed in this way was
lost on no one who knew him.

He shared his physical and philosophical pain with those
who treated him. The orthopedic surgeon who deftly performed
the operation, Dr. Paul Braunstein, remembered Wiesel as a
frail, lonely soul who was caught up in a religious crisis, denying the existence of God but talking about little else. "He was
one of the most religious people I had ever met," Dr. Braunstein wrote.[4]

Because he had no medical insurance, Wiesel's hospital bill
was paid for by someone he had interviewed for a newspaper
article just a few weeks earlier: Hillel Kook, alias Peter Berg-
son, an Irgun icon who had helped save scores of Jews fleeing
the Nazis and arranged entry into the United States for many.
By 1956, he was making a small fortune as a Wall Street stock-
broker and gave Elie blank checks to pay the hospital, asking
only that he turn over any money he might collect from the cab
company's insurer.

Wiesel memorialized his being run over in Times Square
in a novel called *The Accident* in 1962, later renamed *Day* (and

dedicated to Dr. Braunstein) to conform with the titles *Night* and *Dawn*, thereby forming a trilogy whose stories were linked by their Holocaust and post-Holocaust themes. In a preface to *Day*, Wiesel seemed to downplay the idea that he was in any way responsible for the incident, stating emphatically: "The possibility of a suicidal impulse was invented for the sake of the story." Yet he also adds that after Auschwitz, a suicidal impulse was not unreasonable. "Does life have meaning after Auschwitz?" he wrote in the preface. "In a universe cursed because it is guilty, is hope still possible? For a young survivor whose knowledge of life and death surpasses that of his elders, wouldn't suicide be as great a temptation as love or faith?"[5] And in the novel itself his protagonist wonders "why fate has spared *him* and not so many others. Was it to know happiness? His happiness will never be complete. Was it to know love? He will never be sure of being worthy of love."

While in the hospital, Wiesel received a steady stream of journalistic colleagues as well as Irena—his date on the night of the accident—and his sister Bea. Gradually, while still at the hospital, he resumed working, sitting up and writing by hand. When he finally left in a wheelchair and returned to his West Side apartment, the news kept him busy. President Gamal Abdel Nasser of Egypt had nationalized the Suez Canal, and Israel, with covert backing from the British and the French, had begun a sweep across the Sinai to allow the Western powers to re-gain control of the canal. Wiesel was fortunate that the debates over the Suez Crisis were staged at the United Nations. First in his wheelchair and then on crutches he was able to cover the speeches by Abba Eban, and the statements supporting Israel by France and Britain, all of which was manna to his Israeli readers. He also became well acquainted with Golda Meir after she was named foreign minister and visited New York. Meir was moved by this stateless correspondent speaking perfect Hebrew and hobbling about her office on crutches.

Of course, the work was seldom as engaging as it was during the Suez Crisis. In a revealing passage in *Day*, just before the accident occurs, Wiesel describes sending a routine cable this way: "Five hundred words to say nothing. To cover up another empty day. It was one of those quiet and monotonous Sundays that leave no mark on time."[6]

When the year-long visa allowing him to work in America was about to expire, Wiesel learned that to get it extended he would have to travel back to France and wrestle with the notorious French bureaucracy. He decided instead to acquire an American green card, which would allow him to become a resident and apply for citizenship.

He got to see quite a bit of his adopted land in 1957 when Dov Judkowski and his wife, Leah, invited him to join them on a six-week cross-country tour of the United States. Walking much of the time with a cane, which, he said, "made me look rather distinguished," Wiesel was dazzled by the majesty of the Grand Canyon and the Rockies, where the peaks gave him a "sense of being present at a re-creation of the world." Disneyland, which had opened just two years before, awakened the child in him, and he was delighted by Frontierland, the Mark Twain Riverboat, and Main Street, U.S.A. In an article for the Yiddish *Forward*, he told readers, "It's not yet clear to me whether we must thank Him [God] for creating the world, but I am certain all children who visit Walt Disney's paradise will thank Him endlessly for having built Disneyland."[7]

On the other hand, he and the Judkowskis were put off by the glitz of Las Vegas, the "frozen faces and trembling hands" of the gamblers, and the South's "unforgiveable humiliation of its black citizens." On an Indian reservation, they shared a good laugh. The guide who greeted them spoke Yiddish. It turned out he was a concentration camp survivor from Poland who had ended up taking this anomalous job.[8]

9

Writer

LA NUIT RECEIVED favorable reviews in France, Belgium, and Switzerland, with the Paris-based weekly *Le Journal du Dimanche* calling it "an exceptional book" that is "written in a dense and sober style, without one useless word. It is perhaps greater than the poignant and pure *Diary of Anne Frank*."[1] Wiesel flew to France for publication and was interviewed by the cultural journalist Pierre Dumayet. He also had a lunch with Samuel Beckett, appropriately marked by long periods of silence.[2] Despite all the attention, the book sold poorly.

In 1958, Georges Borchardt, a young French literary agent who represented notable foreign authors including Beckett and Marguerite Duras and brought them to the attention of American publishers, received a copy of *La Nuit* from Jérôme Lindon along with a letter asking if he would be interested in trying to get an English-language version published. Borchardt read the book and was deeply moved. He was a Jewish survivor too, although he had grown up in a well-to-do family in Paris (his father was head of the Polydor record company, which produced Édith Piaf's recordings). With the help of a French professor who knew his parents, he had spent the Nazi occupation in plain sight as an unregistered student at a lycée in Aix-en-Provence. Borchardt's mother was killed in Auschwitz and many relatives died in other camps. A former teacher with an elegant manner and a penetrating intelligence, he told me in an interview in 2017, when he was almost ninety, that he realized *Night* would not be an easy sell.

"Nobody wanted to hear about the concentration camps and nobody could have predicted that there would be such a thing as Holocaust studies," he said. Still, he wrote an impassioned letter that he sent to various mainstream publishers, praising the book as one "that I feel more strongly about than any other I ever sent you."[3] *Night* was rejected in short order by Simon & Schuster, Dutton, and twelve other publishers; some of them thought it was more a testimonial to the survivors than a fully-realized literary work. Scribner's said it "had certain misgivings as to the size of the American market for what remains, despite Mauriac's brilliant introduction, a document." The legendary Kurt and Helen Wolff at Pantheon said they had decided not to publish "books of this kind." Blanche Knopf of Alfred A. Knopf said the book was not "going to be for us."[4]

Meanwhile, Borchardt arranged to meet Wiesel, who showed up at his apartment "limping and carrying a cane." The two European-bred bachelors, each roughly thirty, hit it off immediately. They started having dinners at an Italian restaurant on West Fifty-fourth Street and talking about books they were reading or music they enjoyed. The evenings typically went on until Wiesel had to slip away to send his daily cable to Israel.

"It was very casual, the kind of friendship where you call up at six P.M. and say, 'Are you doing anything?'" Borchardt told me. "He was not yet Elie Wiesel and I was not yet a successful agent. Neither of us quite fit in, both of us were struggling, but we were quite happy with what we were doing."

Borchardt noticed that Wiesel ate at places that were not kosher. He "didn't seem particularly religious when I knew him," said Borchardt, who describes himself as a Jew by birth but an atheist by conviction. "He was angry at God for having allowed the Holocaust to happen. Later he became very religious."

"He was very shy. I remember a party we went to. When I left I heard footsteps. I asked him why he didn't stay. He said, 'If you're leaving, I'm leaving.' He didn't like parties. He was a loner."

Still, Wiesel dressed well despite his modest income, Borchardt remembered. "You didn't need that much money in those days. Rents were not that high. I lived on West 55th Street for $225 a month. For $2.40 you could get a seat in the theater and during intermission sneak down to an empty seat in the orchestra." Wiesel could even afford a car and once drove Borchardt and his new wife, Anne, to Idlewild, as John F. Kennedy International Airport was then called.[5]

Finally, in the fall of 1959, an offer was made for the American and Canadian publishing rights of *Night* by Hill & Wang, a small literary house on lower Fifth Avenue. Over lunch, Borchardt had been able to interest its founder, Arthur Wang, in the idea of the book. Ultimately, Wang offered an extremely modest advance: $250, payable in two installments, $100 on signature and $150 upon publication. Once the book was published, Wiesel would receive five percent of the first 1,500 sales, ten percent of the next 6,000, and fifteen percent thereafter. One condition: a British publisher had to be found to share the costs of translation. In an aerogram to Jérôme Lindon to tell him the news, Borchardt admitted that the offer "n'est pas extraordinaire"—an understatement—but given the reluctance of so many publishers to buy the book, he was ecstatic. "Elie est ravi!" ("Elie is delighted!"), he told Lindon.[6]

Night was published in English in the fall of 1960 in a translation from the French by Stella Rodway. Gertrude Samuels appraised the 116-page book in the *Times Book Review* and called it "a slim volume of terrifying power," and "a remarkable close-up of one boy's tragedy."[7] It is telling that Samuels, who had toured the postwar refugee camps in Europe on assignment for the *Times*, opened the review by observing that "for some people it is too early to forget the effects of the Nazis' rule on Europe." The truth was that Americans and Europeans were already trying to put the uncomfortable facts of the Holocaust behind them. A pall of silence and willed ignorance had descended. The word "Holocaust"—originally a Greek term to describe the burning of an animal sacrifice—had been used historically to refer to large-scale slaughter but was not yet used with a capital H to describe the cataclysm that swallowed six million Jews. Wiesel sometimes took credit for first using the word in this context.[8]

There were no courses that focused entirely on the subject. With the exception of a few published testimonies from inmates and resistance fighters, relatively little had been written at that point about the ghettoes and death camps and the slaughter of six million Jews. *The Diary of Anne Frank*, haunting and popular as it was, was really about a precocious girl's two years in hiding in Amsterdam; it did not dwell on her death from typhus in Bergen-Belsen. William Shirer's 1,200-page *The Rise and Fall of the Third Reich* was a bestseller in 1960, but it was a history of the Hitler regime that chronicled the Jewish catastrophe as one of many in a brutal world war. Raul Hilberg's *The Destruction of the European Jews*, published the year after *Night*, is widely considered the first comprehensive study of the Final Solution, but that manuscript was rejected by leading academic presses and finally published by a small house, Quadrangle Books. Even in yeshivas that were filled with refugee children, like the one I attended in the 1950s, almost nothing was said about the near annihilation of European Jewry only a decade earlier. Secular books about the Holocaust were often rejected by Orthodox rabbis because they raised the specter of God's complicity in allowing such unimpeded slaughter of the faithful; an acceptable book, for them, needed to convey the values of *kiddush Hashem* (sanctification of God's name by martyrdom and other acts that spur others to glorify God, a concept sometimes applied to the Jewish victims of the Holocaust).[9] As late as 1974, delegates at the biennial convention of the Union of Orthodox Jewish Congregations of America found it necessary to pass a resolution calling on yeshivas to make the study of the Holocaust a major part of their curricula.[10] The fate of the six million was also absent from many war movies that followed the Allied victory; a film such as *The Pawnbroker*, which told the story of an embittered survivor in New York, was a rarity.

Survivors and American Jews tended not to talk much about the Holocaust either. Commentators who wondered about this void—one that with a few exceptions would last almost a quarter century—theorized that the survivors were either too traumatized, fearful, ashamed, or still gripped by mourning to grapple with what they had been through, or they were too busy raising families and rebuilding their lives.[11] And American Jews, some commentators speculate, were too riddled with guilt for having let such a catastrophe transpire to delve into stories of suffering and unspeakable loss. Or perhaps they simply preferred to ward off painful conversations.

Hasia Diner, a professor of American Jewish history at New York University, published a study in 2009 that sought to refute what her title called "the myth of silence after the Holocaust" in the first two postwar decades.[12] She cited Holocaust observances, survivor gatherings, statements by Jewish organizations, and more. But as Jerome Chanes argued in his review of her book for the *Forward*, whatever took place was "marginal to the core agendas of American Jews, both individually and as a community."[13]

This may explain why, in spite of the glowing review by Samuels, *Night* did not attract much of an audience in the United States. The book sold roughly two thousand copies in the first two years after its publication in English. Indeed, when Arthur Wang died in 2005, Wiesel reflected on how audacious the publisher had been to take a chance on *Night*. "At the time, people didn't want to hear about that period," Wiesel told Dinitia Smith of the *New York Times*. "They said, 'Why should people read such morbid stuff?'"[14]

Between journalistic assignments, Wiesel began working on the novella that became *Dawn*. In *All Rivers Run to the Sea* he spoke of writing as "a painful pleasure" and analyzed his "deliberately spare style." "It is the style of the chroniclers of the ghettos, where everything had to be said swiftly, in one breath," he wrote. "You never knew when the enemy might kick in the door, sweeping us away into nothingness. Every phrase was a testament."[15]

Journalism, though, was still his prime livelihood. A major story in Israel in 1962 was the kidnapping of a Hasidic boy, Yossele Shuchmacher, by his grandfather, who felt the boy's parents were neglecting his Torah education. Ben-Gurion ordered a worldwide search for the boy, and the Mossad assigned the case to Isser Harel, the intelligence operative who had engineered the kidnapping of Adolf Eichmann from Buenos Aires two years earlier. Wiesel learned from a friend in the Mossad that the boy was in Brooklyn, and even though he was not the first to report the boy's recovery, he was the first to land an interview with him. With the parallels in their upbringing, Wiesel found himself dissecting a page of Talmud with the boy, which became the nub of the story he wrote for *Yedioth Ahronoth*.[16]

The novella *Dawn* was an odd choice for Wiesel as his first published book of serious fiction. The story was inspired not by his direct experience but from a philosophical question debated among Holocaust survivors: the morality of revenge, of "an eye for an eye." The plot is relatively simple: A Jewish underground fighter, David ben Moshe, is about to be hanged by the British authorities overseeing Palestine, and the protagonist, a camp survivor and fellow underground fighter named Elisha, has been charged with executing a British captain, John Dawson, as a reprisal. The novel asks: Is a revenge killing a moral act? And, by implication, does the suffering of the Holocaust victims and their desire for a land of their own entitle Jews to inflict suffering on others? The novel has the structure of a morality tale, yet Wiesel infuses the story with enough resonant detail—Elisha's background as a Hungarian boy steeped in Hasidic mysticism and rendered an orphan by the war, Dawson's background as the loving father of a Cambridge student—that the story raises other questions, too: Is an enemy ever faceless? Is there a common humanity that in certain cases nullifies revenge?

In his preface to the 2008 paperback *The Night Trilogy: Night/Dawn/Day*, which he wrote in a post-9/11 world acutely sensitive to international terrorism, Wiesel said he had often mused about what might have happened had he gone to British-controlled Palestine after the war rather than to France. Would he have had the courage to join the resistance? "And if so, could I have gone all the way in my commitment and killed a man, a stranger? . . . How are we ever to break the cycle of violence and rage? Can terror coexist with justice? Does murder call for murder, despair for revenge? Can hate engender anything but hate?" *Dawn*, Wiesel said, affirms that "hatred is never an answer, and that death nullifies all answers. . . . It aims to put on guard all of those who, in the name of their faith or of some ideal, commit cruel acts of terrorism against innocent victims."[17]

In the novella's evocative concluding paragraph, Wiesel describes the moments after Dawson has been shot: "The night lifted, leaving behind a grayish light the color of stagnant water. Soon there was only a tattered fragment of darkness, hanging in midair, the other side of the window. Fear caught my throat. The tattered fragment of darkness had a face. Looking at it, I understood the reason for my fear. The face was my own."[18]

Although Lindon turned down the manuscript, Monique Nathan, an editor at Éditions du Seuil, liked the short work, called *L'Aube* in French, and the house took Wiesel on. The relationship lasted twenty years, and Nathan was his editor for ten of those until her death. Hill & Wang published a ninety-page English edition of *Dawn* in the summer of 1961, with a translation by Frances Frenaye. In his *Times* review, Herbert Mitgang said the book's mood is "Biblical and mystical" but also "frightening and thoughtful." Wiesel, he said, was "unashamedly philosophical in the manner of Graham Greene or our own Robert Penn Warren." He contrasted *Dawn* with *Exodus*, the 1958 bestseller about Israel's creation, saying that "Israelis who found *Exodus* merely a well-intentioned romance would find *Dawn* a book that hits home at the unsentimental heart, a strong morality tale written from the inside."[19]

The *New York Post* serialized *Dawn* and also ran a profile of Wiesel, his first in a significant American newspaper. It was by Joseph Wershba, who went on to become one of the original producers of *60 Minutes*, and it gave Wiesel an opportunity to convey to a relatively broad audience some of his views on the Holocaust. He condemned the complicity of ordinary Germans and their collaborators in France and other occupied countries, rejecting the idea that the Holocaust was perpetrated only by monstrous degenerates. And he took revered world leaders like Churchill and Roosevelt to task for not calling greater attention to the destruction of Europe's Jews. How was it possible, he asked in the interview, that Jews in Hungary in 1944 could board trains headed for Auschwitz not knowing it was an extermination camp when world leaders had known of such camps since 1942?

The timing of this interview was ideal, spotlighting Wiesel

after broadcasts of the 1961 trial in Jerusalem of Adolf Eichmann, architect of the efficient deportation of Jews to the death camps, had riveted the world. The Eichmann trial is often cited as the first of several events that tore away the postwar shroud of silence. In fact, Wiesel covered that trial, having been dispatched to Jerusalem by the *Jewish Daily Forward*.

In his memoir *All Rivers Run to the Sea*, Wiesel talked about the chilling ordinariness of Eichmann, how striking it was that he seemed unmoved at the recitation of his crimes. "It irritated me to think of Eichmann as human. I would have preferred him to have a monstrous countenance, like a Picasso portrait with three ears and four eyes."[20] Wiesel wondered whether he had seen him at Sighet as he took charge of the last deportation, which included Wiesel's family.

But the memoir also makes clear that he felt the competitive rush of a journalist covering a world event on deadline, one that was drawing hordes of other journalists. He describes a few of his rivals, particularly Hannah Arendt, whose coverage yielded her famous "banality of evil" essay for the *New Yorker*. Wiesel found her remote, condescending, and lacking in feeling for the millions of Jewish dead. (The German-born Israeli philosopher Gershom Scholem accused her of lacking "love of the Jewish people," a charge she acknowledged, saying she had never felt love for "any people or collective" and only believed in a "love of persons.")[21] The later revelations that she was the lover of the philosopher Martin Heidegger, a lifelong admirer of Nazi doctrines, with whom she had a five-year affair as his student from 1925 to 1930 and a more ambiguous two-year romance seventeen years later, seemed to accord with the cool dispassion of her observations. Still, there does not seem to be a huge distinction between Arendt's "banality of evil" and Wiesel's observation of how "ordinary" Eichmann seemed.

Wiesel, however, firmly rejected Arendt's view of the Jews having passively gone to their deaths like sheep to the slaugh-

‑ter. In a powerful essay written in the early 1960s, "A Plea for the Dead," Wiesel recalled his own experience as a fifteen-year-old in Sighet, and the delusions that led communities to be overcautious and indecisive rather than passive. Younger people spoke up for an uprising but "older people spoke up against it: God may intervene even at the very last moment; one must not precipitate matters. The argument spread. Then it was too late. The uprising did not take place. And the Almighty did not intervene."[22] As he told Wershba in the *Post*, even in Auschwitz, Jews who thought about escaping knew that the first Pole they encountered would turn them over to the Nazis. "In the end, the Jews accepted death," he continued. "It was their only way of protest. What could they do when the whole world forgot them?"[23]

Clearly, the Germans had learned before the war and in its early years that the West was not eager to save Jewish lives. The United States and Western Europe took few measures against a succession of outrages: the Nuremberg Laws, Kristallnacht, the walling off of ghettoes, the deportations. Even Eichmann scoffed at his trial that he had offered the West the opportunity to ransom the lives of one million Jews, but no country offered to take them in. Yet, as Wiesel noted, it had become fashionable in intellectual circles to blame the victims for their deaths, to say "they are the cause of their own tragedy." Given the moral bankruptcy of those making such judgments, he argued, "let the dead rest in peace."

"Do not ask them the meaning of their death. It might prove dangerous. These dead have their questions and they might well be more disturbing than our own."[24]

10

Survivor

EVEN THOUGH he was a relative newcomer to New York, Wiesel formed bonds with many activist refugees in the area. More than 140,000 Jewish refugees from Europe settled in the United States between 1947 and 1953, the bulk of them in New York City. A corps of these individuals emerged as advocates committed to helping Jews win compensation from Germany for slave labor or reparations for what they had suffered or to memorialize the Holocaust on anniversaries of important events like the uprising by Warsaw Ghetto fighters in 1943. In so doing they began to frame the refugees as an identifiable group: the Holocaust survivors, a term the Americans used and soon adopted.

There were people like Josef Rosensaft, who set up the intricate governing apparatus at the displaced persons camp created after the war in the former military barracks at Bergen-Belsen, with schools, synagogues, hospitals, newspapers, and theaters; Ben and Vladka Meed, two of the underground partisans of the Warsaw Ghetto; Sam Bloch, a partisan who ended up in Bergen-Belsen; and Sigmund Strochlitz, a survivor of both Auschwitz-Birkenau and Bergen-Belsen who, like Wiesel, had lost a younger sister. Beyond their shared scars from the Holocaust, they meshed in other ways, too. Rosensaft, for example, shared with Wiesel a Hasidic background, a sharp sense of humor, and a love of music. All would become successful in America, dealing in real estate (Rosensaft), cars (Strochlitz), or import-export businesses (Meed). By 1963 these survivors were organized enough to sponsor an annual Holocaust commemoration under the auspices of what was then called the Warsaw Ghetto Resistance Organization (absorbed in the 1980s into the American Gathering of Jewish Holocaust Survivors). Rosensaft and Bloch were instrumental in seeing that Wiesel in 1965 was named the first recipient of the Remembrance Award of the World Federation of Bergen-Belsen Survivors Associations.[1] Its purpose, according to Bloch, was to encourage writers to address the Holocaust in their work at a time when the publishing industry avoided the subject.

Wiesel felt a powerful affinity with this group. As he wrote of the survivors in an essay collected in *A Jew Today*, "you will never know the faces that haunt their nights . . . you will never know the cries that rent their sleep. Accept the idea that you will never penetrate the [ac]cursed and spellbound universe they carry within themselves with unfailing loyalty."[2] He was obviously speaking about himself, as well.

In the early 1960s, Wiesel was still a freelance journalist, getting paid by the article and barely scraping by. Yitz Greenberg, deeply impressed by his reading of the then-obscure *Night*, remembers visiting Wiesel on the Upper West Side and finding a young man with a haunted, hungry look. At the time, Greenberg was an Orthodox American rabbi who pushed for formal academic study of the Holocaust. He recalls inviting Wiesel in the mid-1960s to speak about the Holocaust at the

Riverdale Jewish Center in the Bronx. "He is haunting, fascinating, gripping and as a speaker he will change your life," Greenberg remembers telling his congregants. Yet when Wiesel arrived, not many people had showed up to hear him.

"It's a terrible topic. Who wants to come and hear it?" was one reluctant congregant's explanation.[3]

Wiesel was now in his thirties and, whatever his misgivings about marriage and forging a family in a world that could abide the Holocaust, he was plainly drawn to the women he was meeting in New York. Joel Rappel, Wiesel's archivist, told me there are letters from more than a half dozen women with whom Wiesel had close relationships. One was Michal Mishorit Erlichman, a native of Łódź, Poland, whom he had met in France in 1954. She had served in the Palmach during the 1948 war of independence and studied art in Jerusalem. She lived in New York for several years and studied at Columbia University before marrying Nachman Erlichman and returning to Israel. In a 2017 interview with Rappel, Erlichman, then eighty-eight years old, insisted that despite the archive's affectionate letters her relationship with Wiesel was never romantic. Nevertheless, Rappel told me, "He broke the hearts of several ladies."[4]

The English-language edition of *The Accident*, translated from the French by his agent's wife, Anne Borchardt, was published by Hill & Wang in the spring of 1962. The review in the *Times* was not kind, suggesting that Wiesel undermined his themes with shrill dialogue and forced plot twists. Although the reader, wrote reviewer Herbert Mitgang, is persuaded that "man's conscience was defeated at Auschwitz," the New York setting and stagy scenes dilute the novel's moral urgency. "Somehow what is passionate in another time and place becomes falsely melodramatic in familiar surroundings," Mitgang concluded.

If the review was discouraging, Wiesel was not deterred. In the same year the review appeared, his second novel and third book, *The Town Beyond the Wall*, was published in France to favorable reviews and it received the 1963 Prix Rivarol, awarded annually to a French work by a foreign novelist. The following year, the English edition drew an exuberant review in the *Times Book Review* from Daniel Stern, who declared: "Not since Albert Camus has there been such an eloquent spokesman for man." *Newsweek* was just as complimentary: "God-tormented, God-intoxicated, *The Town Beyond the Wall* is a fiction which refuses to be a novel in any usual sense. It is an exemplary tale such as people may in terror and in hope tell one another. It is a legend—archaic, modern, timeless—of an ascent from purgatory to possibility."[5]

The novel contains some of Wiesel's most poetic writing and provocative themes. The details of the protagonist Michael's life match many of the young Wiesel's in his small Hungarian town, in the concentration camps, and during the postwar years. *The Town Beyond the Wall* also includes Wiesel's love letter to Paris: "Autumn had come. Fleeing his haunted room, Michael discovered the beauty of Paris: under a copper sun the city was bathed in an antique yellow glow. Only the horizon suggested any blue. Paris in the fall is more handsome, more sober than in spring. As if the city were allowing itself to be swept along toward winter, but offering a passive, feminine resistance. It is that resistance which gives it its solemn, ripe beauty."[6]

The novel is based on the imagined return of a Holocaust survivor to his hometown. Though Wiesel would make several postwar trips back to Sighet, the first did not occur until a year after *Town Beyond the Wall* was published. Michael, an orphaned survivor, returns in his thirties to the fictional town of Szerencsevaros, behind the Iron Curtain, where he was born and raised. For his own sanity, he needs to confront a neighbor—known only as The Other, "the face in the window—who looked impassively upon the beating of Jews, their near starvation and their forced deportation and did nothing." This Other is the embodiment of the world's indifference to the slaughters and persecutions of our age, and Michael is, as he says, the messenger for "the dead Jews, the women gone mad, the mute children." "I've come to humiliate you," he tells the Other.[7]

Michael's threat elicits barely a quiver of concern in the man's face. The neighbor informs the Soviet authorities, who incarcerate Michael as a foreign agent, and force him to spend three days and nights standing before a wall to reveal who helped him make his way into the town. While undergoing this torture, Michael remembers a series of people and events in his life: Varady, an old mystic who killed himself rather than be killed by the Germans; Millika, who took care of Varady and whom he met in Paris after the war but could not court because he had not recovered sufficiently to feel love; Yankel, a boyish fellow inmate in the camp who was a pet of the guards and instigated Michael's horsewhipping; and Pedro, a veteran of the Spanish Civil War who became his good friend and helped Michael smuggle his way into his hometown. Later, Michael is locked into a cell with a catatonic boy, and in drawing the boy out, Michael seems to recover a sense of purpose, "the necessity of clinging to humanity."[8]

Wiesel's narrative seems to express ideas that had been germinating in his mind since the war, about the apathy of God in the face of suffering and the responses of humanity in such an uncaring universe. Despite the views of Christian theologians who posit that the suffering of the concentration camp victims would "redeem humanity from its own inner tendencies toward self-destruction," the novel, in Michael Berenbaum's distillation, argues that suffering is neither redemptive nor ennobling, nor does it enlighten mankind in ways that would prevent other atrocities. Yes, Michael's willingness to suffer torture saves Pedro from arrest. But in the larger historical scheme, Auschwitz yielded no transformative lessons. It was followed by other genocides and barbarisms.[9]

Although Wiesel would complicate such views in his later

writings—being a witness to atrocity, he later said, does have redeeming value because the witness has the credibility to warn humanity of roads leading to Auschwitz—what is notable is that in his mid-thirties Wiesel was wrestling with questions raised by the Holocaust that he could not let go of for the rest of his life. He was staking out a distinctive place for himself among the survivors, many of whom may have tackled such questions in their own minds but without Wiesel's literary gifts.

In his memoirs, Wiesel confided that his first works were explicitly written for the survivors: "For they have lived in isolation for a long time, locked away, remaining aloof so as not to wound those close to them. Whenever there was talk of the war years, they would clench their teeth and change the subject. It was impossible to get them to let go, to touch wounds that would never heal. They had reasons to be suspicious, to think that no one was interested in what they had to say, and that in any case they would not be understood. With my books and articles I tried to convince them of the need to testify."[10]

Of course, the list of survivors who became eminent writers is impressively long, including Primo Levi, Paul Celan, Aharon Appelfeld, Jerzy Kosinski, and Imre Kertész, among others. While Wiesel grappled with large philosophical and theological questions, Levi, an industrial chemist by profession, focused more on sharp-edged, almost scientifically precise, though often comic, portraits of the inmates, guards, and kapos he encountered at Auschwitz and Buna and, in *The Periodic Table*, the Jewish relatives and friends who made up his world in Turin before the war. Appelfeld, a Romanian-born Israeli who survived the German menace by escaping a labor camp in Ukraine and hiding among hostile peasants, captured the terror of the Holocaust through indirection. In novels like *Badenheim 1939*, his hapless characters go about their lives blithely blinding themselves to ominous developments like a requirement that Jews register. The horrors occur offstage, lending his chilling stories the absurdist gloss of a Beckett play. Kertész, writing in Hungary, was, like Wiesel, orphaned by the concentration camps. He too struggled with the quandaries of living in a world that he knew could abruptly turn insane and barbaric, and he went on to win the Nobel Prize for Literature in 2002. Thane Rosenbaum, a novelist and child of survivors, said of this group of authors, Wiesel among them: "These men testified to what they had witnessed, but they did so as artists."[11]

Two years after *The Town Beyond the Wall* appeared, Wiesel published *Gates of the Forest*, also considered among his best works. His protagonist, Gregor, also shares some elements of Wiesel's biography. He survived the murder of Jews in a Transylvanian town not unlike Sighet, was deeply shaped by a Hasidic grandfather, and had a father whose affection was not always evident. The story begins not in Auschwitz, but in a cave deep in a forest, where Gregor is hiding from the Germans and their Hungarian collaborators. Somehow, the cave is discovered by a mysterious stranger whom Gregor calls Gavriel. Although at first he seems to be another Jewish fugitive, the reader soon recognizes something otherworldly about him. He recounts meetings with Elijah the prophet, and his intuitive wisdom suggests he may be a protective angel or another of Wiesel's messengers or madmen. This mystical aspect enables Wiesel to range widely among the metaphysical questions raised by the Holocaust: How can humans understand God's absence, His abandonment of the Jews? How does one go on living in a world that allows such monstrous evil? Some critics argued that the mysticism at times deflates the tension in an otherwise riveting plot that includes many suspenseful twists: Gregor's eluding his Hungarian pursuers, a plan by anti-Semitic villagers to cut out Gregor's tongue after they discover he is Jewish and has been posing as a deaf mute, and a romance with the lover of a partisan.

Nevertheless, John Wain, in the *New York Review of Books*, praised *Gates of the Forest* as a "neat allegory of the history of the Jews in modern Europe," adding: "To say that this is an important book would be an understatement."[12] And in the daily *Times* review, Eliot Fremont-Smith called the novel a "profoundly moving exploration" of man's struggle with a God who permitted such slaughter to occur.[13]

Wiesel, meanwhile, began cutting back on his freelance work for *Yedioth* and writing more for the Yiddish *Forverts*. Most of his articles were reviews of books by major writers like Camus, Hemingway, and Kazantzakis, which gained him recognition among the *Forward*'s roster of poets, actors, nihilists, Bundists, and Zionists. His stinging reviews, he noted, were especially appreciated by his colleagues at the paper. "Even the angels in heaven are afflicted by jealousy, the midrash tell us," Wiesel wrote.[14]

At the time, Isaac Bashevis Singer was the *Forward*'s star, someone whose translated stories and novels were popular beyond the Yiddish world and respected by literary critics. But according to Wiesel, other *Forward* writers disparaged Singer behind his back. They "complained of his greed, egocentricity and vanity" and of his penchant for populating his fiction with distasteful Jewish stereotypes.

The two *schreibers*—Yiddish for writers—sometimes took the subway together uptown to their respective West Side apartments (Singer was living at the palatial but fraying Belnord on Eighty-sixth Street) and on these occasions were cordial enough. "Bashevis considered me a slightly misguided, inoffensive beginner of little interest to him since I didn't write my novels in Yiddish," Wiesel said in *All Rivers Run to the Sea*. "In fact it is unlikely that he ever read them." The relationship soured at times. In 1958, in the *Forward*, Wiesel wrote what Singer considered a stinting review of his collection *Gimpel the Fool and Other Stories*. Years later, Wiesel said, Singer "took his revenge by writing a lukewarm review of my book, *Jews of Silence*." Wiesel shot back with a satirical article, one that did not name Singer but was clearly about him, and that compared him to the Second Son of the Passover *Haggadah*, the *rasha*, or evil son. He then reinforced that insult with an article in the *Times* that effusively praised the novelist Chaim Grade, Singer's rival for preeminence among that era's Yiddish fiction writers. After that, they barely spoke for years.[15]

Their relationship seemed to have some of the hallmarks of the rivalry in Cynthia Ozick's famous novella *Envy, or Yiddish in America*, in which an aging Yiddish poet, Hershl Edelshtein, is consumed by resentment of the crossover success of another Yiddish writer, Yankel Ostrover. Much of the story's irony and poignance derives from the shrinking world of Yiddish against which this rivalry plays out; so many writers who flourished or would have flourished in that language perished in the Holocaust, and the remnants were now confronting an audience greatly diminished by the ease of assimilation in America. Yet they were fighting with one another.

Wiesel and Singer did meet again when both were famous. Dvorah Telushkin, who served as Singer's personal assistant, recalled a dinner in 1986 for forty-eight Jewish Nobel Prize winners at which Wiesel and Singer, both wearing tuxedos, kibitzed with each other. At a celebration that gladdened many egos, the two recalled the old joke about a rabbi and a cantor competing in synagogue for who was most humble. When an ordinary congregant prostrated himself in heartfelt worship, the rabbi and the cantor turned to each other and said: "Look who's being humble!"[16]

But the tension between the two writers never quite resolved. When Wiesel achieved worldwide fame by confronting President Reagan for deciding to lay a wreath at a military cemetery in Bitburg, Germany, where Nazi SS troops were buried, Singer, according to Telushkin's memoir, told her, "He is making a big *geshray* [outcry]. From all this the vorld [*sic*] becomes our enemies."[17] Interestingly, Wiesel's memoir paints a misleading picture of Singer's funeral in 1991, describing the crowd of mourners as sparse. I happened to cover the service for the *Times*, and the Riverside Memorial Chapel was overflowing with mourners.

When Oprah Winfrey sent sales of *Night* soaring into the stratosphere by selecting the title for her book club, Wiesel mischievously told a longtime friend, "I'm only sorry Bashevis didn't live to see this day."[18]

11

◆◦◆

Return to Sighet

THE TEENAGE WIESEL, after his liberation from Buchenwald, had declined to follow the American officers' suggestion that he return to Sighet. But he could never let go of his memories of his "dusty" hometown, a place that persistently tugged at his soul. In an article in *Commentary* in 1965, he said that his conflicted ties to Sighet explained his postwar wanderings in France, Israel, India, "never knowing whether it was in order to get away from Sighet, or to find it again."

"The town haunted me, I saw it everywhere, always the same as it had been," he wrote. "It invaded my dreams, it came between me and the world, between me and other people, between me and myself. By trying to free myself from it, I was becoming its prisoner."[1]

Sighet, he wrote, was the place "where the world lost its innocence and God lost His mask." When he finally chose to return, the decision was fraught with ambivalence. "Obviously I lived within my anguish," he wrote in a passage that did not make it into the published article. "As in the presence of a mystery I wanted to and did not want to penetrate it." Nevertheless, he sensed it would be a "decisive turning point," just as leaving Sighet as a teenager had been twenty years before, "the closing of a chapter and the beginning of a new one."[2]

Wiesel flew to Bucharest, took a train to Baia-Mare, then hired a taxi to drive him 150 kilometers over treacherous mountain roads. Arriving late at night he glimpsed familiar sights— the main street, the landmark Hotel Corona, the courthouse, the Jews' Street. Little had changed, yet he could not squelch the feeling that "the driver, for his own amusement, had deposited me in a strange town."

That displaced sense began with the hotel, which with his "Jewish child's eyes" he had once seen as a palace reserved for "princes from distant lands" and "fabulously wealthy American women visiting their families." Now it exuded the shabby neglect typical of a Communist enterprise, complete with an icy, rule-bound night clerk. Visiting his old neighborhood, he remarked that the booth of Old Semel the fruit-seller was gone. So were most of the synagogues he had passed as a child and the Vizhnitz *shtibel* he and his father had prayed in. All had been destroyed by the retreating Germans.

The house he grew up in was there, however, as was its fenced-in yard, looking much as when his family was deported. A wooden bucket still dangled from the well and an empty barrel stood near the cellar door. He struggled to find the nerve to enter the gate, but could not go any farther. "I knew the one who was sleeping in my bed would not forgive me for having come back," Wiesel writes. As he walked away, a dog barked, reminding him of those he was taught to fear as weapons of anti-Semites. "Nothing had changed. The house was the same, the street was the same, the world was the same, God was the same. Only the Jews had disappeared."

Wiesel reveals in this essay that after the town's ten thousand Jews had boarded the cattle cars bound for Auschwitz, the
neighbors had descended like "vultures" to occupy every vacated
home. At the time of his return, Sighet still had twenty-five
thousand people, just as it had when the war began, but there
were only a handful of Jews, most of them people who had settled in town after the war. The Jews' Street had been renamed
the Street of the Deported, though Wiesel deduced that no
one cared to differentiate who had been deported and who did
the deporting.

As dawn broke, he continued to wander the streets, remembering his childhood and thinking he might see once familiar
figures—Kalman the Kabbalist, Moshe the Madman, Shmuk-
ler the Prince, Leizer the Fat. He stopped at his grandmother's
house, an uncle's store, a teacher's home. Of course, all these
figures from his childhood were gone. He looked in vain for the
Talmudic students whose chanting over musty volumes always
filled him with joy. The total absence of his childhood world
suggested to Wiesel something like the strike of a neutron bomb
that destroys people but leaves structures intact.

More realistically, he tried to recognize gentiles he might
have remembered from boyhood like Pishta the Swaggerer,
public school classmates, or customers of his father's store. Not
only was no face familiar but he noticed that no one seemed
particularly interested in him—"as if I did not exist. Or rather,
as if I had never existed."[3] He did meet Moshe Kind, a Hasidic
shokhet, a ritual slaughterer who had decided to return to Sighet
while sending his wife and children abroad, because he considered it his duty to provide kosher meat for the few remaining
observant Jews scattered around the region. Overall, Wiesel
had the sense that the town had forgotten its Jews, that it was as
if they had never existed. "Thus, the Jews have been driven not
only out of the town but out of time as well."

There were only two places where his Jewish past became

palpable. One was in the cemetery, because, he wrote wryly, the dead had not been deported. He found his grandfather's grave and lit candles just as the protagonist in *The Town Beyond the Wall* had done. The second place was an abandoned synagogue that now seemed to be used as a warehouse for books and papers salvaged from the town's destroyed synagogues. Wiesel tells how he combed through the trove and miraculously found some "yellowed, withered sheets of paper in a book of Bible commentaries: a commentary on the commentaries I had written at the age of thirteen or fourteen. The handwriting was clumsy, the thoughts confused." The mystical aura is heightened by a description of how in his "madness" leaving the synagogue, he hallucinated a scene of dazed, crippled beggars and wondered if they were "the very last Jewish remnant of what had been the flourishing community of Sighet."[4]

Wiesel did not include in the *Commentary* piece the story of the cherished gold watch his grandfather had given him, which he had buried under a tree a few days before his family was deported. Now revisiting Sighet under cover of darkness, he dug up the watch. It was a little worse for wear but still intact. Then, inexplicably, he put the watch back and covered it with earth.[5]

After twenty-four hours, he found the same taxi driver who had brought him to Sighet and headed out of town. "My journey to the source of all events had been merely a journey to nothingness," he concluded.[6]

12

◆◆◆◆

A Russian Revolution

PERHAPS EVEN MORE than his early writing about the Holocaust, his trailblazing recognition of the struggles of Soviet Jews catapulted Wiesel to prominence in the Jewish world and beyond. His nonfiction book *The Jews of Silence* came out in 1966, just as the United States and Israel were beginning to struggle with the predicament of three million Jews who were locked inside the Soviet Union and could only practice their religion in the most covert ways. The book, as eloquent and stirring as anything Wiesel had written until then, became *the* defining text of a movement that resulted in the emigration of hundreds of thousands of Jews, with most heading to Israel, America, and Europe.

Wiesel made his first trip to Russia in 1965 just before the High Holidays, ostensibly to report for *Yedioth Ahronoth*. "You ought to go and see," Israeli diplomats Meir Rosenne and Ephraim

Tari urged him. "You have been a witness before. Now you must find out the Soviet Jews' true situation and testify for them."[1]

"I went to Russia drawn by the silence of its Jews," he wrote in a preface. "I brought back their cry."

His account is intriguing for many reasons, not least his manner of telling the story. Not until the book's second half does he explicitly detail the oppression Jews were facing, the kind of essential information that a journalist might have telegraphed in a lede. He does not mention until then that Jews could not establish yeshivas or grade schools, that the number of synagogues was limited to a handful of officially sanctioned showplaces, that public displays of religious fervor were limited to a few holidays, that Jewish Bibles and prayer books were difficult to secure, that speaking Yiddish on the streets was officially discouraged, and that any spiritual display could result in imprisonment for the crime of "Jewish nationalism." As a result, young Jews were being forced to assimilate. For instance, Leningrad's large Jewish community, numbering three hundred thousand, was celebrating on average a mere ten weddings and five bar mitzvahs a year.[2]

Instead of taking on the Soviet repression of its Jews as a journalist, Wiesel approached the subject more like an oracle.

"Their eyes—I must tell you about their eyes," the book starts off. "I must begin with that, for their eyes precede all else, and everything is comprehended within them. The rest can wait. . . . their eyes flame with a kind of irreducible truth, which burns and is not consumed."[3]

Wiesel visited Moscow, Kiev, Leningrad, Vilna, Minsk, and Tbilisi. On his first evening in Moscow, he reported, he was approached by a man who murmured riddles in Yiddish about the situation of Jews in the Soviet Union. "There is no time," the man whispered. "We are nearing the end." Wiesel tells us, again in figurative fashion, that he met this man in every city he visited. "Once he thrust a note in my pocket; once he touched my arm without saying a word. Once I caught a secret wink of his eyes."

What struck him most was the fear he detected everywhere, born not of current conditions, which were actually improving, but of the Jews' harsh history. That fear had turned into a reflex, aggravated by the knowledge that there were informers—yes, Jewish informers—scattered in every crowd. In Moscow's Great Synagogue, ten minutes from the Kremlin and the infamous Lubyanka prison, where in August 1952 thirteen Jews had been beaten, tortured, and finally executed over false charges of treason and espionage, he realized by their suspicious looks that other congregants thought he too might be an informer. The reader's sense that Wiesel was traveling alone in treacherous terrain certainly heightened the literary tension. But he pointed out in the introduction to the 2011 reissue of *The Jews of Silence* that he was in fact accompanied by David Bartov, Israel's deputy ambassador.

To get at the distinctive suffering of Soviet Jews, Wiesel drew upon his own more explicitly brutal experience in Auschwitz and Buchenwald, which ceased with the Allied liberation of the camps. "The tortures inflicted upon us were brought to an end somehow, while they remain caught in an unending ring of terror."[4] This climate of fear was particularly evident on his visit to Kiev, the city where more than 33,000 Jews were shot to death by Germans or their Ukrainian collaborators at the Babi Yar ravine during a few days in September 1941. Parents were afraid to teach their children Torah or speak to them in Yiddish, and anti-Semitism was rife among ordinary Ukrainians.

Whatever quibbles a reader may have about Wiesel's reportage—the exaggerated sense of personal danger, the mystical characters who appear and reappear—are outweighed by the lyricism of his description of the tens of thousands of Jews reveling on Simchat Torah—the Rejoicing in the Torah that immediately follows the eight-day Sukkoth festival. For reasons that are never made clear, the authorities under the Soviet leader Nikita Khrushchev decided to look the other way as Jews celebrated that one-day holiday. They let Jews unleash their pent-up religious pride with ecstatic dancing performed while clutching Torah scrolls and the singing of triumphant Hebrew songs, even songs that expressed a yearning for Israel. While such a celebration is taken for granted in Jewish communities around the world, observing it in Moscow thrilled Wiesel. "He who has not witnessed the Rejoicing of the Law in Moscow has never in his life witnessed joy," he wrote, paraphrasing the ancient rabbis.[5]

"Men who had not sung for a year were raising their voices in song," wrote Wiesel. "Men who had not seen a Torah all year long were embracing and kissing it with a love bequeathed to them from generations past. Old men lifted their grandchildren onto their shoulders, saying 'Look and remember.'" Describing the crush of people swaying and whirling on the streets and in courtyards, he writes: "They seemed to hover in mid-air, Chagall-like, floating above the mass of shadows and colors below, above time, climbing a Jacob's ladder that reached to the heavens, if not higher."[6]

The visit deeply moved Wiesel and sparked his anger at Western Jews for not doing more to pressure Soviet leaders to pry open their doors and let the Jews out. He even compared the predicament of Soviet Jews to that faced by the Jews of Hungary in 1944. From an emotional point of view, he wrote, "It is impossible to escape the impression that the two communities have something in common: a sense of total isolation."[7] "What torments me most is not the Jews of silence I met in Russia, but the silence of the Jews I live among today," Wiesel declared in the book's last sentence.[8]

Wiesel's activism did not endear him to some leaders of organizations in the Jewish world, like Nahum Goldmann, the World Jewish Congress president, who believed that behind-

the-scenes diplomacy would be more effective in liberating Soviet Jews than public attacks on Soviet policy. By the time the
book came out, there were already diplomatic overtures to the
Soviets by Israel and the United States, and a sprinkling of Jews
had already been able to get out. But *The Jews of Silence*—and
excerpts printed beforehand in the *Saturday Evening Post* and
France's *L'Express*—helped fire up readers to join the fight for
religious freedom and the right to emigrate. It spurred the creation of the National Conference of Soviet Jewry and helped
generate pressure in Congress to pass trade restrictions—the
Jackson-Vanik Amendment—punishing countries that denied
citizens the freedom to emigrate. By the mid-1970s the movement could claim considerable success. As the British historian
Martin Gilbert tells us in an afterword to *The Jews of Silence* written in 1986, 250,000 Soviet Jews emigrated during the 1970s, with
two-thirds going to Israel and one-third to the United States.

"Thanks to Elie Wiesel's own writing and the work of hundreds of campaigners for Soviet Jewry throughout the free
world, that western silence is no longer what it was, a pitiful gap
in Jewish unity," Gilbert wrote, referring to the silence about
oppression of Soviet Jews that prevailed before Wiesel's first
visit.[9]

Despite the strains in his relationship with Wiesel, Isaac
Bashevis Singer, in a rambling essay that focused largely on his
own thoughts about the misguided Russian Jews who had de-
luded themselves that Communism was the new Messiah, praised
The Jews of Silence as "one passionate outcry, both in content
and in style."[10]

Wiesel returned to Moscow the following Simchat Torah,
this time carrying a copy of his published book. He was accompanied by a friend, Michel Salomon, a doctor and poet. The
visit was marked by the theft of the book from Wiesel's hotel
room, round-the-clock shadowing by the KGB, and three days
of confinement in the Israeli embassy, whose officials were afraid

Wiesel was about to be arrested. Once back in the United States, he immersed himself in the movement he had helped ignite, writing articles, circulating petitions, taking part in demonstrations, and speaking out at conferences and in synagogues.

A few years later, feeling he needed to do more to call attention to the plight of the Soviet Jews, Wiesel wrote a play, *Zalmen, or the Madness of God*, that was produced at Washington's Arena Stage in 1974, and at the Lyceum Theater on Broadway in 1976. It was directed by Alan Schneider, who was the primary American director of Samuel Beckett's plays and had staged Edward Albee's *Who's Afraid of Virginia Woolf?* The great Yiddish actor Joseph Wiseman played Zalmen.

The play is about a small-town rabbi based on, according to Wiesel, the sheepish, weary chief rabbi of Moscow. The actual rabbi had disappointed Wiesel by refusing to criticize the authorities. But the play's rabbi, under the prodding of a half-mad synagogue beadle, does speak out against the oppression of Soviet Jews. Ultimately, he is investigated by the Ministry of Religious Affairs, whose leader decides, as Clive Barnes noted in his enthusiastic *Times* review, that Jews who made no effective protests against Hitler "can be depended upon to remain silent."

"No one," Barnes concluded, "could ever accuse Mr. Wiesel of being a Jew of silence—he is a Jew of golden eloquence."[11]

Indeed the Jewish community responded to the play with an outpouring of affection. American Mizrachi Women presented Wiesel with its Rambam Award—its highest honor—for becoming "the first writer in the West to draw attention to the plight of Soviet Jews."

Wiesel's play and before that *The Jews of Silence* had caught the currents of the political zeitgeist. Slowly, the Soviet Union began opening its gates. Between 1960 and 1970 only four thousand people emigrated, but in later decades more than 1.5 million left. Although the hopeful wave of the 1970s was followed by a period of so-called "refusals"—applicants who sought to leave were more often rejected or fired or demoted from good jobs—the breakup of the Soviet Union resulted in another large exodus of émigrés that brought scientists, engineers, writers, professors, entrepreneurs, and entertainers and enriched the character of the American, European, and Israeli Jewish communities.

It's true that Wiesel wasn't alone in rescuing the Soviet Jews from political oppressions. Scores of Jews put themselves on the line to protest Soviet policy. Starting in 1964, Jacob Birnbaum, the founder of the Student Struggle for Soviet Jewry, Glenn Richter, the organization's national coordinator, and Rabbi Avi Weiss, the leader of a congregation in the Bronx, led demonstrations and grass-roots campaigns to exert pressure on Congress and the president to compel the Soviets to let Jews depart. But Wiesel's *Jews of Silence* and *Zalmen* were crucial in inspiring hundreds to take part in these protests that ultimately forced the Soviets to relent.

13

$\cdot\!\bullet\!\bullet\!\bullet\!\cdot$

Love and War

IN THE MID-1960S, Wiesel was at a dinner party hosted by a French couple when he struck up a conversation with another guest, a beautiful young woman named Marion Erster Rose.

"I liked him," Marion told me in 2017, a year after his death. "First of all he spoke French and we talked about a lot of things, particularly about Paris. He asked me to have lunch with him. He was living at the Masters hotel. It was a nice little apartment on the 24th floor with a magnificent view over the river."[1]

"I wasn't sure what I found most striking about her," wrote Wiesel in his memoirs, "the delicacy of her features, the brilliance of her words, or the breadth of her knowledge of art, music and the theater."

Although she was married to F. Peter Rose, a businessman involved in New York real estate, and the couple had a daughter, Jennifer, it was an unhappy marriage and she was in the process of getting a divorce. Wiesel and Marion—pronounced as the

French would, MAR-yon—had lunch the following week at an Italian restaurant across from the United Nations. "I ordered an omelet and never touched it. I only listened," Wiesel wrote. Sensing that he was "falling in love on the spot," he simply "looked at her timidly."[2]

She told him something of her life and he understood that their friends' effort to introduce them made eminent sense given their wartime backgrounds. Though a grandfather had lived in Lvov (then in Poland, now in Ukraine and known as Lviv), Marion had been born to bourgeois parents in Vienna. After the Anschluss in 1938, when Germany annexed Austria, Marion, her sister, and their parents escaped by hiring a guide who took them to Belgium. There her father was drafted into the Belgian army. When the Nazis invaded and occupied Belgium, the three women fled and wound up in squalid internment camps in southern France, including the infamous Gurs, where people routinely died of hunger and poor hygiene or were shipped off to German death camps. In 1942, the women managed to get out of the camp, rejoin Marion's father, and reach Marseilles. There they bribed a guide to get them to Switzerland, where Marion had an aunt. They survived in that nominally neutral country until the German surrender and stayed on until 1949, when they immigrated to the United States.

As a teenager in Europe, Marion was active in Belgium's Irgun youth movement and occasionally found herself in Paris for the movement as well. She may even have run across Wiesel when he was writing for the Irgun newspaper, though neither could be sure if it actually happened.

After that Italian lunch in Manhattan, Wiesel and Marion saw each other frequently, recommending books to each other, taking in Broadway plays, and, as Wiesel mentions in *All Rivers Run to the Sea*, attending a concert at Carnegie Hall featuring the violinist David Oistrakh. Marion especially loved movies and the theater—she had studied acting at the Herbert Berghof

Studio in Manhattan, though she dropped the classes after realizing "I wasn't going to be a great actress."[3] Like Wiesel, she had a gift for languages and was fluent in no fewer than five.

The friendship blossomed into a romance, though it was not a given that the relationship would develop into something permanent. In his second volume of memoirs, *And the Sea Is Never Full*, Wiesel tried to fathom why he had resisted marriage for so long. "Was I afraid to detach myself from the past and its ghosts? Afraid of a stability I confused with complacency? . . . was there a deeper reason, a general lack of confidence in the future?"[4] Like many survivors, Wiesel had misgivings about bringing children into the world. "My father felt the world is too evil a place for children," their son Elisha told me.[5]

Wiesel discussed this internal conflict with a larger-than-life spiritual figure, Menachem Mendel Schneerson, the leader of the Hasidim who trace their roots to the village of Lubavitch (Lyubavichi in present-day Russia, on the Belarus border). Wiesel first met Schneerson in the early 1960s when Wiesel visited the Lubavitch headquarters in Brooklyn on assignment for *Yedioth Ahronoth*. The Rebbe, as he was called by his followers, instantly made a powerful impression on Wiesel. His sovereign manner and the reverence he provoked in his acolytes were reminiscent of the rebbe of his family's Vizhnitz dynasty. But this rebbe was also a worldly intellectual who had taken courses in philosophy at the University of Berlin, audited mathematics classes at the Sorbonne, and received a degree from a Parisian engineering school before fleeing Nazi-ravaged Europe for America in 1940. Schneerson granted him a private audience, and Wiesel found him congenial in a way that perhaps the Vizhnitzer Rebbe would not have been. Schneerson knew who Wiesel was, having read some of his works in French, and asked Wiesel to explain why he was so angry with God.

"Because I loved Him too much," Wiesel replied.

"To love God is to accept that you do not understand him," Schneerson said.

"How can you believe in God after Auschwitz?"

"How can you not believe in God after Auschwitz," Schneerson responded. He explained that Man had surrendered his right to any primacy, and who else was there to believe in but God?[6]

The two kept up a correspondence, and in 1965, when Wiesel was a thirty-seven-year-old bachelor, Schneerson wrote him a letter urging him to get married and have a child. He argued that despite "how hard it is to free ourselves of those memories and experiences," raising a family was the most forceful response to the Final Solution. "You must make every effort to tear yourself away from your memories and adopt a lifestyle with a stable structure—married life—and establish a Jewish home and a Jewish family. This will certainly bring about Hitler's true downfall—that he was not successful in his attempts at making it that there be one less Vizhnitzer Chassid in the world."[7]

In interviews, Wiesel suggested that the Rebbe's words influenced his own decision to marry and have a child, but when I spoke to Marion in 2017, she said the Rebbe had nothing to do with it. "We discussed this a lot," she said. "He didn't want a child and I did. I changed his mind. I don't think they changed his mind. I told him he would be happy to have a son or daughter."

Wiesel closely followed the turbulent events in the Middle East, not just as a journalist but as a Jew who passionately believed that Israel must remain the Jewish homeland. For him, as he often said, Israel had been an emblem of justice and redemption in the wake of the Holocaust. By the spring of 1967, he read dispatches from Israel with deep apprehension. At stake, as far as he and most Americans understood, was nothing less than Israel's survival. Egypt had blockaded the Straits of Tiran, Israel's sole access to the Red Sea, the passage to Asia and Africa, with dire implications for trade. It had also moved its armies deep into the Sinai, violating the agreement reached after the Suez Crisis in 1956 to demilitarize the peninsula and prompting United Nations peacekeepers to leave. An attack seemed imminent, with the likelihood that the Syrian and Jordanian armies would join in. The major powers were doing nothing to prevent war.

"I remember the outrageous words, the brutal threats of our enemies, and the silence of our friends and allies," Wiesel wrote years later. "And I remember Israel's solitude."[8]

His memoir, written three decades after the Six-Day War, takes a conventional view of it, dwelling on Israel's astonishing victory but passing over the nuances, many of which had become known to diplomats, historians, and journalists by the time the memoir was published. Israel, according to more recent histories based on newly available archival materials, was probably not about to be attacked, since the Egyptians knew it had the superior army and air force. The Egyptians were likely rattling sabers to impress their Arab partners. The United States knew this as well, telling Israeli emissaries that their remarkable military could defeat the combined armies of Egypt, Syria, and Jordan and did not need American help.[9]

The outbreak of fighting on June 5, starting with a preemptive strike by the Israeli air force that knocked out the entire Egyptian air force in a matter of hours, had been something top Israeli generals such as Moshe Dayan, Yitzhak Rabin, Ezer Weizmann, and Yigal Allon had been looking forward to for years. They had long resented the way Western pressure to end the 1948–1949 war had led them to accept an armistice that left Israel with indefensible borders; the metropolitan Tel Aviv region, which holds almost half the population, at some points is only nine miles from the West Bank. This proximity was particularly worrisome for a military largely made up of civilian reserves that take time to be mobilized. When the Arabs gave

the generals the pretext they were looking for—the closing of
the straits—a vacillating prime minister, Levi Eshkol, did not
feel he could rebuff the generals.[10]

Wiesel persuaded the *Forward* to let him cover the war and
managed to get a seat on the last plane to Israel out of Paris. He
arrived at Lod Airport just as Colonel Motta Gur, commander
of the parachutists, was announcing "the Temple Mount is in
our hands," and that his troops had reached the revered Western Wall, the remnant of the Second Temple compound that
had been destroyed by the Romans in 70 C.E. Accomplishing
what he felt was his obligation to be a witness, Wiesel made his
way to Jerusalem's Old City and looked on with pleasure and
wonder as thousands of rabbis, laborers, farmers, and professors
converged on the wall. He was struck by "how awed and con-
templative they looked." An oracular old man told him: "Do
you know how we defeated the enemy? Six million Jewish souls
prayed for us."

"On that day more than ever, I grasped the meaning of
ahavat Israel, devotion to the people of Israel," Wiesel wrote.[11]

Wiesel's first column about the war, published in Yiddish
on June 12, was breathless with disbelief, comparing the victory
to the Hanukkah miracle. In that he mirrored the reaction of
most Jews. "Future generations will never believe it," he began.
"Teachers will have a hard time convincing their students that
what sounds legendary actually occurred."[12]

Yet in his travel diary, as at other moments of triumph or
celebration, he inevitably thought of those who could not be
with him. Wiesel wrote: "Suddenly I thought I saw, intermin-
gled with the living, the dead converge from the four corners of
exile, from all the cemeteries and all the memories. Some seemed
to emerge from my childhood, others from my imagination.
Mute madmen and dreaming beggars, masters and their disci-
ples, cantors and their allies, the Righteous and their enemies,
children dead and immortal, all the characters of my books."[13]

The travel diary, which was written in Yiddish, was in large part a paean to the newly conquered corners of Jerusalem: the Old City's alleyways, "which have made me want to sing like a madman, to sob like a child"; the gold-white stones that "tell tales of Jewish kings and princes of our often glorious, often sad, but always exhilarating past"; the young warriors who died liberating Jerusalem and "bearing Jewish history on their shoulders." He recalls the special place the city had in his childhood and how his mother sang him a lullaby that told of "the widow Zion who awaited her beloved alone on the grounds of the Temple in Jerusalem."[14]

What Wiesel could not know is how the impact of Israel's stunning six-day victory would catapult him to worldwide stature, as pointed out by many of those who have tracked his career. Even more than the Eichmann trial, the surge of jubilation and pride generated by the triumph—in sharp contrast to the degradation, guilt, and despair that followed World War II—allowed Jews to confront the Holocaust in ways they had resisted.

"We were afraid we would see another Holocaust," Yitz Greenberg told me. "Nasser said he would drive the Jews into the sea. When the war ended there was this miraculous reversal of all our worst expectations. So emotionally, for the first time we could deal with the Holocaust—within the framework of Israel."[15]

In the wake of the Six-Day War, Holocaust histories and novels began to be written in profusion, and movies and television programs followed. Suddenly, Jewish organizations, synagogues, and social centers wanted to hear people speak. And when they looked around to find a speaker, no one seemed quite as suited to the task as Elie Wiesel. As a writer, he could shape sentences that shimmered, and he was blessed with an orator's ability to intone his sentences dramatically. His Sorbonne and Talmudic education enabled him to plumb the Holocaust's philosophical and theological implications in an accessible way. His authority was strengthened by the way he had wrestled with the catastrophe in *Night*. The power of his spoken words was enhanced by a tender, musical voice, a furrowed face, and doleful eyes. Most survivors had missed out on the years of advanced education, so there were few who could match his blend of attributes. Soon everyone wanted Wiesel to speak, and so Wiesel became the de facto spokesman for the survivors.

While gazing in awe at the Western Wall during his Israel assignment, Wiesel began sketching out thoughts for *A Beggar in Jerusalem*, his novel that went on to become a bestseller. It tells the story of David, an Israeli soldier who like Wiesel grew up studying the Talmud in a Transylvanian town, was deported with his family to Auschwitz, and survived. As the novel opens, David is sitting with some beggars slumped against the Western Wall that Israel had captured hours before. For Wiesel, beggars are like madmen, imbued with an uncanny wisdom that empowers them to bear prophetic messages. Here, they actually spin tales of how they helped Israel capture the Old City.

David, meanwhile, is consumed with the disappearance of his friend Katriel, another Eastern European survivor. Katriel had vanished during the assault against Jordanians defending the Old City and was last seen within sight of the wall. This occasions a range of musings that obsessed Wiesel after Auschwitz: the importance of the witness, the pull of the past; the reasoning of God; the purpose of survival. The novel ends with the marriage of David and Katriel's widow, a symbolic merging of the haunted past with the uncertain present.

The novel, first published in 1968 in France, was an immediate success there, selling more than 100,000 copies within a single year. When Random House brought out the English-language edition in 1970, it was reviewed on the front page of the *Times Book Review* and propelled Wiesel into the top ranks of novelists writing on Jewish themes. It also won him the Prix

Médicis, a prestigious literary award for a writer in French whose "fame does not yet match his talent."[16]

The *Times* review, written by Manès Sperber, an esteemed Austrian-French intellectual and, oddly, given the newspaper's delicacy about reviews that pose conflicts of interest, a treasured friend of Wiesel's, was glowing. Praising the author's "poetic prose" for its "tender intimacy" and a voice reminiscent of the Talmudic teachers and medieval mystics, he wrote that "Wiesel is one of the few writers who, without any plaintiveness, has succeeded in revealing in the Jewish tragedy those features by which it has become again and again a paradigm of the human condition."[17]

A weekday review in the *Times* by John Leonard affirmed the novel's distinction. "So charged, so subtle, so superb is Mr. Wiesel's prose style, so dangerously lucid (as the 'message' is ambiguous) that his memory becomes our reality; we wake up obliged to live in his bad dream, as beggars asking for an innocence we never earned."[18]

On April 2, 1969, the eve of Passover, Wiesel married Marion in the Old City of Jerusalem. (Her divorce from Peter Rose had come through earlier that year.) Marion had arrived in Jerusalem a few days earlier and telegraphed Elie, who was traveling in Iowa City, to say: "Jerusalem est si belle et calme que j'ai repris espoir. Je sais qu'un jour nous y vivrons heureux tu verras. Laisse la joie revenir. Elle est en moi et elle t'attend." [Jerusalem is so beautiful and calm that I regained hope. I know that one day we will live happily there you will see. Let the joy return. She is in me and she is waiting for you.][19]

The ceremony was held in the Jewish Quarter at the recently rebuilt Ramban synagogue, which was founded in 1267 by the great biblical commentator Nachmanides, Rabbi Moses ben Nachman, known by his Hebrew acronym as Ramban. The ceremony was traditional, including the ritual of the Seven

Blessings for the bride and groom, and was performed by Rabbi Saul Lieberman, a brilliant Talmudist who was becoming Wiesel's scholarly mentor at the Jewish Theological Seminary. Peter Mayer, publisher and editor-in-chief of Avon Books, Wiesel's paperback publisher, was his best man. Both of Wiesel's surviving sisters, Hilda and Bea, were there with their families: Bea's husband, Leonard Jackson, and their children Sarah and Steve; Hilda's son Sidney, as well as a number of cousins and friends. Wiesel's mind often drifted to those who were not there; he found himself feeling sadness rather than joy. He had felt a similar melancholy the Sabbath before the wedding when he was given the honor of blessing the Torah in a small Hasidic synagogue on Manhattan's Upper West Side. At a reception afterward, while the guests sang and danced, Wiesel found he could no longer hold back his tears.

"He saw himself as a child and then as an adolescent, at home far away," he wrote in *All Rivers Run to the Sea*. "He saw his father, head slightly bent, and his mother biting her lip. The night before, he thought that he must go and invite them to the wedding. Custom dictates that before his wedding an orphan goes to meditate at the grave of his parents, respectfully requesting the honor of their presence. But this groom's parents, like millions of others, had no grave of their own. All Creation was their cemetery."[20]

During their weeks in Israel, Wiesel was peppered with requests for newspaper interviews, television appearances, and chats with politicians. So consumed was he by the tumult of Israeli life that Marion had to remind him that he was "no longer a bachelor and that if I don't wish to become one again on the spot, I had better take her away, anywhere." They returned to New York and celebrated their marriage with friends on a Long Island estate so grand it "actually had zoo animals."[21] A bouquet arrived from Menachem Schneerson, with a card extending the Rebbe's blessings.

With the arrival of summer—the summer of Woodstock, Chappaquiddick, and the first moon walk—the newlyweds headed to the French Riviera, renting a house Marion arranged in Roquebrune, then driving down to San Remo on the Italian Riviera to spend time with Yosef Rosensaft and his group of Bergen-Belsen survivors. Wiesel observed something paradoxical about survivors: "They sing and laugh, laugh and sing, even as they evoke their dark memories of long ago."[22]

In the alignment of stars that helped make Wiesel the international icon he became, his marriage to Marion was among the most significant. On the most basic level, said the sociologist Hillel Levine, later his colleague at Boston University, she provided security: "the warmth and comfort that allowed him to be a representative of suffering all over the world. She took care of him and protected him from the travesties of the larger world."[23]

Marion was also gifted in another way. As Elisha told me, "Any understanding of my father as a presence on the world stage has to be considered with my mother in the picture. My mother has a real gift for the scale of things, how to take a small idea and make it have impact. My father had a passion for literature and philosophy but my mother is a woman who knows how to operate in the world and make ideas become reality. You have to look at them as a team." Marion acknowledged as much in our conversation. "My husband was a wonderful intellectual but he was not a very practical person," she said. "I think what I brought to him was a sense of reality of what the world is really like." Sigmund Strochlitz's daughter Romana told me that Marion saw that Wiesel "had this impact on people and the more people he had this impact on the better off the world would be."[24]

Marion encouraged him to take on some of the humanitarian causes he advocated later in his career, but she also helped him turn down some of the countless requests for his time. "My husband was a very kind person and he had difficulty saying no to anything and I shielded him from some of that," she told me.[25] She "got him to look at the world with more appreciation for things he didn't know much about," including theater and the classic movies she loved, such as the Gregory Peck–Audrey Hepburn gem, *Roman Holiday*. With her at his side, he was less reserved; he even laughed more. In *And the Sea Is Never Full*, the second volume of his memoirs, Wiesel described the challenge in marriage to "solder two natures." Like other husbands, he had to adapt to his wife's preferences—for example, accepting her disinclination to spend Saturdays in synagogue. "Around us, our circle of friends becomes larger. I no longer boycott social events with the old determination. With novelists we discuss politics, with politicians we speak of art."[26] Menachem Rosensaft said, "Elie did not allow himself to be intellectually managed. [But] the two of them had a strong partnership. She . . . is a beautiful woman, bright with a sense of humor, and she broadened his circle tremendously. She added a certain flair, which he also enjoyed."[27]

And yet—a phrase that he loved for its evocation of the contradictions of life—Wiesel in the years ahead struggled to overcome what seemed like a bottomless well of sorrow.

"My life now unfolds under the dual sign of change on a practical level and loyalty on the level of memory," he wrote years later. "Inside me happiness and distress seem to spark a fire that is both somber and luminous. Could it be that I fear happiness? . . . I have a wife I love, and yet I write not about love but about solitude. I have a home filled with warmth, and yet I write about the misery of the condemned."[28]

Still, the cocoon of a new family—including Marion's daughter Jennifer and the son he and Marion would soon have—seemed to temper the pain of loss. "In my private life," he wrote, "I discover the vulnerable but dazzling joy of a man who beholds the first smile of his child."[29]

14

***

Transitions

AFTER THEIR MARRIAGE, Elie moved into Marion's two-bedroom apartment on Central Park West. It was in a handsome neo-Renaissance building that featured a doorman, high ceilings, hardwood floors, and a dining room suitable for evening salons. Although the city's perilous fiscal situation and rising crime made such grand apartments affordable to middle-income families, the move put new financial pressures on Wiesel. At the same time, he was increasingly disenchanted with the grind of daily journalism. Much of his work for *Yedioth Ahronoth*, for instance, involved slight, incremental shifts in U.N. policy or operations, and he found too many of his stories formulaic, trivial, or irrelevant and most of the U.N.'s cast of characters uninteresting. But when he turned the U.N. assignment and his bureau desk over to a *Yedioth* colleague he found he had created for himself a large financial hole. So Wiesel became more purposeful in pursuing speaking opportunities. "He felt that he should be more responsible and he tried harder to do well," Marion said.

He also plunged into his personal writing more assiduously than ever, turning out novels and novellas, philosophical essays, book reviews, and collections of Hasidic tales. The American publication of *A Beggar in Jerusalem* shifted from Holt, Rinehart and Winston to Random House when Wiesel's editor moved there. Displeased with the translation, Wiesel turned to Marion to rework it. She rose to the challenge, and although she initially received no credit for her role, the book became the start of her own career as her husband's preferred translator. She eventually translated fourteen of his books.

Wiesel had become so identified with the Holocaust that he could claim in his memoirs that some scholars considered him the first to use the word "Holocaust" to describe the calamity that befell European Jews before and during World War II. Indeed, Primo Levi said as much. "It is a term that annoyed me when it was first used: then I learned that it had been Elie Wiesel who coined it and who later regretted it and wished to withdraw it," he wrote.[1]

In his memoirs, Wiesel explained that he leaped at the word after he saw it used for Abraham's aborted sacrifice of Isaac. The idea of a "burnt offering" suggested "a total annihilation by fire and the sacred and mystical aspect of sacrifice," he said.[2] He first used the term in 1963 in a *Times* book review of *The Terezin Requiem*, a novel by Josef Bor, but came to feel that giving the Jewish catastrophe a singular name contributed to the term's vulgarization.[3] Clearly, Wiesel thought he was the first to coin this usage, given the paucity of works about the Shoah (the Hebrew word for the Holocaust, a term that appears in the Book of Zephaniah to suggest utter destruction). In fact, the Oxford English Dictionary traces this distinctive usage to the early 1950s—before Wiesel was writing in English—and etymological websites have discovered a host of earlier references, including an article in the *Times* on May 31, 1936, that spoke of the "intolerable sufferings of the Jews in the European holocaust."[4]

Continuing to work at a feverish pace, in 1970 Wiesel published *One Generation After*, an eclectic collection of essays, imaginary dialogues, memoir-like sketches, and parables tied to the twenty-fifth anniversary of the end of World War II. Wiesel's attempts in the book to come to grips with the theological and moral significance of the Holocaust contain some of his most evocative writing.

The virtues of civility and culture, he suggests in one essay, may be something of an illusion. Adolf Eichmann, after all, was an exemplary father and considerate husband, "a man like any other."

"It is possible to be born into the upper or middle class, receive a first-rate education, respect parents and neighbors, visit museums and attend library gatherings, play a role in public life, and begin one day to massacre men, women and children, without hesitation and without guilt," he wrote. "One may torture the son before his father's eyes and still consider oneself a man of culture and religion. And dream of a peaceful sunset over the sea."[5]

It is also the first book where he clearly articulates his mission to be both a witness to the Holocaust and a messenger revealing its lessons for mankind, even if that role is riddled with complications and dangers.

"Therein lies the dilemma of the storyteller who sees himself essentially as a witness, the drama of the messenger unable to deliver his message: how is one to speak of it, how is one not to speak of it? Certainly there can be no other theme for him; all situations, all conflicts, all obsessions will, by comparison, seem pallid and futile. And yet, how is one to approach this universe of darkness without turning into a peddler of night and agony?"[6] The writer grappling with the Holocaust, he wrote, will, Icarus-like, "inevitably burn his fingers, and sometimes more." Yet, he concludes, the story must be "told for the sake of our children."[7]

Among the people he consulted about his spiritual struggle was Saul Lieberman, the legendary professor at the Jewish Theological Seminary who had performed his marriage ceremony in Jerusalem. The two had met at a gathering of intellectuals to discuss what might be done to help Soviet Jews. Lieberman was intrigued by Wiesel's suggestion that a Talmud course should be launched in Moscow, with classes much like an impromptu lesson Wiesel had given on his visit to Moscow. Lieberman was so impressed that he attended a generic lecture on the Talmud that Wiesel gave at the 92nd Street Y in New York. That was the beginning of a remarkable friendship that lasted for seventeen years, until Lieberman's death. Wiesel, who considered Lieberman the leading Talmudist of his generation and referred to him as his "master," studied Talmud privately with him twice weekly in three-hour sessions, sitting on opposite sides of Lieberman's desk in his seminary office with dusty volumes open before them. He also enrolled in Lieberman's Talmud course at the seminary.

"My recollection was that when Wiesel entered the class there was a real frisson in the room," said Elliott Rosen, who in 1969 was studying for the rabbinate. "Certainly among rabbinical students, he was quite famous. The other observation I'd make is that there was clearly an emotional bond between him and Lieberman and you could tell they meant something to each other."[8]

One reason for that bond was their shared dedication to confronting the theological conundrums engendered by the Holocaust. Wiesel was mellowing, his anger at God softening, yet he was still gnawed at by existential questions. "What in the world was the Good Lord doing while His people were being massacred and incinerated?" he asked in *And the Sea Is Never*

Full. "What were our ancestors, the patriarchs Abraham, Isaac, and Jacob, doing while their descendants were humiliated and sent to their death? Were they not . . . our protectors and intercessors? Why didn't they shake the celestial throne with their prayers and drown it in their tears?"[9]

Lieberman offered another perspective, one that depicts God as a kind of supervisor forced to preside with a pained heart over a cosmos peopled with deeply flawed human beings, each of whom has free will. Of the characters in Scripture, he told Wiesel, "God is the most tragic. It is not sacrilegious to feel sorry for Him. He, too, needs redemption."

Wiesel's eventual answer to the paradox of God's tolerance of the murder of His chosen people is yet another paradox: "The silence of God is God," he said, a statement that "is both an admission of resignation and an affirmation of hope."[10] He expressed doubts that the human race was "sufficiently worthy to make [the Messiah] come and save a humanity that has doomed itself." He expressed sympathy for those Holocaust victims "who felt the world abandoned them and was not worth fighting for." But by protesting God's "apparent indifference to the injustices that savage His creation," he implicitly acknowledged that he would continue to wrestle with God and that his faith will endure. "I would not be the man that I am, the Jew that I am, if I betrayed the child who was once duty-bound to live for God. . . . It is because I still believe in God that I argue with him."[11]

Rabbi Wolfe Kelman, the executive vice president of the Rabbinical Assembly, which shapes the theology and practices of Conservative Judaism, had discovered Wiesel in the early 1960s through Lieberman, and was captivated by his life story, his erudition, and his writings. He asked Wiesel to address the annual rabbinical convention in Toronto. "None of us who attended will ever forget Wiesel's talk," wrote Rabbi Reuven Hammer, then a rabbi in the Chicago suburbs. "His appearance in itself told a story—young, thin, gaunt, he seemed the very embodiment of the survivor, and his words were equally haunting."[12] Afterward, Wiesel was asked by a series of Conservative rabbis to address their congregations, and invitations from other groups followed. "No major Jewish organization feels it has arrived until it has had Elie Wiesel address a meeting," the Vienna-born Kelman, the scion of Hasidic rabbis, told the *Times* in 1973.[13]

When Yitz Greenberg invited him back to the Riverdale Jewish Center in the early 1970s, the reception was quite different than it had been for his first appearance there several years before. The house was packed. "He had this charisma," Greenberg told me. "He spoke with such force and power, and the fact that he did not get the appreciation he deserved didn't shake his inner conviction of what needed to be done. He mesmerized people. He had this mission, I hesitate to use that term—but he had this inner conviction that he was speaking for the survivors and this was something he had to do."[14] Moreover, as Michael Berenbaum told me, after 1967 "the Holocaust became central to the American Jewish agenda and Wiesel was the paradigmatic survivor. He was young, charismatic. It was a role waiting to happen."[15] Ruth Wisse argues that whether Wiesel carved out the role of spokesman or whether the survivors needed someone magnetic to play that role "is really irrelevant." Like the Yiddish poet H. Leivick, who was smuggled out of Czarist exile in Siberia and landed as a martyr in America in 1913, Wiesel, she said, "radiated the same sense of being the embodiment" of an experience and so was turned into an emblem of the Holocaust.[16]

Particularly significant in his evolution not just as a sought-after speaker about the Holocaust but as a public intellectual were his lectures at the 92nd Street Y, beginning in February 1967, which soon became a semi-annual event. (In a celebration of his nearly half-century of speaking there in 2014, the Y counted 180 lectures by Wiesel.) His first lecture was a reading of and commentary about his novel *The Town Beyond the Wall*, but later talks explored the lives of biblical characters, Talmudic figures, and Hasidic masters as well as more topical subjects like the persecution of Soviet Jews, anti-Semitic documents, the quest for peace, and the state of world Jewry, a subject that he spoke about annually. Wiesel had made a decision to avoid lectures that were explicitly about the Holocaust.

The Y lectures reveal how knowledgeable, witty, and charming Wiesel could be, and what a subtle mind he had. These qualities explain why so many of his appearances were standing-room-only in a large auditorium, and why he could say in one of his lectures in 1981 that "some in the audience have been at every talk since the first one and some of you have met each other at these lectures and married."

An hour-long lecture he gave on the Book of Esther on October 29, 1981, was typical of his remarkable ability to combine deep Jewish and literary erudition with humor and a sense of proportion. In his discursive analysis, Wiesel moved between affection for what he saw as a simple fairy tale that chronicles how "a nice Jewish girl manipulates an old silly king" and a writer's admiration for the complexities woven into a book's characters. Haman, usually seen as a villain of unalloyed wickedness, is also depicted in the *megillah*—the scroll—as a devoted husband and father. Thus, Wiesel said, a smidgeon of pathos can be felt toward a man beset by his blind, seething jealousy of Mordechai. Too-good-to-be-true Mordechai turns out to have a flaw or two, Wiesel pointed out, as when he urged Esther to hide her Jewishness. Similarly, cloyingly sweet Esther turns out, in Wiesel's telling, to have been a canny Machiavellian operator as well; she lies to the king, telling him that Haman tried to seduce her.

Wiesel turns the *megillah* into nuanced literature. Yet he infused his analysis with witty asides that delighted the audience. At a transitional point he asked the audience: "Was all this royal wife trouble good or bad for the Jews?" Rousing laughter can be heard on the Y recording.[17]

In *And the Sea Is Never Full*, Wiesel confessed that he suffered from stage fright and often tired of hearing himself utter well-worn phrases. But he persisted, feeling an obligation to promulgate a message that might ward off another Holocaust.

Wiesel also embarked on a career as a teacher. In the early 1970s, Yitz Greenberg had been asked to assume the chairmanship of a fledgling Jewish studies department at the City College of New York. The department was created as a desperate effort to halt the exodus of Jewish students after an "open admissions policy" brought in hundreds of poorly prepared high-school graduates and diluted the legendary academic quality of what had been "the Harvard of the proletariat." As Greenberg contemplated building a faculty, Elie Wiesel's name came up again and again. Wiesel, however, lacked standard academic credentials. He had no doctorate, not even a formal college degree. Greenberg went to the college president, Robert Marshak, to ask for an exception for Wiesel and Marshak was so impressed by Wiesel's oeuvre that he agreed. In September 1972, Wiesel was named one of nine distinguished professors, a visiting title that was also given that year to the playwright Lillian Hellman, the opera impresario Rudolf Bing, and the novelist Anthony Burgess. The title carried a full professor's salary, which at that time was $31,250, plus a $5,000 annual supplement. The following year Wiesel was appointed full professor. And so, as he was amused to observe, he secured his first full-time job in the United States.[18]

He taught two courses—one on "the literary responses to persecution" and a second, a seminar for twenty students on Hasidic texts. About 150 students registered for his 8:30 A.M. class on persecution literature, a course that at first focused largely on Holocaust works. Although Wiesel felt overwhelmed by the numbers that registered, he turned no one away.

"I put in four hours of preparation for every hour I teach because, for each thing I say, I put my entire career on the line," Wiesel told the *Times*.[19]

It was the beginning of a career that endured until his final years. Indeed, his friends told me that what he most wanted to be remembered for was not his roles as a journalist, novelist, or even Holocaust spokesman but his work as a teacher. He delighted in informing young people about matters they may not have contemplated and stimulating their minds to think more deeply. The students were taken not only with what he taught them but with the teacher himself—his singular intelligence, passion for his subject, ready humor, and the sense that when he spoke it was from painfully lived experience.

He hired Menachem Rosensaft, the son of his good friend and someone who was born in the displaced persons camp at Bergen-Belsen, as his teaching assistant, a role Rosensaft played for the next three years.

"With Elie there was always a human dimension," Rosensaft told me. "I remember his fixing a collar of a college student. Whether with a student or a survivor he listened empathetically. It was that particular authenticity that came across."[20]

In a tribute he gave at Case Western University in 2017 to mark Wiesel's first *yahrzeit*, Rosensaft said he was most struck by how accessible Wiesel made himself to students, no matter how far afield their questions. "This was especially true for those of his students who were sons or daughters of survivors, and who wanted to speak with him not about their studies but about themselves, their relationships with their parents, their efforts to understand what their parents had experienced."[21]

Wiesel often wrote about his students, once vividly recalling a young son of survivors who asked to drop his course. "Visibly ill at ease, haggard, unshaven, he chews his lips and his eyes flee my own," Wiesel wrote. "I've never seen him so distressed. 'You understand,' he says, 'this has nothing to do with you but with me. With my parents.' He stops. It's hard for him to continue. I keep quiet. Wait. 'For a long time I didn't know what they were seeing behind me, and around me. Now I know.' He stops, his eyes brimming with tears. Then: 'I'm the hero of your last novel—his story is my story. My father is silent and sad. His wife and children perished over there. My mother is silent and sad. Her husband and their little girl perished over there. They met after the liberation. I am their son. And each time they look at me, it is not me they see.'"[22]

Many of his City College students were survivors' children. "They come to class, above all, to understand their parents. . . . The parents are silent and their children want to learn, and to relive their life and their death. So for these young people, this is not a matter of some abstract study. Pressing their identities to the limit, they see their parents and grandparents marching toward the common trench at Babi Yar or toward the flames of Treblinka. Sometimes, when they read out loud, they seem to remember events that they had never experienced. Often, after class, they remain seated, frozen, unable to leave the hell they had just visited, to return to their normal life, to get interested again in science or in Elizabethan poetry."[23]

While colleagues sometimes complained about the declining quality of their students, Wiesel was impressed by his students' "thirst to know," and eagerness to devour writings on the Holocaust. "Nothing frightens them, nothing stops them. Wanting to uncover all, they go to the bottom of things. One must explain the unexplainable to them, of how could this tragedy, on such a staggering scale, be possible?"[24]

Yet, as he had with his lectures, Wiesel decided not to teach courses explicitly focused on the Holocaust. Partly it was the elusiveness of the subject—"how can one communicate that which, by its very nature, recoils from words?"[25] But there was also a fear that he was becoming too identified with the subject. At one point, Wiesel confided to Greenberg that he didn't "want to make a living from the Shoah. He didn't want to commercialize it."[26]

Meanwhile, with a regular job and a wife to come home to, Wiesel's life achieved a pleasant domesticity. As Greenberg said: "She got him to break down the wall of isolation."[27] By 1971, Marion was pregnant, and she gave birth on June 6, 1972, to Shlomo Elisha, named after the Sighet grandfather the baby never knew. "A dawn like any other," Wiesel wrote of the birth. "It will mark my existence forever. The little fellow in the arms of his mother will illuminate our life."

Eight days later came the *bris* and it was attended by such notables as the violinist Isaac Stern and Abraham Joshua Heschel, as well as emissaries from the Lubavitch Rebbe. Menachem Rosensaft's mother, Hadassah, who had delivered babies in the concentration camps, carried the newborn in for the circumcision. During much of the ritual, Wiesel was "lost in thought." One of the Hasidim told him to cheer up. "You cannot give in to melancholy, not today," pointing out that Elisha's birth recovered the name of Wiesel's father, an occasion that merited exuberant celebration. Wiesel acknowledged that Elisha assured the continuation of his ancestral line and so he asked his dead parents to protect this infant and "help me sing him lullabies."[28]

"Elisha's birth transforms Elie profoundly, indelibly," Rosensaft said. "For the first time . . . that I've known him, he seems genuinely, thoroughly content."

15

The Israel Conundrum

WHEN THE EGYPTIANS launched a surprise attack against Israeli forces positioned along the Suez Canal in October 1973, Wiesel once again felt the pull to be in *ha'aretz*—"the land," as Israelis call their country. I was on the El Al plane that carried him there two weeks after the initial attack, having been assigned to write about the end of the war and its aftermath for the *New York Post*. Wiesel and his friend Sigmund Strochlitz sat together a few rows in front of me, leaning back in their seats, wearing rumpled shirts and ties and with their shoes off, humming Hasidic melodies to each other. Despite their worries about the perils they would encounter in an Israel under siege, they radiated the joy of two men heading home after a long absence.

Wiesel had learned while at Yom Kippur services at Kehilath Jeshurun synagogue on Manhattan's Upper East Side that the Israeli army had suffered a devastating setback along the inadequately fortified Suez Canal.[1] There had been, he was told, a significant number of casualties. In the following days, he could not focus on writing or teaching. He listened to the radio, watched television, read newspapers to catch the latest developments. His thoughts were elsewhere, "across the ocean, in the land of our ancestors."[2] After two weeks he and Strochlitz were able to arrange a lightning trip—less than two days long—to get a shipment of medical supplies to the soldiers. The announced mission seemed more about boosting morale and public relations than about the delivery of essential medicine. Still, the circumstances allowed Wiesel to fly to Israel at a vulnerable time for the Jewish homeland.

Sitting in the front row of the plane was Abba Eban, the Israeli foreign minister with whom Wiesel was barely speaking. A year and a half earlier, Eban had told the TV interviewer David Frost that after the capture of Eichmann the problem of Nazi war criminals no longer interested him. In the ensuing uproar within Israel, an imperiled Eban asked Wiesel for a statement of public absolution. When Wiesel declined to get involved, Eban claimed that Wiesel had in fact issued such a statement. Wiesel was infuriated and their relationship suffered for more than a decade.

In Israel, Wiesel and Strochlitz found the roads from the airport eerily darkened, as was Tel Aviv itself. Israel had imposed a national blackout. After settling in for the night at the Tel Aviv Hilton, the two men took a bus to Tel HaShomer Hospital, in Ramat Gan, just east of Tel Aviv. There Wiesel visited a seemingly delirious tank officer whose eyes peered out of a bandaged face. "He has read your books," the hospital director told Wiesel. "He wishes to shake your hand."

"I step forward and hold something resembling a hand," wrote Wiesel. "The wounded man's lips are moving. He whispers to me and no words have ever moved me so much."[3]

As Wiesel became a Jewish paragon, he developed something of a tortured public relationship with Israel, even as he loved it passionately. For one thing, he was a target for the disdain that many Israelis express toward Diaspora Jews. Why, they ask, are you as a committed Jew not living in the Jewish homeland? For Wiesel, misgivings also lingered from his first postwar visits to Israel, where he confronted condescension from some native-born *sabras* toward Holocaust survivors for failing to fight back more aggressively against their German persecutors. The initial scorn from *sabras* certainly softened by the 1970s amid annual Shoah commemorations, but for Wiesel that first impression seems to have been hard to shake off.

In 1974, at a time when Israel was roiling from the near debacle of the October 1973 war, he addressed the governors of the Jewish Agency in Jerusalem and put forth some "reproaches" that Diaspora Jews tend to feel toward Israel as they follow events in a country they believe belongs to all Jews.

"Not only do I wish to love Israel," he said, "I wish to admire it, hold it up as an example, find there what cannot be found elsewhere: a certain sense of justice, a certain sense of dignity. I want to find there a society ruled by a vision of probity, justice and compassion. . . . The more we in the Diaspora are prone to materialism, the more we yearn to see idealism flourish in Israel; the more passive we are, the more we would like Israel to be creative; the more earthbound we are, the more anxious we are, the more we would like Israel to be ethereal and sovereign. In short we would like Israel to be what we are not."

"Are we wrong," Wiesel wondered, to ask Israel "to be a model nation? . . . Are we wrong to ask you to adopt a more Jewish attitude toward Palestinian Arabs and, particularly, toward Israeli Arabs? To be less intransigent, more receptive?"[4]

As he moved from a consideration of Diaspora Jews to remarks that were critical of Israel, Wiesel felt the mood in the hall shift, "as if a wind from Siberia had frozen my listeners' features." In an instant, he abandoned his text and improvised some less disapproving words. Still, the next day's newspapers were full of rebukes: How dare Wiesel, an American Jew, preach to Israelis?

Although he stood by his speech, he made a steadfast decision never again to publicly criticize Israel and instead turned his attention to issues like UNESCO's ostracism of Israel and the resurgence of global anti-Semitism masquerading as opposition to Zionism. Wiesel's supportive stance no matter who led the Israeli government did not seem to matter as much to the Israeli left and liberal American Jews when more liberal Israeli politicians like Yitzhak Rabin and Ehud Barak were in power or when Israel took diplomatic initiatives they found congenial. But his refusal to condemn Israel's more controversial actions in the following decades, particularly involving its treatment of the Palestinians, earned him strong disapproval. Those on the left were trying to prod the government to carve out a homeland for the Palestinians or at least stop the expansion of settlements in the West Bank, and they would have liked to have Wiesel's support. In a book published in 1990, Michael Berenbaum, who served as a deputy director of the Holocaust Memorial Commission under Wiesel, pointed out that despite his growing reputation as a spokesman against genocide, he barely mentioned the invasion of Lebanon in 1982 that led to the massacre—not by the Israeli army, but by its allies, the Christian Lebanese Phalangists—of Palestinian refugees living in the Sabra neighborhood and the Shatila refugee camp in Beirut.[5]

When Benjamin Netanyahu came to power in 2009, forging an alliance between the hard-line Israeli right and the Orthodox religious parties, Wiesel again remained a fervent government supporter, even as he gave lip service to President Obama's efforts to push Netanyahu toward a Palestinian deal. When Wiesel took out a full-page ad in the *Times* in 2010 urging Obama to stop pressuring Netanyahu on settlements in East Jerusalem, which Palestinians hoped would be the capital of their state, and then another urging Obama to reject a nuclear treaty with Iran, his standing among both American and Israeli liberals tumbled.

Nevertheless, Wiesel's stance won applause from more conservative observers such as Harvard professor Ruth Wisse, who praised him for his flinty courage in refusing to blame Israel for Palestinian bungling in achieving a state of their own. Wiesel, she said, could have ingratiated himself with what she suggested was America's cultural elite and won prizes from organizations like the writers' advocacy group PEN International or even support for a Nobel literature prize. But "he decided he was not going to pile on," she said. "How easy it would have been for him to say to Netanyahu like he said to Reagan, 'that is not for you to do.' He wouldn't do that. It cost him. He wanted to win the big literary prizes, but they never gave the prizes to him because they are liberals."[6] This is an assessment that Leon Wieseltier, the former literary editor of the *New Republic*, strongly disputes, pointing out that many liberals, from the Nobel committee to Oprah Winfrey, continued to lavish praise on Wiesel despite his well-known views on the Middle East conflict.[7]

Americans continued to esteem Wiesel until his death. That was not as true in Israel, however. There he remained a less celebrated figure and a contentious one. For one thing, an articulate survivor like him was a relative novelty in the United States, where Jewish Holocaust survivors formed less than 1 percent of the population. So his Holocaust-themed speeches and books drew the curiosity or attention of millions of Americans who were not directly affected by that cataclysm or knew little about it. In Israel, the Holocaust was inextricable from the nation's founding, and survivors and their descendants form a major share of the Jewish population. Their impact has become such that at 10 A.M. on Yom HaShoah (the 27th day of the Hebrew month of Nisan) sirens sound and the entire country stops—drivers literally halt their cars on highways—for two minutes of solemn reflection. Someone exhorting the country about remembrance, silence, or indifference—themes that are taken for granted or are much chewed over—would not command the same interest.

In a country where Jews dominate, Israelis do not worry what gentiles will think, are not as circumspect, and are freer to carp at one another without mincing words. Critics could not only accuse Wiesel of being too timid in imploring Israeli leaders to seek a solution to the Palestinian desire for a homeland but baldly accuse him of growing rich off the Holocaust. (They may not have known about his policy of turning over any payments for speeches about the Holocaust to a Jerusalem yeshiva that honors his father.) Joel Rappel, the longtime archivist of the Wiesel papers at Boston University, told me that many Israelis are not even familiar with Wiesel's name even though in the United States he is revered.

"In the States when I mention I work with Elie Wiesel, all doors are open to me," Rappel said. "They tell me, 'We're jealous you work with such a person.'"

16

From Writer to Torchbearer

THE LATE 1970s were a time for Wiesel to catch his breath and build on his mounting reputation. He continued to write prolifically, but the novels he produced in this period are not regarded as among his finest. After *A Beggar in Jerusalem*, many reviews shared the same stinging refrain: Wiesel was fashioning fictional polemics. It was as if his persona as prophetic spokesman of the survivors was infecting his writing, turning natural dialogue into speeches Wiesel might himself deliver.

The Oath, published in French in 1973, tells the story of an old man, Azriel, who early in the twentieth century took part in a communal oath by the Jews of the fictional village of Kolvillag ("every village," if you combine Hebrew and English words) not to tell the story of the pogrom that was about to befall them. Their rationale was an effort, proposed by Moshe the village madman, to end the Jewish preoccupation with the tribe's history of suffering. An oath of silence might stop the suffering itself.

But Azriel, the pogrom's sole survivor, violates this oath decades later when he meets an unnamed young son of Holocaust survivors who is in such despair about what his parents suffered that he wishes to die. Azriel tries to divert him from his self-destructive obsession by, counterintuitively, giving a vivid account of the Kolvillag pogrom. He hopes to turn the young man's depression into defiance and a commitment to raising his voice against evil.

The novel's main theme seems to reflect a quandary that must have weighed heavily on Wiesel at the time: how much to speak out about the Holocaust or whether saying less or even silence was the wiser approach to moving forward with one's life. Wiesel was also becoming conscious of accusations, mainly whispered, by Jewish intellectuals that he was exploiting the Holocaust. *The Oath* can be seen as a defense of the need for perpetuating the memory of what was done to the Jews so that a more vigilant world rises up whenever the prospect of such atrocities looms.

"At his best Elie Wiesel is a remarkable fabulist," wrote Alan Friedman in the *Times Book Review*. Wiesel, he said, "is capable of the most entrancing touches."[1] But much of Friedman's review was critical. Leon Wieseltier, who deeply admired Wiesel, found the writing "pedestrian" and said, "Wiesel's characters are not people captured convincingly in the particularity of their precarious existence." Rather, they are "archetypes of the variety of Jewish pain."[2]

Wieseltier and Wiesel eventually became close friends and studied Talmud and Jewish poetry together. "We loved each other, we had enormous respect for each other," Wieseltier told me after Wiesel's death. Wiesel, he said, never mentioned the harsh review of *The Oath*. "Maybe he forgave me," Wieseltier said.[3]

In his memoir, Wiesel called *The Oath* "the most depressing fictional tale my pen has ever committed to paper," describing it as a "bleak novel, devoid of hope." It was written, he said, when he was depressed without knowing why, since his family and professional life were thriving. Perhaps, he surmised, he sensed disaster looming for his cherished Israel in the months before the Yom Kippur War.[4] As with many survivors, the threats against Israel rekindled fears of annihilation he had felt as a teenager with the German invasion of his hometown. He offered some elaboration the following year in an op-ed published in the *Times* and *Le Figaro* titled "Ominous Signs and Unspeakable Thoughts." In that piece he confessed that he felt personally in danger as a result of a shift in the world's attitude toward Israel. Yasser Arafat, the Palestinian leader whose followers had launched numerous terrorist attacks against Israelis, had been applauded by diplomats around the world. UNESCO voted to effectively exclude Israel from its organization. Eighteen children in the village of Ma'alot in northern Israel were massacred in a horrific terrorist attack. And Israeli commandos had to rescue the passengers of a hijacked Air France plane, including eighty-three Israelis, after they were held hostage at Uganda's Entebbe Airport. A spate of anti-Semitic incidents suggested that contempt for Jews was again becoming fashionable. For the first time since the end of World War II, "Jewish survival is being called into question," he wrote.[5] Yet other events softened his fears, particularly Anwar Sadat's visit to Jerusalem. Wiesel would eventually become the thesis adviser to Sadat's daughter Camelia at Boston University.

Eight years went by before Wiesel published his next novel, *The Testament*. It tells the story of a fictional poet, Paltiel Kossover, awaiting execution as one of the writers and artists purged by Stalin in 1952. The testament he leaves behind for his son is a memoir of disillusion and disenchantment. The idealistic faith in a vision of communism that was supposed to treat Jews as equals had replaced the Orthodox beliefs Kossover absorbed from his parents. But betrayal followed as Jewish writers like Kossover too were seen as threats to Stalin.

In France, the novel was nominated for the prestigious Prix Goncourt, but its reception was mixed in the United States. A reviewer in the *Christian Science Monitor* called the novel "a remarkable experience" and said that "it is a fervent, eloquent and disciplined account of the moral journeys endemic to our times."[6] However, the *Times* reviewer found *The Testament* "the most extreme example of Mr. Wiesel's tendency, evident in other novels, to sacrifice the demands of craft to those of conscience."[7]

A similar point was made by critics with the publication in 1985 of his next novel, *The Fifth Son*, which explores the question of whether children of survivors should avenge the atrocities suffered by their parents. The plot follows the effort of the book's protagonist, Reuven Tamiroff, to complete an act of revenge his stepfather botched: the murder of an SS officer who killed the stepfather's infant son in a Polish ghetto. The writer Frederic Morton, in a review for the *Times*, suggested Wiesel was not "an essential Holocaust novelist" but rather "a first-rate rhetorician." "It's as if Auschwitz had forever tainted his senses, and they were therefore not to be trusted as instruments of the imagination," he said.[8]

By contrast, Wiesel's nonfiction works during this period were almost universally lauded. A superb essayist, he had an eye for essential questions and his intellect was comfortable with contradictions, paradoxes, and dilemmas.

Legends of Our Time, published by Holt, Rinehart & Winston in 1968, is essentially a collection of stories. Wiesel cautions readers at the outset: "Some events do take place but are not true; and others are—although they never occurred." Indeed, some stories are based in fact, like the depiction of his second visit to the Moscow synagogue or his return to Sighet. Some are largely true, like his encounter on a Tel Aviv bus with an Auschwitz barracks chief. And some are wholly imagined, like his receiving a blessing from the old Vizhnitzer Rebbe in

Bnei Brak, the ultra-Orthodox suburb of Tel Aviv. (By 1955, the old rebbe had already died.)[9] With this incongruous collection of fiction and nonfiction, Wiesel was showing readers that he felt free to delve into the realm of *midrash*—stories whose derived truths are more important than the authenticity of the events themselves. Hugh Nissenson, in his review in the *Times*, called the book "a series of brilliantly realized tales."[10]

Souls on Fire, published by Random House in 1972, was a charming introduction to the world of Hasidism. Lively anecdotes and fables about the Baal Shem Tov, the Maggid of Mezeritch, and other Hasidic masters made this arcane religious group accessible to uninformed readers, often for the first time. Wiesel explicated their differences from mainstream Jews and pointed out that, far from being a dark, grim offshoot of Judaism, Hasidism emphasizes ecstatic fervor in the observance of the Jewish commandments, joy and celebration rather than despair in the face of anti-Semitic attacks. In a review printed on the front page of the *Times Book Review*, Charles E. Silberman called the book a "work of genius and of art" and said "it should be read by everyone."[11]

One measure of Wiesel's new prominence was that the *Times* more meticulously chronicled his career, recording his CUNY appointment in 1973 and his collaboration with Leonard Fein and Moshe Dworkin in 1975 to start the Jewish-themed magazine *Moment*. (Wiesel was named the magazine's literary editor.) *Times* editors also began calling on him for reviews and topical essays like the one he wrote assessing the significance of the massacre of Israeli athletes at the 1972 Olympics in Munich. "Dead or alive, Jews are alone," he concluded.

Forsaking his journalist's neutrality, Wiesel increasingly immersed himself in public controversies touching the Jewish community, including that era's often fraught relations between blacks and Jews. In May 1972, Wiesel was one of the Jewish leaders who spoke at an emergency conference called by the New

York City Board of Rabbis to consider what some saw as mounting hostility toward Jews from within the black community. In 1968, in Ocean Hill–Brownsville, a largely African-American school district in Brooklyn that was experimenting with the concept of community control, a dozen Jewish teachers and administrators had been fired, and the clamor to reinstate them was met by several anti-Semitic radio broadcasts and speeches by black nationalists. An effort in 1972 by Jewish and other white residents to block the building of a public housing complex in the middle of the largely Jewish neighborhood of Forest Hills, Queens, also reverberated with racial tensions. These conflicts played out against a backdrop of rising crime in the city that many whites, Jews included, blamed on black residents.

"From the tensions that I feel tonight I'm frightened," Wiesel told the crowd at the emergency conference. "I tell you it disturbs me deeply."

He then related the story of a Jewish taxi driver who considered himself a liberal until he was robbed and had his hand slashed by a black passenger.[12] After a *Times* report on the conference, Wiesel felt compelled to follow up with a clarifying letter that said he was disturbed as much by the hall's angry mood as he was by the incidents that provoked it. "However valid the issues and however serious the anxieties, to counter hostility with more group hostility is not the solution. . . . We must not allow Jews to lapse into 'justifiable' reactionary attitudes. Should this happen it would be a defeat—if not worse—for all of us."[13] It was a long time before Wiesel would once again wade into such thorny social conflicts, where both sides had reasons for anger.

By January he was the subject of a long *Times* profile by Edward Fiske called "Elie Wiesel: Archivist with a Mission." According to Fiske, Wiesel, at forty-four, "has become not only a major force in American letters but also something of a spiritual phenomenon among Jews of all ages. . . . Mr. Wiesel has become a virtual symbol of those who survived the 'holocaust,' . . . at a time when this tragedy is becoming a major theme of Jewish life and literature . . . and his personal odyssey, including his recent marriage and the birth of a son, is seen by many as a symbol of the possibility for hope among Jews today." It quoted Eugene Borowitz, editor of the Jewish journal *Sh'ma*, as saying: "He is the closest thing we have in the Jewish community to a superstar."

The article retraced the story of Wiesel's life, and used the description of a character from *Gates of the Forest* to describe his "sharply defined, handsome, tormented face, . . . and melancholy smile. His eyes two firebrands which sear the flesh and pierce the skin of being. They gaze upon you; you will never be the same." Fiske called the fictional passage a self-portrait of its writer.[14]

The Fiske profile described *Night* as a thinly veiled autobiographical "novel," despite Wiesel's insistence over the years that it was not a novel and was never intended to be one. The article included one other point that chafed. It mentioned that several people had accused Wiesel of "exploiting his identification with the holocaust for personal gain"—a suggestion of large speaking fees and book sales promotions—"but no one does this publicly." The one source backing up that charge was an anonymous quotation (the *Times* ethics code of recent decades discourages unattributed derogatory quotes). In *All Rivers Run to the Sea*, the first volume of his memoirs, Wiesel took on this charge squarely: "At some point in their lives, every writer who has written about the Holocaust has had to defend himself against this sort of accusation, which leaves one feeling smeared and powerless," he wrote. "Yet it is crucial to denounce such malevolence, whose most dangerous and perverse effect would be to make people shrink from speaking of the Holocaust." Survivors like him had a duty to speak and write as witnesses. "In truth, how can anyone fail to see that a witness rendered mute betrays the living as much as the dead?"[15]

Wiesel's preeminence as a spokesman for the survivors was also affirmed in April 1973 when he was called upon for the thirtieth anniversary of the Warsaw Ghetto uprising to address a crowd of over seven thousand people at Manhattan's cavernous Temple Emanu-El—most of them refugees and their relatives—with fifteen hundred others listening through speakers outside. "Let us remember that they lived alone, they fought alone, suffered alone," he said of the six million. "Alone. That is the key word. Desperately alone. We let them down. We let them march alone, fight alone."

In November, a cantata he wrote the libretto for, *Ani Ma'amin, A Song Lost and Found Again*, was performed at Carnegie Hall. The score was composed by Darius Milhaud, with Lukas Foss conducting. Bronx-born Metropolitan Opera soprano Roberta Peters sang, and veteran actors Joseph Wiseman and David Opatoshu took the parts of two of the Patriarchs. The cantata was an expression of Wiesel's spiritual struggle, much of it based on a melody he recalled from his Vizhnitz childhood. But its coda was a forceful declaration of faith: despite the Holocaust and God's indifference to His people's plight, "Ani Ma'amin," "I believe," the singers cried out, words that resonate with Maimonides' thirteen principles of faith.

In August 1974, his sister Bea, just forty-nine years old, died of cancer, the first death among the handful of Wiesels who survived the war. Wiesel was vacationing in Italy with Marion and Elisha when he received the news in a phone call from Bea's husband Leonard in Montreal. He promptly called his other sister Hilda to tell her. When she picked up the phone, he could barely speak. "What is it? What is it?" Hilda cried. Wiesel finally whispered, "Bea."

"Three children from Sighet had been reunited after the war, and now only two are left," Wiesel recalled thinking. "A thought tears through my brain. We had never spoken of her experiences *over there*. Now it is too late."

In a scene described in *And the Sea Is Never Full*, Wiesel finds himself talking to his dead sister and telling her she will soon see their parents. He remarks that mourning her was the first time he had been able to sit *shiva*. "Certain midrashic texts suggest that the soul of the dead floats through the house during shivah. And I can indeed feel my sister's presence." Wiesel would visit his sister's grave whenever he returned to Montreal. On her tombstone, he tells us, are engraved "the names of those dear to us who never had a grave of their own."[16]

17

A Boston Professor

IN JUNE 1975, Wiesel accepted an endowed chair at Boston University at the invitation of President John Silber. For the next thirty-seven years, he was the Andrew W. Mellon Professor of Humanities at the large urban university. The BU position was a far more lucrative one that only required him to teach one course a week, rather than the two he was teaching at City College. But as he later admitted, he had miscalculated; his weekly trips to Boston took twice as long as the six hours he had spent at City College.[1] He had become disenchanted with the academic atmosphere at City College, however. The open-admissions policy that admitted virtually any high school graduate to the once selective college was discouraging Jewish students, who less than a decade before had been a majority of the enrollment, from applying. Wiesel, like Yitz Greenberg, worried whether the Jewish Studies Department at City College could survive in such circumstances.[2]

By all accounts, Wiesel was an unforgettable teacher, and he continued teaching until 2013, when he was already past eighty and had written his final novel. Ariel Burger, his teaching assistant between 2003 and 2008 who went on to write *Witness: Lessons from Elie Wiesel's Classroom*, remembers him saying: "Teaching will be the last thing I'll give up." Martha Hauptman, his personal assistant for twenty-seven years, estimates three thousand students took his classes at BU.[3]

Ilene Semiatin, a business development consultant, audited one of Wiesel's first courses at BU—"The Literature of Memory"—in a banked lecture hall and found him a magnetic teacher. "He had a very gentle and yet very intense presence," she recalled. "He spoke very beautifully. He was a very human person. He emoted. He moved around a lot. He seemed very passionate to me. Some of his classes were very, very depressing, but he wasn't couching things in ways that made it easy for students to cope. And yet he as a person didn't seem dark. When people asked questions, I remember he was very personal. He looked at the person—it was a personal conversation with the person who asked the question."[4]

Wiesel arranged to teach future courses as seminars, so that he could sit with students around a table. Though "The Literature of Memory" remained the overall title of many of those courses, each had a different subtitle, such as "The Jewish Response to Persecution," or "Memory and Conscience." He also taught courses on Hasidism and on literature by Jewish women. The reading lists of various courses included Hannah Arendt's *Origins of Totalitarianism*, Emil Fackenheim's *God's Presence in History*, and Simon Dubnow's *History of the Jews in Russia and Poland*. The required novels, in addition to Wiesel's own, tended to have philosophical themes: Camus' *The Plague*, Kafka's *The Trial*, Goethe's *Faust*, and Aeschylus' *Prometheus Bound*. A modern addition was Milton Steinberg's *As a Driven Leaf*, a historical novel whose main character—named Elisha like Wiesel's son—

is a leading Talmudist in the Palestine of 100 C.E. who becomes skeptical of an omnipotent God after witnessing an undeserved tragedy. "It is all a lie," he proclaims. "There is no reward. There is no Judge. There is no Judgment. For there is no God." Such passages were certain to provoke probing conversations about questions Wiesel himself was still wrestling with, and that was precisely what he sought.

Only once did Professor Wiesel teach a course explicitly on the Holocaust, and afterward he was so emotionally drained that he never taught the course again. "I remember Elie saying that he had to leave it to younger scholars because it took too much out of him," Martha Hauptman, who had been a student in his first Boston class before becoming his assistant for twenty-seven years, told me.

Ariel Burger said Wiesel would sometimes use "obscuring language" when talking about the Holocaust. "He wouldn't say Auschwitz; he would say 'that place,' or the 'Kingdom of Night.' Not that he couldn't be direct but he was worried about discussion of the Holocaust becoming banal," Burger said. In fact whatever the subject, the professor and the students inevitably found themselves talking about the Shoah. Another former student, Rabbi Jeffrey J. Sirkman, said Wiesel made clear to the class that the "Holocaust was woven into everything" as were the haunting existential questions it raised.

In his seminars, Wiesel roamed widely across the landscape of his preoccupations. In his class on the Jewish response to persecution, for instance, he would start out with Jeremiah, whom he called a prophet of persecution and suffering, but then would bring in the Fascist bombing of the Basque village of Guernica, the German massacre of Jews at Babi Yar, and the Warsaw Ghetto uprising. He would suggest that like Jeremiah, Emanuel Ringelblum, the historian who documented life in the Warsaw Ghetto, felt abandoned by God and forsaken by mankind. "He foresaw the destruction of Polish Jewry for a few months until his own execution and suffered guilt that he was still living while others died," reads a student's notes citing the professor's comments.[5]

Professor Wiesel made a strong impression on his students, many of whom were not Jewish, according to Burger. One student, David Bell, described Wiesel as "physically quite small" and said he "spoke barely above a whisper." But "the tormented expression which never escaped his face," he wrote, "jolted me into the reality of a very powerful physical presence in our midst."

Sirkman, who went on to become the long-serving rabbi at Larchmont Temple in Westchester County, recalled that "The Literature of Memory" course he took demanded that its fifteen students study a different novel by Wiesel every week. For the first half of the three-hour class, a student would read a paper analyzing a particular novel, and for the second half Wiesel would offer his own perspective. What was so beguiling, Sirkman told me, was the professor's teaching style, which relied more on anecdote and allegory than on a recitation of facts. He "unlocked the secrets" of his books, Sirkman said. "Being in the room with him was like being with a biblical prophet or a great Hasidic rebbe."

Wiesel was so steeped in Jewish history that he seemed to relate personally to biblical and Talmudic figures, as if they were old friends. When he talked about the sages he profiled in *Souls on Fire*, students felt as if they were meeting the great Hasidic rebbes themselves. "He imbibed the person he was speaking about," Sirkman said. "He became Rabbi Levi Yitzchak of Berditchev. When he spoke of Abraham or Moses, there was a depth there where he seemed to understand these figures as if they were in the room."[6]

Wiesel typically opened the semester by having each student explain why he or she was taking the class. One Orthodox young man said he did so to understand why the Shoah happened. Wiesel, gripping his pen like a Gitanes cigarette, told the student in so many words: "Perhaps this is not the class you hoped for because I can't tell you why. Nobody can tell you why."

Sirkman also recalled how Wiesel openly let his students know of his affection for madmen. One time a disheveled man with a wild-eyed demeanor stood on Commonwealth Avenue, preaching that the end of the world was approaching. Wiesel listened to him attentively. When his students wondered why he would waste his time doing so, Wiesel replied, "Who knows who's a prophet?" "Madness is the only way you can cope with a world that's gone insane," he said, making that somber statement with what Sirkman described as "a beautiful, radiant smile."

Sirkman came to understand how Wiesel could be furious at God yet pray to him with the regularity of any other observant Jew. "Being angry is a relationship," Sirkman told me. "If you're angry you care." As he put it, "To be a Jew is to ask a question: Why and how can we survive in a world which negates us?" "You couldn't walk away from his class without being enveloped by the emotional, psychic and social power of being with this man."[7]

Professor Wiesel would forge many personal connections in the classroom, making a point of meeting one-on-one with each student and welcoming correspondence long after the semester was over. Sometimes he would inform a student of an upcoming speech or meeting with a notable figure and solicit the student's thoughts about what he should say. There were times many years after taking the class when Sirkman, as a rabbi, encountered Wiesel, who would warmly remember details about Sirkman and his wife, Susan, and their lives. Then he would ask, "When are you going to come back and learn with me?"

"No question he was the most transformational teacher I ever studied with and I have had great teachers," Sirkman told me. "As a teacher I try to model the way he taught."

Ariel Burger, now a teacher and artist, told me Wiesel's passion for teaching never flagged, even late in his career when Burger was his teaching assistant.

> When he walked into the room there was often a hush. Students would feel suddenly alert in a way that was rare. . . . His presence invited students to bring themselves to the conversation beyond the materials we were studying.
>
> There was something about his presence that I've only perceived with Hasidic rabbis. . . . He really celebrated questions. . . . Sometimes he would allow questions to build on one another. After five or ten minutes there was a tapestry of questions. Then he would respond—with his own questions. He always welcomed . . . personal questions, derived from the kind of baggage people were carrying.

In one class, Burger recalled, there were several students from Germany, some of whom were wrestling with the dark legacy of their grandparents. One young woman, the granddaughter of a German SS officer, asked Wiesel: "What would you say to my grandfather if he were here now? Could you forgive him?" The class became silent, sensing, as Burger remembered, that "something special was happening and curious how Wiesel would respond."

"It's not my place to forgive," Wiesel said, "but whatever guilt your grandfather had doesn't extend to you. We don't believe in collective punishment."[8]

Another time, on the last day of class, when the professor typically welcomed any questions still gnawing at students, a student in the front row raised his hand and hesitantly asked: "Can you show us your number?" The class fell silent. This was what Burger called "a dangerous moment," and students weren't sure whether Wiesel would react angrily or with embarrassment. At this point in his life, Wiesel was being assaulted on the internet by Holocaust deniers who claimed that he had never been in Auschwitz and therefore had no number tattooed on his left forearm.

"Without a word," Burger recalled, "Professor Wiesel took off his jacket, rolled up his shirtsleeve and swiveled his arm so the whole class could see. Then he rolled his sleeve down, put on his jacket and said, 'Next question.' The student turned bright red, but Professor Wiesel saw it was a sincere question. He felt students needed to be witnesses to his reality. Every student could then tell that story."

Beyond engendering understanding for those who went through the Shoah, Wiesel hoped that through his teaching "students would be sensitized to suffering, that they would not pass a homeless person without giving some money and a smile," Burger said. "People who were in medical school told me their mission shifted from being a successful practitioner to wanting to be the kind of doctor who made sure patients were treated with dignity, or law students who shifted their focus to human rights. Some became clergy because of Wiesel—Jews and Christians. Some became more religious, immersed themselves in Hasidism and mysticism. I encountered ministry students who became comfortable with doubt and more connected to the Jewish roots of Christianity."

18

The Holocaust and the Arts

As the Holocaust became a cultural phenomenon—to a
large extent as a result of Elie Wiesel's own influence—he chafed
at various depictions of it. Over four nights in April 1978, tens
of millions of Americans were glued to NBC-TV for a nine-
and-a-half-hour miniseries about what befell the Jews of Europe before and during the Second World War. Starkly titled
with the single word *Holocaust*, the miniseries traced the history
of the persecution and mass slaughter of Europe's Jews through
the stories of two fictional families, one Jewish, one German.
Its screenplay was written by the novelist Gerald Green and it
had an all-star cast that included Meryl Streep, James Woods,
Fritz Weaver, Rosemary Harris, John Houseman, David Warner, and Sam Wanamaker. According to NBC, as many as 120
million Americans saw all or part of the miniseries, with one
episode having been seen by half of all TV viewers that night,

or one-third of American homes with televisions.¹ It was a major TV event.

The miniseries should have been a validation of Wiesel's work, confirming his admonition that the Shoah be remembered. But he was appalled by the show. He was asked by the *Times* to write a review, and his assessment in a long essay in the Sunday Arts and Leisure section was withering. "Untrue, offensive, cheap: as a TV production, the film is an insult to those who perished and to those who survived," he wrote. "It transforms an ontological event into soap opera. Whatever the intentions, the result is shocking. Contrived situations, sentimental episodes, implausible coincidences; if they make you cry, you will cry for the wrong reasons."

Wiesel was repelled by what he considered the docudrama's cavalier treatment of the facts. For example, inmates were shown inside Auschwitz opening suitcases and studying family pictures, items they were in fact not allowed to keep. He objected to the portrayals of the Jews and their German tormentors as stereotypes. The Jewish family's members were improbably shown as being involved in every signature event from Kristallnacht to the confinement of the Warsaw Ghetto, to the massacres at the Babi Yar ravine in Kiev, to Auschwitz, and even to the Sobibor revolt. The same license was taken with the main German protagonist, who appeared at every milestone of the Nazi regime's rise and fall. Not only would a viewer unfamiliar with the history be misled about what really happened and what was fictionalized, but such distortions, Wiesel suggested, undermined the credibility of those devoted to telling the accurate history. That was a dangerous outcome in a world already containing Holocaust deniers.

"Thus, I object to it not because it is not artistic enough, but because it is not authentic enough," he wrote. "The witness feels here duty-bound to declare: What you have seen on the screen is not what happened there."

Wiesel was not wrong to lament the series' tawdry qualities and to fault the artistic choices. But ultimately his standards may have been impossible to meet. "Auschwitz," he wrote in the *Times* essay, "cannot be explained nor can it be visualized. Whether the culmination or aberration of history, the Holocaust transcends history. Everything about it inspires fear and leads to despair. The dead are in possession of a secret that we, the living, are neither worthy of nor capable of recovering."

"How is one to tell a tale that cannot be—but must be—told?" Wiesel asked, addressing the conundrum head-on. "I don't know. All I know is that the witness does not recognize himself in this film. The Holocaust must be remembered, but not as a show."[2]

The piece drew scores of letters, including one that the *Times* chose to print at length—from Gerald Green himself, the author of the miniseries. He acknowledged some inaccuracies, disputed others, and pointed out that inserting the story's Jewish and Nazis families into a series of historical events is an accepted literary device. He vehemently objected to Elie Wiesel's setting himself up as the sole arbiter of which Holocaust works merited public attention.

"Is Elie Wiesel to be allowed a monopoly on the subject, to be self-anointed and the only voice of the Holocaust?" he asked. He predicted—quite presciently—that "the viewing of *Holocaust* will create a surge of new interest in the subject. . . . More of Elie Wiesel's books will be sold than ever. There will be more lecture bookings and seminars for him. . . . And I will be the first to rejoice."[3]

Although he had reservations about the miniseries, Yitz Greenberg, Wiesel's friend and teaching colleague, helped the show reach a wider audience. Greenberg produced a study guide for NBC in which he called the show a "breakthrough." It would "deepen our understanding of the incomprehensible," he wrote, and "tens of millions will see with their own eyes and experience in their own homes a shadow of the incredible and un-precedented total assault on Jews and humanity."[4]

When I interviewed Greenberg in 2017, he told me of fruit-lessly trying to negotiate a truce of sorts between Wiesel and Green. Still, Greenberg said he did not regret helping to pro-mote the show. "It was self-evident this would spread the idea in ways none of us could have dreamed of," he said.[5] And of course it helped enlarge Wiesel's reputation in ways he himself could not have dreamed of.

Thane Rosenbaum, a son of survivors who wrote *Second-Hand Smoke* and other Holocaust-related novels, acknowledged that the TV series compelled more of the public to confront the Holocaust's reality and what it said about human iniquity, yet felt credit should be given to Wiesel for insisting that "while memory is important the quality of memory is too, and it's not helpful if you're trivializing it and misrepresenting it."[6]

In his memoir, Wiesel said he was "partial" to Holocaust documentaries like *Shoah*, *The Eighty-First Blow*, *Night and Fog*, and *The Partisans of Vilna*. But almost every fictional depiction on screen and stage "was tainted by either the images or the lan-guage." He panned the television series *The Winds of War* based on Herman Wouk's novel, and the film (not the book) *Sophie's Choice*. Nevertheless, his comments caused a falling out with William Styron, the author of *Sophie's Choice*.[7]

The argument over trivialization was one he would be tan-gled in for the rest of his life. In 1989, he wrote still another *Times* essay about cultural exploitation, disparaging films like *Seven Beauties* and *The Night Porter*. The essay opened starkly with a quotation from Wittgenstein: "Whereof one cannot speak, one must not speak" (other translators render the sentence as "Whereof one cannot speak, thereof one must be silent") and argued that Auschwitz "defeated art because just as no one could imagine Auschwitz before Auschwitz, no one can now re-tell Auschwitz after Auschwitz. The truth of Auschwitz remains hidden in its ashes. Only those who lived it in their flesh and in their minds can possibly transform their experience into knowledge." Clearly, his comments resonated with Theodor Adorno's famous remark: "There can be no poetry after Auschwitz." In a period of "general de-sanctification of the Holocaust," Wiesel wrote, Hollywood and Broadway were producing simplistic melodramas with doses of sex, sentimentality, and suspense along with a "dash of theological rumination about the silence of God and there it is: let kitsch rule in the land of kitsch, where at the expense of truth, what counts is ratings and facile success."[8]

He was particularly harsh toward a recent play, *Ghetto*, about the Vilna Ghetto in Lithuania, resorting to the use of words like "blasphemy" and "profanation." Its author, the Israeli playwright Joshua Sobol, responded in kind, calling Wiesel's insistence on artistic silence "monopolistic" and "authoritarian." Wiesel, after all, had written not only *Night* but novels that dealt with concentration camps, deportations, and mass shootings; he seemed to reserve this territory for himself and other witnesses. Sobol argued that researching events in the Vilna Ghetto taught him to be skeptical about those who claim to possess the truth about what happened.

"I learned that there are almost no two concurring testimonies about one single important event," he wrote. "My work taught me that the zone of silence of one witness is sometimes the unhealed screaming wound of another." Insisting on silence, his letter concluded, will only yield ignorance.

Wiesel's published reply to the letter said that Sobol had mischaracterized his point, that he did not endorse silence since he wanted survivors and their children to speak out, teach, and bear witness. What he was objecting to was vulgarization.[9]

Despite Wiesel's admonitions, Holocaust movies, books, and plays appeared with increasing frequency. Among these were such honored films as *Life Is Beautiful* (three Academy Awards, including best actor), *Schindler's List* (seven Academy Awards, including best picture), *The Pianist* (Academy Awards for best director, actor, and adapted screenplay), *The Reader* (Academy Award for best actress), *Europa, Europa* (Golden Globe, best foreign film), *Son of Saul* (Academy Award, best foreign film), *Enemies, A Love Story* (three Academy Award nominations), and *Denial* (British Academy Award nomination for best British film). By 2021, Rich Brownstein, a lecturer at Yad Vashem's International School for Holocaust Studies, had produced a book that catalogues and analyzes four hundred Holocaust films. Eventually Wiesel's views mellowed, or perhaps he tired of appearing to be a purist and a scold. In 2013, producer Harvey Weinstein (four years before his downfall for sexual abuse) presented Wiesel with a "Warrior for Truth" award at a celebration for the Yiddish newspaper *Algemeiner*.

"I think there would be no *Schindler's List*, no *Life Is Beautiful*, no *Reader*," Weinstein told the assembled. "So many of the movies that us in the industry have been involved in, . . . about the Holocaust, came from that first seminal book which was *Night*, which continues to inspire me." Wiesel responded, without addressing the movies Weinstein mentioned, some of which had offended him: "You made me love films. It is only thanks to you, really. . . . I was not part of films. My life was books. Because at one point you came in my life and now I like films too, especially those that you make."[10]

Perhaps Wiesel also realized that his original argument was one he could never win. He may have come of age as a writer during a period of reticence about the Holocaust, but by the 1980s survivors were often eager, even desperate to have their stories told before they died—a goal Wiesel encouraged. The children and grandchildren of survivors also started producing fictionalized works drawn from their own experiences, and some of these were adapted for film. They included Jonathan Safran Foer's *Everything Is Illuminated*, a national bestseller that was made into a film directed by Liev Schreiber and starring Elijah

Wood, Nicole Krauss's *The History of Love*, Thane Rosenbaum's *Second Hand Smoke*, and Sonia Pilcer's *The Holocaust Kid* and *Teen Angel*. A generation or two removed, these authors did not see the subject of the Holocaust as unapproachably sacred. Hallowed as the dead were, the unfolding of the Holocaust nevertheless involved human beings engaged in human activities with all the granular detail and ambiguities that novelists and filmmakers seek out. If these descendants did not consider it wrong to grapple with the Holocaust, why couldn't a Jew with no particular wartime legacy, or a non-Jew for whom the catastrophe had a particular resonance tackle the subject as well? Indeed, more than seven decades later, the Holocaust continues to challenge writers, artists, and filmmakers.

Of course, the great irony is, as Gerald Green predicted, that all the works of art that Wiesel disdained helped elevate his own stature as a Holocaust authority. "With the passage of time, he accommodated himself to reality," said Rabbi Greenberg. "These forms of commercialization made breakthroughs possible. He was a human being and eventually human beings compromise with reality."

19

Museums and Memory

THE TREASURED U.S. Holocaust Memorial Museum in Washington had its genesis in one president's political headache.

In 1978, President Jimmy Carter had persuaded Congress to approve the sale of a fleet of F-15 fighter jets to Saudi Arabia. He also agreed to sell the Saudis all-weather spy planes—known as AWACS—because he wanted to empower an ally after the Soviet invasion of Afghanistan and the outbreak of war between Iran and Iraq.[1] Jewish organizations, already dismayed by Carter's call for a Palestinian homeland, were furious, worried that the jets and spy planes could eventually be used against Israel.

Fearing a backlash that would deny him votes and donations for his 1980 reelection campaign, Carter realized he needed to do something to demonstrate his concern for the Jewish people. He asked Stuart E. Eizenstat, his chief domestic policy adviser and a committed Jew, for ideas.

Eizenstat had long been disturbed by the rise of Holocaust revisionists and, as it happened, he and two other administration officials, Ellen Goldstein and Mark A. Siegel, had developed a proposal for a monument or memorial to victims of the Holocaust on federal land. It had languished, but Carter's inquiry allowed Eizenstat to revive the proposal. According to Greenberg, the first director of the council charged with building the memorial, Carter leaped at the suggestion. He was aware of the enormous popularity of the *Holocaust* television miniseries two years before and thought the proposal "would carry great Jewish resonance," Greenberg told me.[2] Carter revealed his vision for a monument or memorial to an ecstatic audience of visiting rabbis in the Rose Garden in June 1978.

To determine what kind of memorial would be appropriate, Eizenstat needed to assemble a commission, and he asked Greenberg, whose work with the National Jewish Center for Learning and Leadership (CLAL) he knew, to recommend a chairman. Greenberg urged Eizenstat to name Wiesel. Michael Berenbaum, who would become Greenberg's deputy, told me Eizenstat's first choice was actually Arthur J. Goldberg, the former Supreme Court justice. But Goldberg had declined, telling Eizenstat that "if it's Holocaust-related it had to be Wiesel."[3]

Wiesel was in a hotel room in Israel chatting with Shimon Peres, the head of the opposition Labor Party, about a new book by Peres when the telephone rang. It was Eizenstat wondering why Wiesel was not returning his calls. Wiesel explained that he thought the telephone messages purporting to come from the White House were a prank. When Eizenstat got around to laying out his proposal, Wiesel candidly—and as it turned out accurately—replied that he did not think a political position like chairman of a federal commission suited him. But eventually Greenberg and Wiesel's friend Sigmund Strochlitz persuaded him to reconsider. "If you refuse," argued Strochlitz, "some politician or other will be nominated. Who knows what he'll do with our memories?" Before committing himself, Wiesel asked for a meeting with Carter.[4]

In the Oval Office, Carter was warm and welcoming, even quoting lines from Wiesel's writings (Wiesel suspected they had been excerpted by an aide). At one point, he showed Wiesel the White House's Auschwitz file containing photos of the camp taken in daylight in 1944. To Wiesel's mind, the photographs proved that FDR knew about the horrors occurring at Auschwitz and yet declined to bomb the camp or the adjacent railways. The inmates, Wiesel said in his memoirs, had prayed for such an act. (Berenbaum told me, however, that Wiesel may have misremembered, that the Auschwitz photos were only developed out of raw film long after Roosevelt's death, so the president never saw actual pictures from the camp.)[5] When Wiesel expressed dismay at Roosevelt's failure to act, Carter shrugged and said, "What can be done now?" He then turned to the reason for their meeting. "We must fight oblivion," he said. "Isn't that the purpose of all your work?"

Wiesel was disarmed and right there told Carter he would accept his offer to serve as the commission chairman. Nevertheless he let Carter know that Jewish tradition did not glorify monuments. Perhaps he was thinking of a passage by his friend the theologian Abraham Joshua Heschel, about memory as the truest way to honor past events. "Jews have not preserved the ancient monuments, they have retained the ancient moments. . . . With sustaining vitality the past survives in their thoughts, hearts, rituals."[6] Other survivor friends like Sigmund Strochlitz "thought the idea of a monument was a complete waste," said his daughter, Dr. Romana Strochlitz. "Their mission, Wiesel's and my father's, was to teach and remember. They wanted a living memorial. They wanted history to be preserved and [to] have it serve as the basis for the idea of 'Never again!' Not just for Jews but for the wider world."[7] So Wiesel told Carter he would rather have some kind of "teaching project" or "teaching institution" and a National Day of Remembrance than a monument. If such a day were to be held, Carter replied, he would show up at the first ceremony.

On November 1, 1978, Carter publicly announced the establishment of a President's Commission on the Holocaust with Elie Wiesel as its head. The thirty-four members of the commission were an eclectic group, including U.S. senators, historians, religious leaders, and survivors. Well-known members included Arthur Goldberg, Isaac Bashevis Singer, the Holocaust historians Raul Hilberg and Lucy Dawidowicz, Senator Henry "Scoop" Jackson, Notre Dame president Theodore Hesburgh, and the civil rights leader Bayard Rustin.

From the start four questions emerged that would shape the commission's deliberations: What kind of memorial should there be—a monument, a museum, a research center, a school, an advocacy organization? How Jewish or how universal should the memorial be? How Jewish should the membership of the council—the successor to the commission as the group that would actually design and build the memorial—be? And who would pay for the project?

The issue of how Jewish the memorial should be struck the commission emphatically within six months of its formation. When Carter appeared at the first Holocaust commemoration in the U.S. Capitol rotunda on April 24, 1979, he spoke of eleven million victims. Wiesel approached him afterward and asked where he learned of this figure. Carter told him that it came from the writings of Simon Wiesenthal, the fabled Nazi hunter who would eventually become a nemesis of Wiesel's. Wiesenthal had been imprisoned in Mauthausen in Austria, where many inmates were not Jewish, and he preferred to universalize the toll. (Historians have since said that he arbitrarily added five million in an effort to draw wider sympathy to Jewish suffering, though the larger number has sometimes had the opposite effect.) As Wiesel explained to Carter, many of the non-Jewish victims were anti-Semites and sadistic criminals whom the Germans released from prison to help supervise the camps. Other groups of victims such as the Gypsies, Poles, and the disabled were never pursued as relentlessly as were the Jews, and only the Jews were singled out for extermination. Suggesting an equivalence with non-Jewish victims was a distortion. Carter never used that figure again.[8]

That first Holocaust commemoration in the Capitol was also notable for Wiesel's outspokenness before an audience that included an American president, leaders of Congress, and prominent non-Jews. More than offering generalities about genocide and the horrors of the Holocaust, he explicitly took the United States and its allies to task for their failures before and during the war to rescue Jews. "The world knew and kept silent," he declared in the rotunda. "Jewish victims were disowned by the whole world. Not one bomb was dropped on the railway tracks to the death factories." If critics like Naomi Seidman were justified in faulting Wiesel for pulling his punches in the English edition of *Night* regarding the world's indifference, the speech in the Capitol demonstrated that by 1979 he was forcefully confronting such passive responses.

Taking the helm as chairman, Wiesel wisely realized that a necessary first step, one that would be enlightening and set an appropriately somber tone, was for the commission to visit what he called "the capitals" of the Holocaust—the Warsaw Ghetto, Majdanek, Treblinka, Auschwitz, and Babi Yar. That fall, ten commission members along with their relatives and a team of advisers—forty-four people in all—set out on that journey. Wiesel brought along Marion and seven-year-old Elisha.

Like Wiesel, the other survivor members were revisiting sites where they had suffered or lost relatives: Ben Meed at the Warsaw Ghetto's Mila 18 address, Miles Lerman at Treblinka, Hadassah Rosensaft in the Cracow Ghetto, Sigmund Strochlitz in Auschwitz-Birkenau. "One had to be there in order to understand that there are some kinds of loneliness that can never be overcome," Wiesel said.

In both Poland and the Soviet Union, the commission's hosts soft-pedaled the inescapable fact that most of the Nazis' victims were Jews, emphasizing the victims' nationalities rather than their religion. The Poles wanted the delegation to start their tour with a visit to Warsaw's monument to Poles who had been slain in a bloody revolt in 1944, a year after the Warsaw Ghetto uprising. Meed, who had been a courier for the ghetto fighters in 1943, was uncomfortable with the arrangement but nevertheless consented, angering Wiesel. Taking matters into his own hands, Wiesel told the Poles that if the delegation could not visit the Warsaw Ghetto monument first, they would cancel their tour of the city. The Poles relented. In various talks he gave while in Poland, Wiesel pointedly said that although Poles were also victims of the Germans and while individual Poles did hide Jews, thousands of Poles aided the Germans or reveled in the slaughter of their Jewish neighbors. "We were the victims of the victims as well," he said.[9]

"Jews were murdered because they were Jews, not because they were Poles," he wrote afterward in a *Times* essay. "They, and they alone, were fated to total extermination not because of what they had said or done or possessed, but because of what they were."[10]

Wherever the commission members went they were confronted with the dispiriting fact that Poland and hundreds of towns in the Soviet Union had been stripped bare of Jews. That year, Poland had just six thousand Jewish citizens; before the German invasion in 1939 it counted 3.5 million Jews. The community so powerfully evoked by Isaac Bashevis Singer, Chaim Grade (when Lithuania was part of Poland), and the photographer Roman Vishniac had largely shrunk to a handful of wizened men and women. The rich Jewish matrix of synagogues, yeshivas, political clubs, theaters, and Yiddish newspapers had vanished or lay in ruins.[11] "It is only natural, therefore, that a Jew feels out of place in today's Poland," Wiesel wrote of his visit. "He looks for his brothers and he fails to find them; he fails to find them even among the dead."

Treblinka, with all evidence erased of the single-purpose death factory that killed 925,000 Jews in just fifteen months, had been replaced by a graveyard-like constellation of austere stones, each with a name of an eviscerated town or city etched into it. The haunting scene, memorializing places many of the American visitors had grown up in, left them speechless. "We shall never understand," Wiesel wrote. "Even if we manage somehow to learn every aspect of that insane project, we will never understand it: How could men have done that to other men?"

The visit to Auschwitz and Birkenau was Wiesel's first since his own imprisonment. As he viewed once again Blocks 11 and 17 where he had been consigned and which have been preserved as part of what was now a "museum," the memories flooded back: of hunger, skeletal bunkmates, the barking of dogs, the screams of parents, the cries of children, the heaps of ashes, the ubiquitous corpses. It was striking, he wrote, to gaze now at the beautiful forested landscape around Birkenau, "the contrast between God's creation and human cruelty."

"Dante understood nothing," he wrote. "Hell is a setting whose serene splendor takes the breath away."[12]

Although the camps looked strangely peaceful on that sunny August day, the scene on the day in May when his family arrived in Auschwitz was still vivid in his mind. "It was cold," he wrote so many years later in *And the Sea Is Never Full*.[13] "Hilda and Bea were silent. Jumping down from the cattle car, a small golden-haired girl put on her coat. 'Button up,' said her mother. The little golden-haired girl, so beautiful, so calm, obeyed. My eyes followed her. I see her still, through my tears. I see her carried away by the crowd, disappearing into the distance, the well-behaved little girl, so very well behaved, with a poignantly beautiful smile, a little Jewish girl with a dreamy but worried face, a shining light high above a shipwreck."

"I see them moving forward, holding hands as if to reassure each other. I will see them that way, walking away, to the end of life."

When they came upon the rubble of the gas chambers and crematoria in Birkenau, Wiesel and the other delegates locked arms and said the "Shema Yisrael": "Hear O Israel, the Lord is our God, the Lord is One." They sensed that most of the victims must have recited that core Jewish prayer as they headed toward their deaths. Yet with all the solemnity, Wiesel could not help but notice the Disneyland-like presence of guides, souvenirs, and postcards: "This way to the bunker, a jail within a jail, this way to the crematorium." This may explain why he was at first somewhat skeptical about the value of creating a museum in Washington. "As the years go by I have less and less confidence in museums as sanctuaries of memory," he wrote in his memoirs.[14] Yet he had to concede that the preserved Auschwitz did validate, for visitors unfamiliar with the story or susceptible to Holocaust deniers, that "crimes against the Jewish people and against humanity were committed here," that "Auschwitz really existed."[15]

"So be it then," he wrote. "Visit the museum—as long as it remains unaltered, authentic."

At Babi Yar, the ravine where in 1941 more than 33,000 Jews were machine-gunned in two days between Rosh Hashanah and Yom Kippur, the delegation was pleased that Soviet officials had finally erected a monument. Wiesel found the work— a Stalinesque ramp of uneven brown stones crowned by a huddle of men, women, and children at the point of being shot—pompous, banal, and vulgar. He was outraged that its engravings spoke of "100,000 citizens of Kiev" killed by the Fascists, never mentioning that the majority were Jews.

Wiesel had to remind himself that he was representing the

president. But when he was called on to lay a wreath at the foot of the monument he audaciously let his hosts know his feelings about the glaring omission. "Now there is a monument at Babi Yar," he said. "But what kind of monument is it? We all had hoped to find a memorial for all the Jews who died as Jews, as well as for the others who died here. But the Jews are not being remembered."[16]

One bright spot in the European tour was Wiesel's return to the Moscow synagogue where he had first seen otherwise repressed Jews dancing rapturously with Torahs on the Simchat Torah holiday. Elisha was fussed over by the worshipers, "longingly as though he were a prince from a faraway kingdom." "It had been years since they had seen a little Jewish boy saying his prayers in the synagogue," Wiesel wrote.[17]

It was on this trip that perhaps unwittingly Wiesel also assumed some unfamiliar roles—those of diplomat and negotiator. No longer just a freelance journalist or novelist, he now had to be politic. Wiesel boldly asked Soviet leaders to release four "prisoners of Zion." Denied permission to emigrate, these so-called refuseniks had been dispatched to a gulag for campaigning on behalf of Jews seeking emigration to Israel. Among the four were the scientist Anatoly Sharansky and the Jewish activist Yosef Mendelevich. Soon a meeting was arranged with the Soviet attorney general, Roman Rudenko, who had been a prosecutor at the Nuremberg trials. As the encounter approached, Wiesel worried that his demand to see the four prisoners might have created a contretemps that would embarrass President Carter.

After a formal meeting with commission members seated at a boardroom table, Wiesel asked Rudenko if they could speak privately. When Rudenko imperiously asked the reason, Wiesel replied Talmudically: "In order to explain to you why we need to be alone." Rudenko relented and in their tête-à-tête, Wiesel began by saying he was not a political person. Rudenko, having read the dossier on Wiesel's writings and speeches, laughed off this attempt at humility, but accepted the list of four refuseniks that Wiesel handed him. He finally told Wiesel he would agree to seek the release of two of the four. Wiesel says in his memoir that Rudenko kept his word, but it is obvious who the two were. Mendelevich was released in 1981, and Sharansky in 1986.[18]

During this painful European tour, it became increasingly clear to Wiesel that the majority of commission members favored the idea of erecting a "memorial." A mere symbol or marker would not do. But Wiesel still had his misgivings. Menachem Rosensaft, the Second Generation leader who served on the council, said Wiesel found even the notion of a museum too concrete.[19]

"How are we going to 'show' the Tragedy, when it is impossible almost to speak of it?" Wiesel wrote in *And the Sea Is Never Full*, betraying as he often did his own inner conflicts about morally complicated subjects with serial questions. "Could images be more eloquent? More effective? And what images? Those taken by the enemy?"[20]

Meanwhile, several influential Jews opposed the idea of any Jewish presence on the Mall in Washington, whether a museum or monument. Among them was Henry Kissinger, the former secretary of state and a refugee from Nazi Germany. He worried that a museum might ignite anti-Semitism. "I remember the conversation," Yitz Greenberg, the commission's director, told me. "Kissinger pleaded that Elie not go ahead with this. 'No one is going to come. It will become a white elephant. And no one is interested. People will say this shows that Jews control Washington and control the national agenda.'"

But Wiesel overcame his doubts, insisting only, as his son Elisha suggested to me, that what they conceive be a "living museum"—one that encouraged education, research, documentation, and reflection.[21] The forty-page report to President Carter on September 27, 1979, largely drafted by Berenbaum with an introductory four-page letter by Wiesel that had been translated by Lily Edelman, endorsed the creation of a museum. It served as a blueprint for almost everything the museum ultimately became.

"The museum would present the Holocaust through pictorial accounts, films and other visual exhibits within a framework that is not merely reportorial but analytic, encouraging reflection and questioning," the report said. The chief focus would be the slaughter of the six million Jews; it would also include other victims such as the Poles and the Gypsies. It would depict the Jewish culture that was destroyed by the Nazis. It would examine the American role in liberating the concentration camps, but also chronicle the failure of the American government to act more swiftly and admit more imperiled Jews into the country. It would speak of the heroism of rescuers like the people of Denmark, who together saved 92 percent of that nation's Jewish population, and Raoul Wallenberg, the Swedish diplomat who saved 30,000 Hungarian Jews.[22]

The working out of this vision was severely strained by the differing views of commission members, by Washington politics, and by ethnic sensitivities. In addition to Kissinger's dissent, Arthur Goldberg and Lucy Dawidowicz wanted the museum to be built in New York, "the center of the Jewish population," and Dawidowicz worried that too grand a building would seem to celebrate rather than memorialize the Holocaust. So ardently did she feel that she alone among the commission's members declined to sign the commission's final report.[23]

In the end, Congress turned over to the museum almost two acres of land among the iconic buildings of the National Mall, including three late nineteenth-century structures—annexes actually—that had once been known as the Auditors Building Complex. The annexes intrigued Wiesel. To him they evoked the brick barracks at Auschwitz, and he argued that any design for a museum should retain those buildings. But Raul Hilberg and others felt that the museum should be as stately as the other edifices on the National Mall lest the dead be disrespected by a second-rate building and the museum be short of space for its ambitious plans. Experts in construction told Wiesel that two of the buildings were structurally unsound, in danger of collapse. Ultimately, Annex 3, a Romanesque brick fortress, would be refurbished to create administrative offices (as it still is used today), but the other annexes were demolished and replaced by the classical limestone and brick edifice, with a prominent curved front on Fourteenth Street, that is today the core of the museum.[24]

It is worth asking why Congress and a succession of presidents would consider allocating resources for a museum on the coveted National Mall devoted to the systematic slaughter of European Jews before one depicting the history of African-Americans. There were some halting efforts; as early as 1915 black Union Army veterans of the Civil War sought such a national museum. But however much racial prejudice may have been a factor, there was no groundswell in Congress until planning for the Holocaust museum was well along. The civil rights leader John Lewis, as a first-term congressman from Georgia, did not introduce a bill to create such a museum until 1988. He faced implacable opposition from the staunchly conservative senator Jesse Helms of North Carolina, and his legislation did not bear fruit until 2003, when President George W. Bush signed the Lewis measure and directed the Smithsonian Institution to select a site. The National Museum of African American History and Culture opened in 2016.[25] Government officials were also aware that prosperous American Jews, Holocaust survivors included, were ready to open their pocketbooks to finance such a project and thus minimize the federal burden.

In the wake of the commission's report a full-blown United States Holocaust Memorial Council was appointed, with sixty members and three non-voting members—representing the departments of State, Education, and Interior, federal agencies with which the museum would regularly need to engage. The ethnic politics of an election year seemed to drive the council's composition. President Carter, still pressing for universalizing the Holocaust, insisted on adding a member of Polish descent, and then a Ukrainian, a Hungarian, and a Lithuanian were imposed as well, all to the chagrin of Wiesel and other survivors who knew that many nationals of those countries collaborated with the Germans. Wiesel selected an Armenian-American, Set Momjian, a retired Ford Motor Company executive and the U.S. representative to the United Nations who had contributed $1 million on condition that any museum exhibit on other genocides include a thorough explanation of the Turkish deportations of Armenians between 1915 and 1923 and the resulting 1.5 million deaths. The Turkish government objected, threatened to rethink its relations with Israel, and said it might "no longer guarantee the safety of Jews in Turkey." Ultimately, the council resisted Turkey's threats.[26] But to further complicate matters, the inauguration of a new president, Ronald Reagan in 1981, meant that the council would have to add Republicans to its team. So the council was forced to grapple with backroom, ward-heeler politics, which was not something Wiesel relished.

The thorniest issue both the commission and its successor council had to face remained how Jewish to make the museum. Wiesel would have to persuade a federal government concerned with ethnic sensitivities that the slaughter of Jews was unique even amid the devastation of World War II; expressing that reality in words and pictures, he felt, had to dominate the museum's exhibits. At the start Wiesel came up with an artful formula: "Not all victims were Jews, but all Jews were victims" and wanted his staff to abide by that.

When Berenbaum, the commission's young deputy director, wrote a letter to a Polish-American stating that the Polish experience would be represented along with the Jewish experience, Wiesel, according to Berenbaum, interpreted his language as suggesting an equivalence between the two. Berenbaum insisted equivalence was not his intent at all. He simply thought the museum ought to recognize that many Poles—as well as Gypsies, homosexuals, Jehovah's Witnesses, and others—were also exterminated. The museum eventually chose to take note of these other victims but it also made clear, as Wiesel insisted, that the mass murder of Jews was unparalleled in history. Only Jews were destined for extermination no matter where they lived, what status they held, what work they did, or whether they had converted to Christianity. Nevertheless, Wiesel, according to Berenbaum, had Monroe Freedman, the commission's first executive director and the dean of Hofstra Law School, fire Berenbaum. "He was afraid the Israelis would attack him for de-Judaizing the Holocaust."[27] However, Wiesel, in *And the Sea Is Never Full*, makes clear that beyond any Israeli objections the centrality of the Jews as Nazi victims was a deeply held conviction he would not allow to be diluted.

During the long planning stage, as the potent symbolism of a Holocaust memorial in Washington sank into the minds of world leaders affected by its narrative, Wiesel had to contend with a number of sensitive diplomatic issues, particularly in his dealings with Germany. Helmut Kohl, then the leader of Germany's Christian Democratic Union party, complained that a museum would reduce Germany's history to the dozen years of Hitler's rule. He dispatched Peter Petersen, a member of the Bundestag, Germany's parliament, to meet with Wiesel. As a teenager, Petersen had been an enthusiastic member of the Hitler Youth, but he now worked to cleanse Germany of fascist ideologies. Petersen urged Wiesel to include exhibition panels chronicling Germany's efforts at contrition through its aid to Israel and its reparation payments (then totaling 100 billion Deutsche marks). Wiesel was receptive. Indeed, Petersen found his subsequent dealings with Wiesel so rewarding that he helped recruit eighty members of the Bundestag to support Wiesel's nomination for the Nobel Peace Prize.[28]

The council was charged with determining how the museum would be financed and it decided that, except for the federal gift of land, money for construction would come from private donations, with fund-raising aimed largely at the Jewish community. Appealing for federal funding, it was felt, would not be good for the Jews' public image. Wiesel also rejected suggestions that the council tap German reparations and fought against naming museum spaces for donors. He was to lose that battle; the 500-seat auditorium, for example, is named for Wiesel's successor as chairman, Harvey Meyerhoff.

By 1986, after seven years of deliberations, the council had grappled with many philosophical issues underlying the project, but little progress had been made in actually getting a building off the ground. The council, some complained, was turning into a debating society. It became increasingly obvious to the members—and to Wiesel himself—that his lack of experience in management, fund-raising, and construction was a problem. Any neophyte who has ever undertaken a small home renovation would understand that the countless decisions that have to be made in a construction project are both daunting and, for a man of Wiesel's intellectual bent, tedious. Imagine what was involved in the construction of a national museum.

"Wiesel solved basic issues with words, not with reality," Berenbaum told me. "We needed a developer . . . [someone] who knows how to develop property: get a piece of land and hire an architect."[29]

In his memoirs, Wiesel did not dispute the criticism. Rather, he emphasized his own predilections as chairman. "I find it exciting to watch men and women of every background gathered around a table exchanging ideas, learning from one another just what it is that makes each of us unique," he wrote in 1999.

"Dialogue: philosophical debates, religious discussions—if the Council had served only that purpose, *dayyenu*—it would have been enough."[30] Wiesel loathed the "intrigues and quarrels, overt and covert conflicts and clashes between personalities and ambitions, [and] thirst for the pitiful power that supposedly is ours to give."[31] One measure of the council's fecklessness in that period: it went through five executive directors in four years.

Recognizing her husband's frustration, Marion urged him to give up leadership of the museum project. Why did he need the aggravation? But Wiesel hung on even as the battles for power flared. Eventually, the council brought in Albert (Sonny) Abramson, a Bronx-born developer of apartment houses, office buildings, and malls in the Washington, D.C., area. Besides his expertise in construction, Abramson knew how to drum up funds and could subsidize the project with his own wealth. He could also exploit his connections to influential congressmen, particularly Sidney Yates, the long-serving Illinois representative who sat on the House Appropriations Committee and could ensure substantial funding for the museum's operations. Abramson also had the support of a friend he brought along, Harvey "Bud" Meyerhoff, a wealthy Baltimore developer and philanthropist whose wife was active in national Republican politics and had been rewarded with a ceremonial U.N. position by the Reagan White House.

Abramson seemed a godsend. Frustrated by the slow pace of raising money and the absence of architectural designs, he complained that the museum's board had produced only "talk, talk, talk" and led the way for the council to make several firm decisions.[32] As chairman of the building committee, he persuaded the council to scrap its original design—which would have maximized the use of the federal annexes that had reminded Wiesel of Auschwitz. Abramson argued that those buildings limited the opportunities for innovative exhibits and persuaded the council to start over by razing two annexes. Despite having worked through several architects without settling on a design, he urged the council to hire yet another architect, bringing in James I. Freed, a partner in the esteemed I. M. Pei architectural firm who had fled Nazi Germany with his parents as a nine-year-old.

The episodes that culminated in Wiesel's decision to step down started with clashes between Abramson and Wiesel's friend Sigmund Strochlitz, head of the development committee. Then a key council fund-raiser, Miles Lerman, a Polish Jew who had been a resistance fighter during the war and had appeared to be a Strochlitz ally, turned against Strochlitz, and became a supporter of Abramson and Meyerhoff.

Exhausted, Wiesel realized the project could not succeed without Abramson and Meyerhoff, but he did not have the heart to embarrass Strochlitz. There was only one solution, he said in his memoirs: he had to resign. Before that year, 1986, was out, and after he received the Nobel Prize for Peace, he submitted his resignation to Ronald Reagan, telling the president that the council needed someone with expertise in management, finance, construction, and programming, areas beyond his realm of expertise.[33]

The museum, which cost $168 million to build, finally opened on April 19, 1993, the anniversary of the Warsaw Ghetto uprising. Along with President Clinton, Wiesel was invited to speak at the dedication. He was so anxious that he might be associated with a flawed, potentially embarrassing project that before visiting the museum he asked Strochlitz to preview the exhibits and make sure their main focus was still the destruction of European Jewry. Strochlitz reassured him and he attended the dedication. It was a drizzly day and he found it difficult to read the wet pages of his speech. He therefore spoke extemporaneously, his words filled with themes he had sounded many times before—especially the importance of bearing witness and of remembering the dead. But he also spoke movingly of the murder of his mother and sister at Auschwitz.

"To forget would mean to kill the victims a second time," he told the eight thousand guests gathered outside the Capitol. "We could not prevent their first death; we must not allow them to be killed again."

Importantly, he tied the Holocaust to other genocides of the day, particularly the Serbs' murder of Bosnian Muslims in horrific acts of "ethnic cleansing." Turning to address Bill Clinton, he issued what some saw as an admonition. "Mr. President," he said, "this bloodshed must be stopped. It will not stop unless we stop it." That courageous moment is sometimes cited as the goad Clinton needed to intervene in that genocide, although he did not do so until two years later, in August 1995, after more than 7,000 Bosnians had been massacred in Srebrenica, mass murder on a scale not seen in Europe since World War II.

Elie Wiesel did not publicly reveal his feelings about the museum until the publication of *And the Sea Is Never Full*, in which he said he would have preferred "a more sober, more humble edifice, one that would suggest the unspoken, the silence, the secret. . . . Here the sense of mystery is missing."[34] On subsequent visits, he tempered his assessment, pronouncing the photographs and maps magnificent, and the depiction of the rise of Nazism and the failure of the allies to do more to save Jews, admirable.[35]

In the end, the museum turned out to be a colossal success. Borrowing a quote from Wiesel, that the Holocaust "defies language and art, and yet both must be used to tell the tale," Herbert Muschamp, then architecture critic of the *Times*, lauded Jim Freed for designing "a work of such enormous power that it, too, defies language." Between its dedication in 1993 and 2018, it counted approximately forty-four million visitors, eleven million of them schoolchildren, making it one of Washington's most visited sites. The museum calculates that less than ten percent of those visitors are Jewish. So with the Western Hemisphere's single largest collection of Holocaust research material—

approximately 21,000 artifacts (including striped camp uniforms, survivor diaries, passports belonging to the doomed Jewish passengers of the ship *St. Louis*, and the like), 111 million pages of archival documents, more than 1.1 million photographs, and 19,000 oral testimonies—the museum is indisputably accomplishing its mission of compelling visitors to reckon with the cataclysm that befell Europe's Jews.

By 1996, Wiesel was reconciled enough with the museum to accept another appointment to the council, this time from President Clinton. As Abramson himself said, without the inspiration of Wiesel and other survivors on the council, the museum would never have gotten built. Abramson understood that Wiesel could not be scorned for failing to transform an idea into a practical reality. "Building a project of this complexity was something beyond [his] experience—just like writing a book would be beyond mine," he said.[36] Indeed, more than anyone else, Elie Wiesel deserved the credit for infusing the project with his spiritual power and for making sure the museum primarily memorialized the destruction of Europe's Jews, and was not simply a monument to the idea of genocide, broadly defined. More than anyone else, Wiesel wrote the books and articulated the sentiments that propelled the Holocaust so prominently onto the nation's agenda and persuaded American presidents to realize that this shameful history had to be permanently memorialized on the National Mall.

20

✦◆✦

World Stage

As MUCH AS HE identified himself as an ardent Jew, Wiesel
was always cosmopolitan in outlook, never insular. Early on in
his advocacy for the survivors of the Holocaust, he recognized
that he could not genuinely condemn the world for its indifference to imperiled Jews if he remained indifferent to the suffering of other peoples. The chairmanship of the council offered
him a platform to become an international spokesperson for
many groups under siege.

Wiesel had been moving in that direction even before his
appointment. In May 1972, for example, he gave the commence-
ment address at Manhattanville College in Westchester County,
which had been founded as a Catholic women's college but had
become nondenominational and co-ed. He had been chosen by
the senior class, whose predominantly Christian students were
taken with his writings and lectures. He spoke to the 337 graduates and their families not just about the Holocaust but also

about the still-raging Vietnam War, the conflict in Northern Ireland, and the racial tensions at home. "I pity you," he said, "because the world which is not yet ready to receive you is full of horrors, full of violence, full of absurdity." Never, he said, "has society been so dehumanized as it is now. Words mean nothing. What is even worse, . . . lies come out as words of truth."

"My idea in my story telling is to make Jews better Jews, and Christians better Christians, and in general, if possible at all, make man a little bit warmer, so he will not feel crushed by his own solitude," he said. "I have learned that in extreme situations, those who were good become better, those who were bad become worse. . . . I have learned the value of tales that have to be transmitted, and we are all carriers and messengers of tales from one to another."[1]

Wiesel visited South Africa in 1975 to witness the workings of apartheid first-hand. Ten years later he wrote an op-ed for the *Times* in which he admitted that as a white man he felt shame visiting the shantytowns of the black township of Soweto outside Johannesburg because "South African law has declared him superior. . . . Racism itself is dreadful but when it pretends to be legal and therefore just, it becomes altogether repugnant."

In 1977, the French government, after appeals from the Palestinian Liberation Organization and Arab governments, freed Abu Daoud, the terrorist who had masterminded the massacre of eleven Israeli athletes at the Munich Olympics five years earlier, and put him on a plane to Algeria. Wiesel, again capitalizing on his rising stature, arranged for a full-page ad in the *Times* written as an open letter to President Valéry Giscard d'Estaing assailing France's decision. "I owe France my secular education, my language, and my career as a writer. Liberated from Buchenwald, it was in France that I found compassion and humanity. . . . France, to me, represented humanity's highest values in a sterile and cynical society." But the freeing of Abu Daoud "betrayed its own traditions."

"Why was he allowed to leave Paris in the comfort of a first-class airline seat, when eleven Israeli athletes left Munich in coffins?" the ad said.[2]

The protest was genuine, but the ad's lengthy appreciation of France omitted a glaring crime: the collaboration of high French officials with the Nazi government in deporting Jews to the death camps. In *And the Sea Is Never Full* Wiesel follows the Abu Daoud episode with a reminiscence of an encounter he had fifteen years later with Giscard d'Estaing on an airplane in which the two discussed the terrorist's release. The former French president explained that France had been ready to extradite the Palestinian to Germany, but that Germany did not want him. Wiesel does not ask why France nevertheless did not find a way to hold Abu Daoud or extradite him to Israel.

In June 1979, the world's front pages and television news shows were saturated with pictures of Vietnamese so desperate to flee the Communist regime that they risked their own lives and those of their children to cross turbulent seas in flimsy, overcrowded junks and trawlers. They hoped these ill-suited boats would take them to safe havens in other Southeast Asian countries. The United Nations estimated that between 200,000 and 400,000 Vietnamese "boat people" perished at sea. Wiesel was reminded of the frantic attempts by Jewish refugees to flee the Nazis' menace and, bolstered now with his stature as chairman of the Holocaust commission, he called on all countries to open their borders and extend asylum. The Carter administration should take the lead and "learn from the history of the Holocaust not to err again," he said.

"We are outraged at the sight of people set adrift with no country willing to welcome them ashore," he said. "We are horrified at the imposition of quotas which exclude women and children in the full knowledge that such a policy of exclusion can be a sentence of death."[3]

Though it is impossible to measure the impact his voice had, the following month the United Nations convened an international conference that produced a more orderly resettlement process. Several countries agreed to provide temporary asylum, Vietnam promised to create an "orderly departure program" that allowed Vietnamese to apply for resettlement in other countries rather than risk a random trip in a small boat, and the United States and several Western countries agreed to take in more refugees as permanent residents.

The following February, Wiesel traveled to the dusty Thai border village of Aranyaprathet with a delegation of a hundred Americans and Europeans—including Bayard Rustin, Joan Baez, and Liv Ullmann—in a symbolic effort to deliver twenty truckloads of food to Cambodia. Under the Khmer Rouge regime that had already killed between 1.5 million and 3 million of its own citizens through mass executions, torture, and disease, Cambodia was now plagued by widespread famine. The delegates, organized by the International Rescue Committee and Doctors Without Borders, stood at a bridge on the border shouting through a bullhorn at the uniformed Cambodians on the other side to accept the food and distribute it to the Cambodian people. But the soldiers watched impassively. The food was eventually delivered to the Thai Red Cross for distribution to Cambodian refugees there.

Later, the delegation held a vigil in which the civil rights anthem "We Shall Overcome" was sung, and Wiesel and Rabbi Marc Tanenbaum, director of international affairs for the American Jewish Committee, chanted the Kaddish together with a minyan formed with eight other Jews they corralled among the activists, journalists, and doctors.

In an interview with the Pulitzer Prize–winning reporter Henry Kamm, who helped make up the minyan, Wiesel explained that that day was the *yahrzeit* of his father's death so Kaddish was entirely appropriate. But given the innumerable Cambodians who had died at the hands of the Khmer Rouge, the prayer was especially fitting. He reminded Kamm, himself a refugee who had fled the Nazis as a child, of his own experience in Auschwitz and Buchenwald and said: "I came here because nobody came when I was there."

"One thing that is worse for the victim than hunger, fear, torture, even humiliation is the feeling of abandonment, the feeling that nobody cares, that you don't count."[4]

In 1984, Wiesel, who never learned to swim, even traveled by canoe through jungle rivers in Honduras to protest the expulsion of Nicaragua's Miskito Indians by the Ortega regime. Why was he making these far-flung journeys to places that were not part of the actual Holocaust landscape? *And the Sea Is Never Full* contains a succinct explanation: "As for me, I believe that when human beings suffer I have no right to be elsewhere."[5] He acknowledged that speaking out against other genocides enhanced the legitimacy of his primary mission to foster the memory of the six million, even as it helped transform a world that permitted such massacres to happen.

"How can I criticize those who were indifferent to Jewish suffering during the Shoah, if I do nothing when confronted with the suffering of innocent people today?" he told the editor of *Reform Judaism* magazine in 2005. "We Jews suffered not only from the cruelty of killers, but also from the indifference of bystanders. I believe that a person who is indifferent to the suffering of others is complicit in the crime. And that I cannot allow, at least not for myself."[6]

Wiesel had come to realize that, when called on by human rights activists, he could leverage his reputation and moral standing for causes other than the Holocaust. A cynic might say that Wiesel was being exploitative. But there was a strong argument that he and the organizations he supported were being pragmatic, aware that his name could help their work gain traction.

On some diplomatic visits, the moral calculus proved tricky.

In 1987, when he and Marion visited Hiroshima, laid a wreath at a cenotaph containing a registry of atomic bomb victims, and met with survivors of the atomic bombing, he unsettled his Japanese hosts by telling them: "I shall never forget Hiroshima, but you in turn must never forget Pearl Harbor." Wiesel admonished journalists against making "cheap comparisons" between the bombings of Hiroshima and Nagasaki, which together killed almost 200,000 Japanese, and a genocide like Auschwitz. The bombings were a strategic assault against an enemy in a war that the enemy had started; they were responses to Japanese aggression, not acts of aggression themselves. Still, he noted that the bombings did shadow all of humanity with the prospect of future destruction and the issues they raised called for profound exploration, debate, and reflection.[7] He also used the visit to warn the Japanese about budding anti-Semitism spurred by a spate of popular books that blamed Jews for the despised Japanese constitution imposed by the postwar American occupation.

In June 1982, Wiesel was asked to chair a conference in Israel on genocide. The conference progressed fairly smoothly until Turkey objected that one of the genocides cited was the killing of 1.5 million Armenians between 1915 and 1923. It warned that if Armenian killings were taken up, the conference would jeopardize diplomatic relations between Israel and Turkey. Its language also seemed to threaten the lives and livelihoods of eighteen thousand Turkish Jews. Concerned that Turkey might carry out its threats, Wiesel asked colleagues to postpone the balance of the conference and move it out of Israel. "One life is more important than anything we can say about life," he told the *Times.* But he insisted that the Armenian genocide remain part of the conference agenda. He had a clever explanation for his steadfastness on this point. Hitler, he remarked, justified the persecution of Jews to some of his generals by saying, "Look, who remembers what happened to the Armenians?"

"I would like to show that I remember the Armenians," Wiesel said.

Ultimately, the stalemate was resolved in a way that couldn't have been satisfactory to Wiesel: Israel dropped its status as an official participant and he surrendered his role as conference chairman.[8]

Later that year, Wiesel found himself embroiled in a far more disturbing event. More than eight hundred Palestinians, including many women and children, had been massacred in the Sabra and Shatila refugee camps that were then under Israel occupation. The atrocities were carried out by Lebanese Christian militias, who had been allowed by their ally, Israel, to clear the sites of remaining terrorists. Israeli commanders, learning that a wider massacre was in progress, failed to stop the killings. The Israeli commanders were ultimately reprimanded by the United Nations and by Israeli investigators for their failure to anticipate what the Christian militias might do. As a leading voice—perhaps the world's leading voice—against genocide, Wiesel was asked to comment; he said the event had resulted in "the darkest Rosh Hashanah for me since World War II."

"It is not that I accuse or indict anyone, and surely not the people of Israel, but I felt sadness, incommensurate sadness," he said. "I believe now that 'a gesture' is needed on our part. Perhaps we ought to proclaim a day of fasting, surely of taking stock."[9] Critics thought he could have been tougher on Israel and explicitly reproached its leaders and generals.

Inevitably, Wiesel returned to the theme of the world's complicity in the Holocaust through indifference, silence, or outright bigotry. In September 1986, he was asked to speak at the dedication of a site near Battery Park in Lower Manhattan for another Holocaust museum, the Museum of Jewish Heritage. The organizers made sure to place the stage against a stunning symbolic backdrop: the Statue of Liberty with its upraised torch that had welcomed so many immigrants to New York harbor.

In this setting, Wiesel harkened back to a period when the United States was not so welcoming and had shut its gates to thousands of European refugees seeking to escape the gathering Nazi inferno.

"Why did the State Department not give out all the visas that were available?" Wiesel asked. "Why was this harbor closed to so many Jews who could have come?"

21

◆⬩◆

"To Help the Dead Vanquish Death"

WHILE PROJECTING HIMSELF into the public sphere during the 1970s and '80s, Wiesel managed to continue to write at a staggering pace: novels, nonfiction, essay collections, a children's book, more than two dozen books in all. Although he had mastered English well enough to become an eloquent speaker and riveting teacher in the language, he continued to write in the French he had learned as an orphaned teenage refugee. As Marion told me, "He didn't want to lose it. You have to cherish it. You have to take care of it."

Meanwhile, by his own account, writing for Wiesel became "more difficult, more exhausting, more pressing." "I become acutely aware of the ambiguity of words," he wrote. "Always the same questions, the same doubts. How to express that which eludes language? I erase. I rewrite. I fill the wastepaper basket with superseded drafts. Will I be discerning enough to know when the well runs dry?"[1]

His son described his work routine. "He would wake up early, 5:30 or 6, make a cup of instant coffee. Where everybody had sophisticated coffee-making machinery, he still liked Sanka or Nescafé with lots of sugar—he liked everything very sweet. Once he had his coffee and half a muffin, he would start working for a few hours. He used to write on a typewriter, though the first draft was always by hand. Then later he got an electric typewriter and in the early '90s he started using a computer. It took some adjustment."[2]

Wiesel could have limited himself to a full-time career as a speaker and human rights activist on top of his work as a college professor, yet he could not stop writing. The emotional and metaphysical fallout from the Holocaust drove him, no matter what quibbles critics might have. He made that clear in an essay called "Why I Write," which was as ardent and raw as anything he wrote. First published in 1978, it was adapted by the *Times Book Review* in April 1985.

> Why do I write? Perhaps in order not to go mad. Or, on the contrary, to touch the bottom of madness. . . .
>
> There are easier occupations, far more pleasant ones. But for the survivor, writing is not a profession, but an occupation, a duty. . . .
>
> . . . I never intended to be a philosopher, or a theologian. The only role I sought was that of witness. I believed that, having survived by chance, I was duty-bound to give meaning to my survival, to justify each moment of my life. I knew the story had to be told. Not to transmit an experience is to betray it. I owe them [the dead] my roots and my memory. I am duty-bound to serve as their emissary, transmitting the history of their disappearance, even if it disturbs, even if it brings pain. Not to do so would be to betray them, and thus myself.[3]

Even though "all words seemed inadequate, worn, foolish, lifeless, whereas I wanted them to be searing," his obligation to the dead demanded that he set down what he had endured. "The fear of forgetting remains the main obsession of all those who have passed through the universe of the damned," he wrote. "We had all taken an oath: If, by some miracle, I emerge alive, I will devote my life to testifying on behalf of those whose shadow will fall on mine forever and ever." Wiesel would have preferred "to stop mourning the past," to "sing of love and its magic," to shout "I too am open to laughter and joy," but as a survivor he must remain faithful, owing "everything to the dead."

The one million murdered children, his seven-year-old sister Tzipora among them, haunt his writings. "I shall always see them," he wrote, his phrases and rhythms echoing passages from *Jeremiah*. "They are thirsty, the children, and there is no one to give them water. They are hungry, but there is no one to give them a crust of bread. They are afraid, and there is no one to reassure them."

"Why do I write?" he concluded. "To wrench those victims from oblivion. To help the dead vanquish death."[4]

In *Messengers of God: Biblical Portraits and Legends*, based largely on his sold-out lectures at the 92nd Street Y, Wiesel explored seven biblical figures—Adam, Cain, Abraham, Isaac, Jacob, Joseph, and Job—describing them as "the distant and haunting figures that molded him." Through their struggles, he sought to probe his own relationship with God. Could he complain to God, question God, rebuke God, defy God as those characters sometimes did? "Wiesel's concern with the imponderables of fate seems to move from strength to strength," *Kirkus Reviews* said. But the *Times* reviewer suggested that Wiesel twisted his stories tendentiously to reach comforting conclusions. "From Adam to Job, there is always a life-affirming message to be deduced," he wrote.[5]

One might ask, what was the alternative? Should Wiesel have promulgated a message of despair, of retreat from human encounters? Shouldn't he be praised for having the resilience to move from Auschwitz to hope?

A Jew Today, published in 1979, was a collection of articles Wiesel had written for magazines that he augmented with a variety of new essays and imagined dialogues. One notable section expressed rancor at Christians and Christian institutions for failing to stop or protest the persecution and slaughter of Jews before and during the war. Wiesel hedged at the outset by noting that he felt close to Catholics like Pope John XXIII and François Mauriac, but he went on to write, "what I am about to say will surely hurt my Christian friends. Yet I have no right to hold back."

> How is one to explain that neither Hitler nor Himmler was ever excommunicated by the Church? That Pius XII never thought it necessary, not to say indispensable, to condemn Auschwitz and Treblinka? That among the S.S. a large proportion were believers who remained faithful to their Christian ties to the end? That there were killers who went to confession between massacres? . . .
>
> In Poland, a stronghold of Christianity, it often happened that Jews who had escaped from the ghettos returned inside their walls, so hostile did they find the outside world; they feared the Poles as much as the Germans. This was also true in Lithuania, in the Ukraine, in White Russia and in Hungary. How is one to explain the passivity of the population as it watched the persecution of its Jews? How explain the cruelty of the killers? How explain that the Christian in them did not make their arms tremble as they shot at children or their conscience bridle as they shoved their naked, beaten victims into the factories of death?[6]

Those statements, in an essay that first appeared in *National Geographic*, are crucial in evaluating Wiesel's record because, as was shown earlier, he has sometimes been scorned as someone soft-pedaling his anger so he could win widespread affection as a universal altruist, a "secular saint." In 2017, the writer Ron Rosenbaum took him to task for the revelation that he had edited out of the French and English versions of *Night* condemnations of Christians, ordinary Germans, and other Europeans that had been included in the Yiddish and Hebrew versions. Although it is probable that Wiesel, as a novice writer, excised a few passages to improve his chances of getting published— and we will never know if he did so deliberately—he spent much of his life making sure that Christians and predominantly Christian countries were made aware of their guilt for the Holocaust. Even a cursory examination of Wiesel's work would have told Rosenbaum, who published the gratuitously nasty article in *Tablet* a year after Wiesel's death, that he was off target.[7] Moreover, Wiesel had confronted several American leaders about the nation's failure to do more for the imperiled Jews. In April 1983, when Vice President George Bush presented him with a symbolic key to the Washington museum yet to be built, Wiesel praised the American army for liberating the concentration camps, but pointedly asked: "Why did they come so late? . . . Why didn't the Allied forces bomb the railways going to Auschwitz? . . . In those days, ten thousand people died daily."

The 1980s brought singular moments of affirmation for Wiesel and the survivors—a massive gathering of five thousand of them plus two thousand of their relatives in Jerusalem in 1981, followed by smaller gatherings in Washington in 1983 and Philadelphia in 1985. Wiesel did not conceive or organize the gatherings; he did not enjoy "mass productions," Menachem Rosensaft told me.[8] But they would not have taken place without his steady focus on the Holocaust as a moral challenge to humanity and his attaining for the survivors the recognition they deserved.

The idea for the gathering in Jerusalem came from Ernest Michel, who had survived two periods of confinement in Auschwitz and went on to become executive vice president of the United Jewish Appeal in New York. Michel was a seasoned organizer who knew how to draw a crowd of seven thousand people from around the world and put them all up for four days filled with memorial events. He was joined by other talented organizers, among them survivors like Ben and Vladka Meed, and Norbert Wollheim, an accountant who had successfully sued Germany for his unpaid wages at an I.G. Farben construction site in Auschwitz. Michel was also skilled in managing the egos of the prominent and, for example, could anticipate that Israel's prime minister, Menachem Begin, needed to speak before Wiesel at the closing ceremonies so that he would not have to follow a legendary orator.

I filed reports on the Jerusalem gathering for *Newsday* and was profoundly moved by the sight of all those once-emaciated refugees gathered in swank hotels. Identifiable by their ill-fitting suits, outdated ties, newsboy caps, and ragged speech, they boasted of their children's achievements, laughed at some of the ironic and incongruous events they had lived through, and often shed tears for all those they lost.

Almost forty years later, many still hunted desperately and futilely to locate prewar friends in the crowds and in some cases brothers, sisters, even children. Some wore T-shirts inscribed with the names of missing relatives, or their hometowns and the camps in which they were last seen, hoping another attendee might have some useful information. Others searched a computerized registry of postwar survivor lists or thumbtacked notices on billboards. My father was one of those posting messages, writing a heartbreaking note in his spidery script that began: "My name is Marcus Berger and I am missing my six sisters, Gittel, Rivka, Sura, Chava, Leah, Miriam." (It is evidence of the difficulty so many survivors had discussing with their children what they had suffered that the Jerusalem gathering may have been the first time my father ever told me his sisters' names.)

The climax of the four-day gathering was the assembly at the foot of the Western Wall. The survivors positioned themselves in front of the two-thousand-year-old remnant of the

Second Temple compound, holding candles or torches in the gathering dusk, a muffled sob here and there shattering the silence. When it was his turn to speak, Wiesel, silhouetted against the ancient gold-hued stones, began by comforting his audience, implying that whatever guilt survivors might feel over losing their families, whatever so-called sages may say about Jews submitting too easily to their persecutors, they—the Jews—were not to blame. Nor were the dead at fault.

"We shall remember those who fought and those who did not, those who resisted with weapons and those who did so with prayers. Even the victims were heroes, even the heroes perished as victims," he said.

"We have come here," he continued, "to draw strength from our memories. For we have been alone—and we have remained alone: only the quality of our loneliness has changed. Remember! When we emerged from the ghettos and forests and the death camps, hopelessly determined to invoke hope and tell the tale, few were willing to listen. . . . Survivors were understood by survivors alone."

"Have we, survivors, done our duty?" he asked.

Something went wrong with our testimony; it was not received. Otherwise things would have been different. Look, look at the world around us: suspicion again, violence everywhere, hatred everywhere, organized state-sponsored terror, racism, fascism, fanaticism, anti-Semitism. Had anyone told us when we were liberated that we would be compelled in our lifetime to fight anti-Semitism once more, or, worse, that we would have to prove that our suffering was genuine, that our victims had indeed perished, we would have had no strength to lift our eyes from the ruins. If only we could tell the tale, we thought, the world would change. Well, we have told the tale, and the world remained the same. . . .

And yet, we shall not give up, we shall not give in. It may be too late for the victims and even for the survivors—but not for our children, not for mankind. Yes, in an age tainted by violence, we must teach coming generations of the origins and consequences of violence. In a society of bigotry and indifference, we must tell our contemporaries that whatever the answer, it must grow out of human compassion and reflect man's relentless quest for justice and memory.

These were of course themes that he had sounded before. Yet in Jerusalem he did so lyrically and with an exquisite genuineness that drew strength from his awe at seeing thousands gathered in "the sovereign land of our dreams" just as they had once "been together in the kingdom of night and nightmares."[9]

22

◆I◆I◆

The Bitburg Fiasco

It SHOULD HAVE BEEN an uneventful exercise in diplomacy.
President Ronald Reagan, after five years in office and still enormously popular after a landslide reelection, was planning to visit
Germany to reaffirm a sturdy forty-year political alliance. But
Germany was no ordinary country. In the minds of many Americans, it had not entirely faced up to its record of systematic
slaughter during World War II. It also had not brought about
a reckoning from those perpetrators still living—and in most
cases thriving—among the general population. So every detail
of the visit would be closely watched.

At first, Wiesel and other survivors were upset that the Rea-
gans' itinerary did not include a stop at a concentration camp
like Dachau or Bergen-Belsen. But Reagan brushed off that
omission at a press conference on March 21, 1985. "Since the
German people have very few alive that remember even the war,
and certainly none of them who were adults and participating in

any way, they have a feeling and a guilt feeling that's been imposed on them," he said. It was a profoundly ignorant statement from a president, let alone one celebrated as the Great Communicator. There were in fact tens of thousands of Germans in their sixties, seventies, and eighties who were adults during the war, many of whom had participated in the mass killings or were aware of what was happening and said or did nothing. At first, Wiesel made no public protest. He understood that Chancellor Helmut Kohl was trying to put the country's past behind it—to "normalize" Germany, in Kohl's phrase.

But on April 11, the announced details of the Reagan trip stunned the American Jewish community. The president, it was disclosed, would lay a wreath at a military cemetery at Bitburg to pay his respects to the Wehrmacht, the German army. Such ceremonies between former enemies were not uncommon. But as Wiesel and other survivors noted in their agitated telephone conversations, the Wehrmacht was no ordinary army. Yes, it was a professional corps doing the bidding of a crazed führer, but it had also provided important logistical support for the SS-led *Einsatzgruppen* (task forces) and local collaborators who shot to death hundreds of thousands of Jews in western Russia, Ukraine, Lithuania, and Poland in places like the Babi Yar ravine outside Kiev (33,000 Jews massacred) and the fuel storage pits in the Ponary forest outside Vilna (70,000 Jews massacred).

Jewish leaders registered their dismay. But soon there was an even more shocking revelation: The Bitburg cemetery contained the tombstones of forty-nine members of the Waffen-SS, the armed wing of the Nazi Party's protective corps. Waffen-SS units had perpetrated many of the war's atrocities—the *Einsatzgruppen* killings and the crushing of the Warsaw Ghetto uprising, and its members had constructed the gas chambers at Auschwitz and served as camp guards.

Telegrams flooded the White House and phone calls tied up its switchboard—from Jewish leaders, human rights leaders, union bosses, veterans groups, and hundreds of distressed individuals. Both the leaders of the conservative Moral Majority and the liberal NAACP signed a letter saying the visit "dishonors the sacrifices of millions of American and Allied soldiers who fought and died to liberate Europe" and "mocks the suffering and death of millions of innocents, including six million Jews." Fifty-three senators, including eleven Republicans, signed a letter asking the president to cancel his visit, and 257 members of the House of Representatives urged Helmut Kohl to withdraw the invitation. Newspapers highlighted an act of protest by army staff sergeant Jim Hively, who mailed in the Silver and Bronze Stars he'd won for his bravery during World War II. Polls showed Reagan's approval rating plummeting.

Most distressed were those who had suffered at the hands of the SS, whose relatives had been murdered either directly by the SS or at death factories the SS had set up. Their eyes turned again to the one survivor who was increasingly seen as a standard-bearer. There were other leaders of Holocaust organizations, but only Wiesel had the eloquence, the voice and stature as the author of a Holocaust classic and the head of the U.S. Holocaust Memorial Council, to implore the president to shift his itinerary.

Wiesel liked Reagan personally. He had been at the president's side during the annual Holocaust commemoration in Washington that year—held at the White House because Reagan was still recovering from an assassination attempt—and had noticed how genuinely moved the president was by the ceremony, even saw tears in his eyes.

Wiesel told the *Times* he was "baffled by the announcement," and could not believe the president "would visit a German military cemetery and refuse to visit Dachau or any other concentration camp." "I know that the president is a sensitive man," said Wiesel, "and do not understand how he could show such insensitivity."[1]

But even that mild objection put the White House on edge, as was apparent when Henry Kissinger, the former secretary of state under Presidents Nixon and Ford, called Wiesel at his Upper East Side apartment. As a teenager Kissinger had been a Jewish refugee from Nazi Germany whose family settled in Manhattan's Washington Heights; he had credibility on Holocaust issues. As a civilian, he was an unofficial adviser to President Reagan. Speaking to Wiesel in his gravelly Germanic accent, he sounded uncommonly sheepish, as if reluctantly doing someone's bidding on an assignment he found embarrassing. He told Wiesel he had received a call from Reagan and that the president would like Wiesel to desist from criticism and marshal Jews to support him. Wiesel bluntly told him that he could not do that. Kissinger did not press the issue as he once might have with foreign leaders on controversial matters, telling Wiesel he understood.

Meanwhile, the White House summoned a group of influential Jewish Republicans—Detroit philanthropist Max Fisher, his friends Gordon Zaks and Richard Fox, and Kenneth J. Bialkin, president of the Conference of Presidents of Major Jewish Organizations—for a sit-down. Wiesel, though not a registered Republican, was invited too. On the White House side were Donald Regan, Reagan's chief of staff, Patrick Buchanan, his communications adviser, and Ed Rollins, his political adviser. The Jews in the room expressed their opposition to the Bitburg ceremony visit, though Fisher argued that it was too late to turn back. More important than Jewish sensitivities, he informed the group, was the pragmatic American need for air bases in Germany where short-range tactical weapons could be placed. Embarrassing Kohl would cause a diplomatic contretemps that might trigger some unforeseen payback.

For Wiesel, the debate recalled the paralysis among Jewish leaders during World War II as word of the mass exterminations leaked out and they deliberated how to confront FDR. "I sit there thinking to myself that this is doubtless how things happened during the Holocaust," he wrote in his memoir; "the Jewish leaders were here to plead for European Jews but wound up saying the same things as their hosts."[2]

Buchanan chimed in with his own viewpoint, one that dovetailed with a number of controversial statements he made years later that critics considered anti-Semitic. He argued that Reagan could not give the appearance of buckling under Jewish pressure. Bialkin was stunned to notice that Buchanan kept scribbling on a yellow pad the words "Jewish pressure, Jewish pressure."

"That is what obsessed him in this whole affair, that is what he is afraid of," Bialkin later told Wiesel as they returned to New York on Fisher's private jet.

After some more back and forth, Donald Regan proposed what he thought would be a breakthrough: the president could visit Bitburg *and* Bergen-Belsen. But Wiesel chafed at this.

"Give up Bitburg *and* Bergen-Belsen," he told Regan. Regan declared he could not agree to those terms, and the conference broke up.[3]

That might have been the end of the affair, with the president going through with his Bitburg itinerary and Jewish leaders left fuming. But the episode instead hurtled toward a dramatic climax because of a remarkable coincidence. It happened that Wiesel had been named a recipient of the prestigious Congressional Gold Medal, in his case for "humanitarian leadership in documenting and preserving the memory of the Holocaust." The medal, though co-sponsored by at least two-thirds of both houses of Congress, is almost always conferred by the president. The ceremony was set for April 19 at the White House. That meant Wiesel and Reagan would encounter each other in a public ceremony just two and a half weeks before the president was due to leave for Germany.

The Holocaust Memorial Council, meanwhile, decided to hold a special session the day before the medal ceremony to consider a resolution put forward by Sigmund Strochlitz, that the members collectively resign to protest the Bitburg visit.

If Wiesel had any thought of offering the White House a face-saving resolution, it was shattered on the way to the council meeting by what he heard on his car radio. Reagan, at a press conference, made another tactless statement, one that enraged Wiesel and other survivors. Speaking of the soldiers buried in Bitburg, he told White House reporters: "They were victims just as surely as the victims in the concentration camps." Equating German soldiers with the murdered innocents was too much for Wiesel.

"I heard the comments and I couldn't believe it," he told a reporter.[4] Other Jewish leaders did not hold back either. Even the judicious Alexander Schindler, president of the Reform movement's Union of American Hebrew Congregations, called Reagan's remarks a "distortion of history, a perversion of language and a callous offense to the Jewish community." Menachem Rosensaft, chairman of the International Network of Children of Jewish Holocaust Survivors, predicted that the photograph of the president laying a wreath at a cemetery that includes the graves of SS officers will be "exploited by revisionist historians and neo-Nazis as proof that the president has forgiven the SS and it is now all right to forget."[5]

At the Holocaust Council, Wiesel supported the motion for a mass resignation. But most members, it turned out, were reluctant. They decided there was still time for Reagan to change his plans and merely issued a statement expressing their dismay. They appealed to Reagan to cancel the Bitburg visit because of the anguish it would cause survivors. Michael Berenbaum considers it fortunate that the council did not resign en masse, because if they had, the museum would never have been built. "It would have been a powerful gesture, but a stupid one," he told me. "The ultimate revenge was [to] get the museum built."[6]

At a press conference, Wiesel was asked point blank if he

would resign as chairman, and he replied: "I don't believe that will be necessary. I don't believe the president will be going to Bitburg." He could not accept that the leader of the world's foremost democracy would do anything to whitewash the savage record of the SS.

Aware of the potential for embarrassment, the White House began maneuvering. It moved the ceremony from the East Room, which can accommodate three hundred people, to the Roosevelt Room, which can squeeze in just forty. Given only a handful of seats, Wiesel had to cancel invitations to survivor friends and others in Congress, Europe, and Israel. In addition to Marion, Elisha, and Strochlitz, he shrewdly chose to bring two powerful journalists, Abe Rosenthal, the executive editor of the *Times*, and Arthur Gelb, its managing editor. Per Ahlmark, a former deputy prime minister of Sweden and a poet and writer known for speaking out against anti-Semitism and for his vigorous support for Israel, was invited by the Wiesels to spend the days around the ceremony with them.

As the clock wound down, the White House sent more emissaries to persuade Wiesel not to embarrass the president. It dispatched Marshall Breger, the president's Jewish affairs adviser, then Arthur Burns, the ambassador to Germany and himself a Jew, who contended that as long as the Bitburg visit was balanced by a visit to Bergen-Belsen, he could assent. Ambassador Burns reminded Wiesel of the military and diplomatic importance of sustaining Helmet Kohl's good will. "To me it's a question of Jewish memory," Wiesel replied. "Bitburg will taint that memory." Senator Frank Lautenberg of New Jersey, a son of Jewish immigrants and a staunch advocate for the emigration of Jews from the Soviet Union, called with yet another argument for going along: Reagan's support would be needed in any Israeli crises to come. But none of these arguments would dissuade Wiesel.

Out of courtesy, Wiesel arranged to have a copy of his

speech dropped off at the White House in advance of the ceremony, and requested to see the president privately before it began. He spent a sleepless night, unsure whether to even attend and what to say. Marion had recommended a few changes to the speech and Wiesel also made some edits, making the language more direct.[7]

When Wiesel arrived at the White House on the morning of April 19, Breger buttonholed him, urging him to shorten the speech to three minutes and remove the critical passages. Wiesel rebuffed him. Then, in a private corner of the White House, he conferred with Rosenthal and Gelb. What, he asked, should he do if an attempt was made to either eliminate his speech or finesse the program so he could not deliver it? Rosenthal advised him that in that case he should stage a press conference after the ceremony and read his text.

Shortly after 10 A.M. Wiesel was summoned to the Oval Office. Donald Regan greeted him warmly in an outer office, and Wiesel asked whether he had read the speech. He had, Regan said, and had no objections. Wiesel was then escorted into the Oval Office itself, where the president was chatting with Peggy Tishman, an energetic philanthropist for Jewish causes who organized the merged UJA-Federation of New York and would soon serve as its first president. She was obviously there as a buffer.

Reagan opened the conversation by recalling photographs of the concentration camps he had seen at the war's end, noting that the images were still imprinted on his mind. Wiesel replied that he appreciated how much Reagan understood the survivors' pain and the importance of memory. That is why, he said, the president should cancel his visit to Bitburg. It was not too late, he said, and he urged the president to do so at the award ceremony that was just minutes away.

In his memoir, Wiesel described what he said to the president during their twenty-six-minute meeting that morning.

"Imagine for a moment the following scenario: You deliver your remarks. You hand me the medal. I respond. You already know my response. When I finish speaking, you return to the microphone and simply say: 'Very well. I shan't go.' Do that, Mr. President, and people everywhere, Jews and non-Jews, young and old, Republicans and Democrats alike, will applaud your decision. They will say: 'The president of the United States doesn't really need advisers; *he* decides.'"[8]

Surely Wiesel was aware that state visits are not changed on the spur of the moment. But a soupçon of naïveté was part of his charm. Indeed, Reagan had confided to him that he had just spoken with Chancellor Kohl, who had affirmed that a cancellation of the Bitburg visit would be nothing less than a "national catastrophe."

Minds unchanged, Wiesel left and headed to the Roosevelt Room, now crammed with the maximum number of guests and a cluster of television cameras, two of which—from NBC and CNN—were broadcasting the ceremony live. The president strode to the lectern and showered Wiesel with praise for memorializing the Holocaust and for his advocacy on behalf of Israel, Soviet Jews, and all of humanity. He compared him to a biblical prophet whose words "will teach humanity timeless lessons."

"He teaches about death, but in the end he teaches about life," Reagan declared.

When he was done, Wiesel approached the rostrum and Reagan handed him a gold medallion designed by Wiesel's friend the artist Mark Podwal. It was emblazoned on one side with a likeness of Wiesel adapted from a Roman Vishniac photograph that was set below the words AUTHOR, TEACHER, WITNESS. On the other side were the words "If I Forget Thee O Jerusalem." Wiesel, fifty-six years old at the time, wrote later that during the ceremony he felt himself to be a little boy in Sighet again, a boy on his way to synagogue on a snowy morning, anxious that he could be assaulted.

He began his remarks by graciously returning Reagan's compliments, calling him a man who has always shown an "understanding for Jewish concerns," someone who had "learned that in extreme situations when human lives and dignity are at stake, neutrality is a sin."

Wiesel then turned to his subject. He reminded the president that that day—April 19th—was the anniversary of the Warsaw Ghetto uprising. He recalled how the world stood by while ragtag fighters armed with a few handmade or smuggled firearms took on the German forces; that the world stood by while a million Jewish children perished in the Holocaust. "If I spent my whole life reciting their names I would die before I finished. The Jewish children, Mr. President. I saw them. I saw them being thrown into the flames alive." He sounded themes he had sounded before about the dangers of indifference and silence. Then he launched unequivocally into the part of his speech Reagan was hoping he would not have to hear.

> I wouldn't be the person I am, and you wouldn't respect me for what I am, if I were not to tell you also of the sadness that is in my heart for what happened during the last week [since it was revealed that there were SS men buried at Bitburg]. And I am sure that you, too, are sad for the same reasons. What can I do? I belong to a traumatized generation. And to us, as to you, symbols are important. And furthermore, following our ancient tradition—and we are speaking about Jewish heritage—our tradition commands us, quote: "to speak truth to power."
>
> So may I speak to you, Mr. President, with respect and admiration, of the events that happened. We have met four or five times, and each time I came away enriched, for I know of your commitment to humanity. And, therefore, I am convinced, as you have told us earlier when we spoke that you were not aware of the presence of SS graves in the Bitburg cemetery. Of course, you didn't know. But now we all are

aware. May I, Mr. President, if it's possible at all, implore you to do something else, to find a way, to find another way, another site.[9]

Although several commentators, including Chris Wallace, then of NBC, said he lectured the president like a professor with a student, the video of the event found on YouTube makes clear that Wiesel spoke with a voice that was more often mournful and pleading than hectoring.

"That place is not your place, Mr. President," he declared, in a simple but memorable line that resonates to this day. "Your place is with the victims of the SS."

No one could remember anyone so forcefully admonishing a president in so public a forum in his own house. The Bitburg visit, Wiesel continued, "is not a question of politics but of good and evil. And we must never confuse them. For I have seen the SS at work. I have known their victims. They were my friends. They were my parents. Sons watched helplessly their fathers being beaten to death, mothers watched their children die of hunger. There was terror, fear, isolation, torture, gas chambers, flames, flames rising to the heavens."

He stared at Reagan, his voice cracking. "I understand you seek reconciliation. We all do. I too wish to attain reconciliation with the German people. I do not believe in collective guilt nor in collective responsibility. Only the killers were guilty. Their sons and daughters are not. I believe, Mr. President, that we can and we must work together with them and with all people. And we must work to bring peace and understanding to a tormented world that, as you know, is still awaiting redemption. I thank you, Mr. President."

He walked off briskly, not waiting to take in the applause that followed. Several of the listeners were in tears. Still, the ever jaunty Reagan and Vice President Bush greeted him with handshakes and warm smiles as if nothing charged had just happened. In another room Donald Regan thanked him for the moderation of his speech. He even had the chutzpah to invite him to join the president on his trip to Germany, Bitburg included. Incredulous, Wiesel interrupted him: "Mr. Regan, I don't understand what you're saying. I desperately don't want the president to go there, and you want me to go there with him?"[10]

Afterward, there was an impromptu press conference, and White House correspondents asked Wiesel if he was afraid to have been seen as lecturing the president. He replied: "No, no, I am not a moralist. I am a teacher. I am a storyteller. I have words. Nothing else. I represent nobody. All I did was give him a few words."

In the limousine to his hotel with Marion and a *Times* reporter, Wiesel could not quite digest the events and sat silently for a long time. Marion spoke first. "If there is one primary emotion, it has been disbelief," she told the reporter, Phil Shenon.

"Disbelief, yes," Wiesel said. "We couldn't believe it. We couldn't believe it. . . . It has been such a horrendous week. It's a nightmare, going on and on."[11]

The confrontation generated front-page headlines around the world, with some newspapers reprinting Wiesel's speech in full. He was inundated with mail and realized that he had, "in just a few minutes, touched a thousand times more people than I had with all my previous writings and speeches."[12] The attention compelled the White House to announce that Reagan would indeed go to Bergen-Belsen during the Germany trip, a small but significant victory for Wiesel. Yet, according to Gil Troy, a professor of history at McGill University and a former graduate student of Wiesel's who visited him a few days after the speech: "Rather than being pleased with himself for heroically defying the pressure from Reaganites and Jewish community worrywarts to keep quiet, Professor Wiesel looked terrible. . . . Having been born in freedom as an American, I had not appreciated the superhuman courage it took for this con-

centration camp survivor, this European refugee, this natural-
ized American, to confront the popular American President, in
the President's own home, before the world."[13]

Marion Wiesel told me as much. "He was very steadfast,"
she said. "He knew he had to say something, and he said what
he had to say."[14] In a later conversation with me, she added:
"He was doing the right thing. I got a confirmation that he was
doing the right thing a day or two later when I took a taxi and
the driver said to me, 'That was terrific what your husband
did.'"[15] But Elisha Wiesel emphasized how much confronting
the president took out of his father. "I didn't think my father
wanted to be in a spotlight saying powerful words that he would
be remembered for," Elisha said in an interview with Nadine
Epstein, editor of *Moment Magazine*, on the fourth anniversary
of his father's death. "He didn't want to humiliate a sitting president. He didn't want to humiliate anyone."[16]

Ultimately, Reagan did go to Bitburg, on May 6, and laid
a wreath there, though at a strategic distance from the tombstones of the SS men. And he did visit Bergen-Belsen. Still, the
fiasco cast a permanent shadow on the president's legacy and
underscored the continuing tone-deafness of American officials,
not just to the enormity of the Holocaust but to the plight of
brutalized people all over the world.

As with the Eichmann trial, Elie Wiesel's remarks about
the Bitburg visit amplified the public attention given to the
Holocaust and helped elevate remembrance to a national obligation. Even more than before, Holocaust themes were emphasized in school curricula, on reading lists, and in cultural programs. It was no coincidence that little more than a half year
later, in January 1986, Wiesel himself visited Germany. This
was his first trip back since Buchenwald and the visits he made
after the liberation to see his sister Bea in a displaced persons
camp. The trip was most notable for what Wiesel had to say on

the still vigorously debated subject—at least within a Jewish community where many refused to buy Volkwagens or Leica cameras—of whether Germans and Germany were worthy of forgiveness after so many years and acts of repentance, including the tens of millions of dollars paid in reparations.

"With whom am I to speak about forgiveness?" he asked. "I, who don't believe in collective guilt. Who am I, to believe in collective innocence?" That was as far as he was willing to go then, but as he told reporters afterward, "I have fervent hope for these people. I found here people who reminded me of good names," such as Dietrich Bonhoffer, the Protestant pastor who resisted the Nazis.[17]

While visiting West Berlin, Wiesel took a haunting side-trip to the palatial villa in the suburb of Wannsee where senior Nazi officials had cobbled together the blueprints for "the Final Solution to the Jewish Question." He was shaken and said afterward: "In our Jewish tradition we listen to objects, to trees, to clouds, to pebbles. I wanted to listen to those walls, to ask them: what do they remember?"

In the years that followed, Wiesel made several more trips to Germany and his remarks chronicle his evolution on questions of German guilt. Were all Germans—even those born after the war and those yet to be born—to be regarded with suspicion and contempt? His analysis of the issue, in a speech he gave in November 1987 at a Kristallnacht commemoration held at a conference center built into the shell of the ruined Reichstag, evinced the fine distinctions of a man imbued with Talmudic reasoning and comfortable with philosophical debate. It also produced some of his most stirring and memorable words.

He began his speech by reading a Yiddish lullaby written in the Vilna Ghetto by Shmerke Kaczerginski, in which a mother tells her baby to hush: "Crying won't do us any good; the foe will never understand our plight."

"Yiddish in the Reichstag?" he asked in English. "There

is symbolism using this warm, melancholy and compassionate language in a place where Jewish suffering and Jewish agony—some fifty years ago—aroused neither mercy nor compassion." There was indeed irony—and justice—in his speaking from the very rostrum where Hitler decreed the death of all Jews. Still, he was not going to placate the crowd with bromides that blamed only doctrinaire Nazis. Hitler's "poisonous words," he pointed out, did not make him unpopular with Germans. Few Germans sheltered Jews during Kristallnacht or tried to extinguish synagogue fires. Few objected when society's laws were twisted and perverted. "It was made legal and commendable to humiliate Jews simply for being Jews—to hunt down children simply because they were Jewish children." How could a people that had produced Goethe and Schiller, Bach and Beethoven, "put its national genius at the service of evil," become so bloodthirsty that their lust to kill extended to old men and women and a million children?

But on the matter of guilt there was some parsing to be done: "I have no right to forgive the killers for having exterminated six million of my kinsmen," Wiesel said. "Only the dead can forgive, and no one has the right to speak on their behalf. Still, not all Germans alive then were guilty. . . . Only the guilty were guilty. Children of killers are not killers but children." Yet, he said, "today's generation" should be held "responsible not for the past but for the way it remembers the past. And for what it does with the memory of the past. . . . We try to remember the dead. You must remember those who killed them."

It was Wiesel's call to the Germans to "help your own people vanquish the ghosts that hover over its history. . . . Salvation, like redemption, can be found only in memory. . . . 'Remember' is the commandment that dominates the life of young Jews today. . . . Let it dominate yours as well."[18]

Later, in 2000, Wiesel addressed the full German Bundestag on International Holocaust Remembrance Day and again took note of the "irony and justice" of his commanding a rostrum "where my own death, and the death of my family, and the death of my friends, and the death of my teachers and the death of my entire people, was decreed and predicted by the legally elected leader of Germany." Yet, he said, there can be reconciliation, and remembering is the key. "Challenged by memory, we can move forward together," he said. "Opposed to memory, you will remain eternally opposed to us and all we stand for."[19]

As Michael Berenbaum has observed, Wiesel lost the battle with President Reagan over Bitburg insofar as the president made the trip, "but clearly he won the war for memory, especially in Germany." In the aftermath of his Bitburg speech, Germany required its youth to study what had happened during the Third Reich and the Holocaust. It built monuments to the victims and museums that told their story in graphic detail. It produced exhibitions on many aspects of the Holocaust, including the cooperation between the Wehrmacht and the murderous *Einsatzgruppen*. Although the book's thesis stoked a vigorous debate in their country, many Germans spoke of how mortified they were to read Daniel Jonah Goldhagen's damning *Hitler's Willing Executioners*, which argued that it was "ordinary Germans," not just the fanatics of the SS, who persecuted, rounded up, and killed Jews.

"A new generation of Germans has come into being willing to ask questions that their parents—the children of perpetrators—were afraid to ask *their* parents," Berenbaum wrote. "Consequently, Helmut Kohl's wish that the Holocaust recede into the distant German past has not come to be realized."[20]

23

Family Time

WHILE GROWING into his role as a revered public figure, Wiesel continued to be plagued by nightmares—about the camps and especially about his father's death. At times, it was hard for him to experience elation, so small did daily life seem in a universe that permitted the atrocities he had experienced. Yet the embrace of his family kept him from despair.

Wanting their son to have a strong Jewish education, the Wiesels sent Elisha to Ramaz, an Orthodox Hebrew day school on Manhattan's Upper East Side with a vaunted reputation for both secular and religious studies. Elisha attended Ramaz all the way through high school. His father, locked into a teaching schedule that kept him in Boston from Monday evening until Wednesday afternoon, was not always home to hang out with him. But he always made sure to be home for Shabbat dinner, where he would chant the Kiddush over wine. He would keep the twenty-five hours of Sabbath sacrosanct, praying at the morning service at a synagogue near his home, often with Elisha at his side. When he traveled the world, he often took Marion and Elisha along and immersed them in whatever subjects he was dealing with. Elisha remembered "continually being pulled out of school" for trips to Washington for the planning of the museum, to Treblinka and Auschwitz for somber tours there, to Sighet for a rendezvous with his father's past, to Moscow and Kiev to meet with refuseniks.

As a young child, Elisha did not understand or appreciate what his father had achieved. A classmate might boast of a father who was a doctor or a pilot in the Israeli Air Force. But when Elisha was asked what his father did, he would reply self-consciously, "He's a Holocaust survivor."

"At a time when you want to say 'My Dad can beat up your Dad!,' my six-year-old self could only comprehend that he was a victim," Elisha said. 'I didn't understand what he had done from that platform that was so incredible. That was beyond me at a young age."[1]

Wiesel was already in his fifties when Elisha was approaching his teenage years, and as the product of a Hasidic community where Torah study was prized above all, sports and athletics were remote from Wiesel's passions. He didn't even know how to swim (though following a rabbinic tradition that parents teach their children to swim, he arranged for Elisha to have an instructor).

"I had to teach him how to pitch so we could play catch together," Elisha said. "But he did it. Would he rather that I was studying the Talmud? Yes. Did he love it? No. But he did it for me."[2]

There are photos of Wiesel and a friend in Central Park pulling a sled with Elisha on it. And, after his father's death, Elisha offered an unexpected anecdote. When Elisha was in the seventh grade, he and a friend, instead of studying for a test, were playing soccer outdoors. "If I take both of you on in soccer and score a goal, will you go study for your test?" Wiesel asked them. Elisha, thinking this was going to be no contest, agreed, and was quickly flabbergasted. "He turned into this super-amazing soccer athlete who was dancing rings around us and scoring goals."[3]

Yet like many children of immigrants eager to be seen as Americans, Elisha was aware of how entangled his father was in his *shtetl* past. Around the house, he sang Russian army songs or hummed Hasidic melodies, not pop tunes of the 1980s. He didn't know how to pump gas or keep score in baseball. Many of his tastes were throwbacks to poorer days. When the adult Elisha offered to make his father a cup of rich French press coffee, Wiesel declined, saying, "I like my instant."[4]

While he often reminisced about his childhood "willingly and openly," he seldom spoke about his parents and never about his seven-year-old sister, Tzipora. "I can't think of his ever bringing her up," Elisha told me. Like many other survivors, Wiesel sought to protect his children from absorbing the anguish of his own losses and his dehumanizing ordeal. "He was respectful in not jamming it down my throat," Elisha said. "I was getting a lot of it given the places we were going. But he never asked me to read *Night*. I picked it up on my own." It is notable that Elisha's daughter, Shira, has the middle name of Tzipora.

Around the age of fifteen and lasting almost a decade afterward, Elisha's relationship with his father grew strained. Of course, this is not at all unusual for a teenager trying to carve out a separate identity for himself. But Elisha, particularly after Bitburg, had to grapple with a father who had become a global icon. Elisha felt he was not seen for who he was but only as an offshoot of his father.

"I was a very shy, introverted small kid with big glasses who liked computers," he said. "I was desperately trying to fit in and be cool and impress my peers. It's hard just to be known as Elie Wiesel's son. It seems ungrateful, I know. What a gift it was to be with my father. But it was difficult just to be known as some-one's shadow."

Not surprisingly, there was a divergence of political views between a father deeply grateful for the refuge and freedoms America provided and a young man who grew up with those virtues as his natural backdrop. In 1990, when the free speech–based right to burn an American flag was at issue before the U.S. Supreme Court, Elisha provoked his father's fury. "Full of the confidence and liberal values of a college freshman, I told my father that the right to burn the flag was a more profound American asset than the flag itself," Elisha recalled. "He pushed back his chair and gave me the darkest look I could ever remember. 'If you had been there when that flag arrived in Buchen-wald,' he told me, 'carried by men who had lost their brothers fighting to rescue us, you would never say anything so beneath you again.'"

As a freshman at Yale, Elisha sported a Mohawk, at times purple, at times green, blue, or red, and told his parents he wanted a career in video games. He showed more interest in his electric guitar than in his studies and favored heavy-metal bands like Metallica. Later, he took part in a challenging train-ing program offered by the Israeli military. Then, he took up skydiving, terrifying his parents. At one point, his father offered to do a single skydive if Elisha would give up the sport.

Yet Elisha's father gave him a wide berth. "I love you and would walk down the street with you at any time," he told his son with the purple hair. "I am not embarrassed. I would take you to shul like this and out to dinner. You are my son." But there was one condition: "You can do anything you want as long as you marry Jewish."

A shift seems to have occurred in Elisha's mid-twenties when he and his cousin, Dr. Steve Jackson, joined his father on a trip to Sighet that included stops at Auschwitz and Paris. He was particularly shaken by their visit to Sighet. "You felt it was a town where there were no more Jews, where there had been a vibrant community," Elisha told me. "It felt haunted. It was very emotional. I would walk down a street and I would have in my mind's eye a picture of my father as a young person running around for an encounter with Jewish learning. I felt the relatives he had—his parents, grandparents and sister—and I felt their absence in a powerful way."

It was on this trip that Wiesel suggested a way for his son to get back on a more conventional path. Elisha had worked for a summer at Goldman Sachs, and Wiesel urged him to call his old boss and "rejoin Wall Street." Elisha followed through. Long obsessed with computer games, programming, and algorithms, Elisha worked in Goldman's securities division, was made a partner in 2004, and became the firm's chief information officer in 2017. After twenty-five years at the bank, he announced in September 2019 that he was leaving, saying he would take time to contemplate his next role, though it probably would not be in banking. One initial adventure: he joined the quixotic 2020 presidential campaign of Michael Bloomberg as a volunteer on a digital data team.

While at Goldman, he married—yes, a Jewish woman, Lynn Bartner (now Bartner-Wiesel)—and gave his parents two grandchildren, Elijah and Shira. Shira attends a Jewish day school, Elijah a school focused on science, tech engineering, and math.

Meanwhile, Marion was exercising her own influence. Wiesel, it can be said, was something of a *luftmensch*, more preoccupied with ideas than with the practicalities of advancing his career. Marion gently nudged him out into the world of influential people who might support his work and find ways to get more of the world to pay attention. Dr. Romana Strochlitz, the daughter of Wiesel's close friend Sigmund, recalled that as Wiesel's fame grew he was often reluctant to do interviews with television personalities or newspaper reporters. "Marion helped him see the importance of doing that and supported him unbelievably. To make the public more aware, that was her vision as well as his, and she helped him do more public things. She saw that he had this impact on people and the more people he had this impact on the better off the world would be."[5] His appearances on television with Oprah Winfrey or at fund-raising dinners, his travel writing for the *New York Times*, or his frequent televised conversations with ABC's Ted Koppel doubtless owed much to Marion's management. On his own, Wiesel was not one to insist on the speaking fees he received in later years—$25,000 was not uncommon—though the amounts were not out of line with those that other famous speakers received. And, as was mentioned before, whenever he spoke about the Holocaust the honorarium would be turned over to a yeshiva and "house of study" in Jerusalem founded by Menashe Klein, who had been in Auschwitz, Buchenwald, and the Écouis and Ambloy orphanages with him. The yeshiva is dedicated to Wiesel's father.

"Marion has a very good business head," Wiesel's friend the cantor Joseph Malovany told me. "The idea of exposing him to the larger world came very much from her. She has very much to do with the fact that he became well-known. She felt he should connect with the general public, with non-Jews" as well as Jews.[6]

When Marion met Mark Podwal, a Manhattan dermatologist who fashioned a second career as a prominent illustrator of Judaica, she suggested that Wiesel and he collaborate on a Passover *haggadah*. Wiesel would write the text explicating and commenting on the *haggadah* service and Podwal would create the drawings. In 2019, that book was in its twentieth printing and going strong.[7]

Thane Rosenbaum told me about an evening at the theater in 2005 that he and a girlfriend spent with the Wiesels. The play was *Primo*, a one-man show at Broadway's Music Box theater based on Primo Levi's memoir, *Survival in Auschwitz* (originally published in Italian as *If This Is a Man*). Seeing the play must have been emotionally difficult for Wiesel. He was friends with Levi and they had spoken by telephone not long before his apparent suicide in 1987. After the curtain fell, Marion wanted to stretch the evening out by attending a cast party at Sardi's. Wiesel was reluctant, preferring to go home and process his thoughts. But at Marion's insistence he went, and once there was sought out by a stream of celebrities. The specter of Elie Wiesel at Sardi's was "surreal," Rosenbaum said.

"I remember she [Marion] saw Lynn Redgrave and the two were hugging and kissing," Rosenbaum recalled. "Elie was not culturally cosmopolitan. He didn't have a clue who John Turturro was. He didn't know George Clooney. Elie was not reading *Variety*."

In his three decades as a journalist, Wiesel had befriended such world leaders as François Mitterrand and Golda Meir and certainly understood the power that media wielded in the shaping of public opinion. Yet he also understood that the dazzle of power and fame can be blinding, and that he too could stumble under their spell. When *The Pianist*, the Academy Award–winning film about the Warsaw Ghetto, opened in 2002, Wiesel went to the press screening, despite his own misgivings about the film's historical verisimilitude. To Rosenbaum he said, "This film makes you think that had the Germans only had more classical music in their lives, there would be no Holocaust." When the mega-producer Harvey Weinstein fawningly introduced him at the screening as "my all-time favorite hero," Rosenbaum pointed out to Wiesel: "This is how you get used."[8] Despite Rosenbaum's caution, Wiesel and Weinstein went on to appear together at a number of galas, including the one in 2013 mentioned earlier in which Wiesel returned the flattery by publicly telling Weinstein: "You made me love films." (Actually, it was Marion, who for many years attended the annual festival in Cannes, that had a true passion for film.)

The strong partnership between Elie and Marion kept him

in the public eye. She translated fourteen of his books and made sure he chose lectures and other engagements that enhanced his stature. Some friends found her overly possessive, felt she blocked or cut short meetings with friends she did not like. But whatever truth there is to that impression, Wiesel was appreciative of the touch of glamour and excitement she brought to his world.

In the early 1970s, Marion bought a summer place in Amagansett on Long Island for the family, and she transformed what her husband described as a ruin into a beautiful country house. Elisha remembered that when he was three or four years old his father rescued a bird that had fallen out of a tree there.[9] But the long weekend drive to the Hamptons, with stop-and-go traffic much of the way, exasperated Wiesel, so after a few years Marion sold the Amagansett house and bought a new one, first in Deal, New Jersey, then in Greenwich, Connecticut.

Marion even got her husband to warm to her cats. "He learned to love them because of me," she told me in 2020, as her cat Moishe glided across the armchair I was sitting on. "At first he said, 'No, no, no. No cats, no dogs.' Then one morning I woke up at five A.M. and I saw him feeding them. 'He was hungry and I fed him,' he said. He cried when one of them died."

Every weekday morning and on Sundays, Wiesel would chant his morning prayers while wrapping his forehead and upper left arm in the leather straps of the *tefillin*. Wiesel was following the commandments stated in Exodus and Deuteronomy: "And you shall bind them as a sign upon your arm, and they shall be as *totafot* [a synonym for *tefillin*] between your eyes." Asked once by Ted Koppel why he continued to perform Jewish rituals after all the Jewish suffering he had witnessed, Wiesel replied: "I didn't want to be the first member of my family to stop."[10]

On Shabbat he would walk over to the Fifth Avenue Synagogue, a few steps from Central Park in the Sixties. He would arrive around 9 A.M. just as the Sabbath service was starting, talk briefly with the rabbi, then take a seat in the synagogue's front row facing east toward Jerusalem and begin to pray, his eyes sometimes shut, his brow furrowed in the intensity of his appeal to God. Cantor Malovany, whose mother had grown up in Sighet and who today is regarded as one of the world's leading cantors, became his good friend and was often struck by Wiesel's fervor.

"No one could distract his attention," Malovany told me. "He loved the whole concept of *tefilah* [prayer]. To see him *davening* [praying], closing his eyes, and concentrating on prayer was an experience all by itself. What prayer meant was a double header. One was about a rediscovery of God. And two, he was always concerned about continuing the Jewish chain of life."

Cantor Malovany attributed Wiesel's evolution into an observant Jew to his experiences among the Jews of the Soviet Union, who yearned to draw closer to their God despite their government's denial of religious freedom.

"When he saw that in spite of their tragedies, Holocaust survivors and Soviet Jews were fighting as much as possible to retain their religious life, then perhaps God was putting into people the will to worship Him," Malovany said. "And therefore Elie realized that if Jews were fighting so hard to retain their Jewishness by going to synagogue, then he needed to make some changes in his relationship with God."[11]

Elisha remembered his father insisting on the family keeping a kosher home with separate dishes for meat and dairy. The family ordered meat from a kosher butcher, and Wiesel would not drive or travel on the Sabbath. But he did not always wear a yarmulke in public as most Orthodox men do, and there were sometimes compromises made because Marion was not as observant. "If it was a choice between *shalom bayit* and Orthodox observance, he'd give in to *shalom bayit*," Elisha told me, using the Hebrew phrase for "peace in the home," a religious concept. "He had his parameters and his flexibilities."

Yet there were times during the Jewish calendar when Wiesel seemed transported by the prescribed ritual. On Rosh Hashanah—the Jewish Day of Judgment when observant Jews believe that God decides, as the holiday's keystone prayer states, "who shall live and who shall die"—Malovany chanted a prayer beseeching God for mercy. "Almighty, You don't want people to die, you want people to repent," it begins in Malovany's translation. Malovany sang the prayer to a melody he learned from his Sighet relatives. And Wiesel, who had sung in the choir of Sighet's main synagogue, "sang along from his seat" with an expression of intense yearning.

On Simchat Torah, where the end of one cycle of the Five Books of Moses and the start of another is celebrated with seven exuberant rounds of dancing around the altar, often while cradling large Torah scrolls, Wiesel would follow the first round with an ardent prayer, "*T'zavei, T'zavei, Yeshuas Yaakov*" ("Order the salvation of the children of Jacob"). He would sing it to a particular Hasidic melody also derived from Sighet, while holding the scroll tightly to his chest and dancing with high spirits alongside Malovany. Inevitably, the congregation encircled them, joining in the revelry.

Every year, on the Sabbath before the date chosen to mark the anniversary of the deaths of Wiesel's parents and his little sister Tzipora, Wiesel would read the *haftorah*—a supplemental selection from the Prophets that is added to that week's Torah portion. The anniversary, or *yahrzeit*, has particular meaning for Holocaust survivors because they often do not know the precise date of their relatives' deaths. Wiesel did not know the date of the deaths either, but after the war he was told by rabbis to mark the anniversary on the date the transport carrying his family arrived at Auschwitz—the second day of the Hebrew month of Sivan. Wiesel honored his parents by reading the passage to a melody sung by the Vizhnitzer Hasidim of Sighet.[12]

In short, Wiesel, like many Jews, was eclectic in observance, in his case allied with a Modern Orthodox synagogue, observing most of the commandments and deepening his prayer with borrowings from his Hasidic roots, but ignoring some traditions in his public role as a teacher and speaker. And always he seemed locked in a vigorous, sometimes heated, dialogue with his God.

Although he was not a professional theologian, Wiesel, in his novels and essays and in his public talks, influenced the ways many Jews conceive of God. His ideas sometimes paralleled those of contemporaries like Emil Fackenheim and Richard L. Rubenstein, the latter perhaps the most compelling Jewish voice in the "Death of God" school of the 1960s. (As America and the world grew increasingly secular in practice and outlook, several Protestant theologians abandoned their faith's traditional visions of a commanding deity—that God was dead, they suggested— and devised new paradigms for understanding the divine role in the universe.) Rubenstein was seen as allied with that school because in *After Auschwitz: Radical Theology and Contemporary Judaism* he discarded his Jewish notion of a God who controlled the cosmos and directed human history. He did so by raising up the specter of the six million.

"How can Jews believe in an omnipotent, beneficent God after Auschwitz?" he wrote. "Traditional Jewish theology maintains that God is the ultimate, omnipotent actor in the historical drama. It has interpreted every major catastrophe in Jewish history as God's punishment of a sinful Israel. I fail to see how this position can be maintained without regarding Hitler and the S.S. as instruments of God's will."

"To see any purpose in the death camps," he continued, "the traditional believer is forced to regard the most demonic, antihuman explosion in all history as a meaningful expression of God's purposes. The idea is simply too obscene for me to accept."[13]

Night is laced with glimmers of such ideas. Indeed, a plausible interpretation of Wiesel's narrative of the hanging scene at Auschwitz is that the God who safeguards Jews as his Chosen People is mortally hanging in the gallows and a different conception is now needed. Since *Night* was published in English six years before *After Auschwitz*, it is likely Wiesel arrived at this viewpoint on his own. True, the incident was observed by a fifteen- or sixteen-year-old yeshiva boy exposed almost exclusively to the Jewish canon and unlikely to fixate on so sophisticated an observation. But *Night* was written ten to fifteen years after Auschwitz by a young man who had studied philosophy at the Sorbonne with existentialists and agnostics and who likely reworked earlier experiences through a more expansive lens.

The maturing Wiesel, like Rubenstein, always recoiled at rabbis who viewed the Holocaust as a punishment for sin; for Joel Teitelbaum, the grand rabbi of the Satmar Hasidim, it was the sin of fervently advocating the creation of an Israeli state in the absence of the Messiah. Wiesel also did not accept the viewpoint that God stood back and allowed the Holocaust to proceed in order to pave the way for an independent Jewish homeland or to teach the world lessons about the consequences of racial animus and the price of indifference.[14]

"Nothing has been learned," Wiesel argued in *One Generation After*. "Auschwitz has not even served as warning. For more detailed information, consult your daily newspaper."[15]

Nevertheless Wiesel remained a believer, preferring to ask challenging questions but leaving them unanswered. When he conducted a press conference after the announcement that he had won the Nobel Peace Prize, I asked him how he can explain to himself why God allowed the Holocaust to occur, and he replied: "I have not answered that question, but I have not lost faith in God. I have moments of anger and protest. Sometimes I've been closer to him for that reason."

There were periods when Wiesel did forsake the Orthodox rituals that affirmed his faithfulness; he did so in Auschwitz and Buchenwald and as a new immigrant in America. As a writer, Wiesel created characters in his early novels—Michael in *The Town Beyond the Wall* and Gregor in *Gates of the Forest*—who at moments express some of his cynicism toward a God that would allow the pointless death of innocents. Yet as the years went by, whatever his rational mind told him, it became a comfort to observe the Jewish rituals he had absorbed as a child, the same rituals that his father and grandfather performed before him, and to bask in the camaraderie of a synagogue and the tribal bonds of the wider Jewish community.

The notion of a ubiquitous God who created and oversaw the universe was bred in his bones, absorbed as an impressionable child in a daily immersion in the Five Books of Moses and, as a teenager, the Talmud and Midrashim. It was strengthened by the devotion he saw in his parents and grandfather and the plainspoken Jews of Sighet. These emotional attachments would exercise far more influence on Wiesel than all the philosophers, existential or otherwise. Although he delved deeply into theological works, his visceral intuitions weighed as much in his thinking and in composing his novels as his cerebral reflections. His theological musings were in line with a shrewd observation of Rubenstein's: the theologian is more like a poet than a scientist, "communicating an inner world he suspects others may share."[16] Moreover, Wiesel grew up on stories of the biblical luminaries—Adam, Abraham, Jacob, Moses, Job—and he often borrowed lessons from their stories in stitching together his own religious view.

As much as any biblical figure, Wiesel identified with Jeremiah, the reluctant prophet who foresaw the Babylonian Exile. "I love the Prophet Jeremiah because he is the one who lived the catastrophe before, during and after and knew how to speak about it," Wiesel told a conference of social studies teachers in 1977.[17] Like Jeremiah, he saw himself as the survivor "who could not speak but must speak," as a messenger whose message was not heard and so was profoundly lonely. At a point of near despondency, Jeremiah wondered in *Jeremiah* 15:18 whether God would "be unto me as a deceitful brook, as waters that fail?" Wiesel too could quarrel with God, even suspect him of treachery. Why, he wondered, was God silent when the inmates of Auschwitz or Buchenwald or Treblinka cried out for Him to intervene? Although Wiesel may offer no answers or speculative ones, he nonetheless affirmed God's majesty and firmly believed, as Robert McAfee Brown wrote, "that to quarrel with God is to pay God the supreme compliment: it is to take God seriously."

In the discordance of theologians Wiesel carved out his own distinct views. Fackenheim might have been a great admirer of Wiesel, yet Wiesel would not concur with a view of a binary Deity who either saved his followers or instructed them with painful lessons. At Auschwitz, Fackenheim wrote, God's "commanding presence" in essence ordered survivors not to give Hitler another victory by despairing and forsaking their Judaism. Yet this God let more than a million Jews die there. Nor could Wiesel accept Fackenheim's assertion that "Jews are forbidden to despair of the God of Israel lest Judaism perish." Wiesel could certainly despair, of God and of humanity, though significantly he tried to transform that despair into new conceptions of God's role in the universe even if he never quite arrived at a definitive vision.

Like Rubenstein, Wiesel rejected the notion of a God who intervenes in human history for the ultimate benefit of Jews. Where was such a God at Auschwitz? Yet Rubenstein, who developed his Judaism late in his youth because his parents had offered him little training, not even a bar mitzvah, proposed an almost godless alternative: Jews could still define themselves by

coalescing into a supportive and congenial community that iden-
tifies itself by timeless rituals and rites of passage. This was a
solution Wiesel also could not accept. Though paradoxical, even
mystical, Wiesel's outlook emphatically kept God at the center
of his beliefs. True, it was a God he often found baffling and
infuriating, a God he often rebuked, yet it was a God he loved
with all his being and would grapple with until the end of his
life. His anger at God did not require that he stop believing
in Him or abandon keeping Shabbos or donning *tefillin*. He
could no more extract from his soul his belief in God or his desire to perform the traditional rituals than he could pluck out a
vital organ.

Wiesel loved listening to music. Mark Podwal, who sometimes acted as his medical consultant in addition to serving as
his resident illustrator, liked to drive him to events or appoint-
ments just to spend time with him. During these rides, they
would often play CDs of classical or klezmer music. Wiesel
would spend many evenings at home listening to, say, the second movement of Beethoven's Seventh Symphony or almost
anything by Mozart. Matthew Lazar, director of the Zamir Chorale in New York, was amazed to see among Wiesel's shelves of
CDs and tapes the complete works of Josquin des Prez, a now
obscure sixteenth-century Franco-Flemish composer of poly-
phonic vocal music.

Wiesel loved to sing, and as he got older and more comfortable in the public eye, he would snatch opportunities to
break into song or lead others in singing. At the 92nd Street Y,
to celebrate various anniversaries of his lecture series, he sang a
Hasidic version of "Ani Ma'amin" with the Zamir Chorale. And
in 1992, at a program at Carnegie Hall celebrating the twenty-
fifth anniversary of Jerusalem's reunification, Wiesel, once the
teenage leader of an orphanage choir, conducted the Zamir Chorale and three hundred other singers from the National Jewish

Chorale in several pieces. And he did so with panache. When he visited the Jewish Primary Day School in Washington, D.C., in 2008, where his friend Leon Wieseltier's son Matthew was in kindergarten, he surprised his hosts by breaking into a Hasidic liturgical tune, "[He] who remembered us in our lowliness." The children were delighted.

No performance was more moving than a concert of seventeen songs performed before a sold-out auditorium at the 92nd Street Y in 2010. In a shaky voice but one deep with feeling, Wiesel, then eighty-two, sang such Yiddish classics of his childhood as the lullaby "Rozhinkes mit Mandlen" ("Raisins with Almonds") and "Oyfn Pripetshik" ("In the Fireplace" of the *cheder*, or Yiddish schoolroom). "I hope you don't expect a late-life career change," he joked. "I'm doing this only once."

Toward the end, he sang the Holocaust lament "Es Brent!" ("It Is Burning"), about the destruction of a *shtetl*. "Each time I hear this song it breaks my heart," he said. "And I think of the world today, in danger, and what are we doing about it."[18]

As often as possible, Wiesel found time to pore over passages of Talmud, sometimes asking a friend such as Abe Foxman, the longtime national director of the Anti-Defamation League, or Wieseltier, then literary editor of the *New Republic*, to study with him. He kept an entire set of the sixty-three tractates of the Babylonian Talmud in his home and another at the Madison Avenue offices of the Elie Wiesel Foundation for Humanity, which he started with Marion after he won the Nobel Peace Prize. He could rattle off hundreds of Talmudic legends and allegories and pluck just the right one out for a speech or a conversation.

"His religion was a mixture of intense intellectuality with intense romanticism," Wieseltier told me. "He was truly a Hasid in some ways. He liked to think but he also liked to be transported emotionally, transported by a spiritual state, high and low, joy and despair."[19]

He was a ferocious reader, and his apartment was filled with thousands upon thousands of books. Near his desk he always kept a haunting photograph of his family's thatched-roof house in Sighet. "Whatever I do, if I get too full of myself, I want to remind myself every day where I came from," he told the publisher of *Lifestyles* magazine.[20] In another interview, with PBS for the documentary *Elie Wiesel: First Person Singular* (2002), he articulated a similar thought about the photograph with a fine but significant distinction: "With all that has happened to me," he said, "it is essential for me to remember that place."

Deep into middle age, Wiesel loved to hear homespun stories and jokes, even those that elicited groans from others, and he loved to laugh. When Cantor Malovany's mother visited her son in 1982, Wiesel chatted with her in Yiddish, and enjoyed some of her earthier jokes. According to the cantor, he convulsed with laughter at one she told about an insane asylum where two residents had been involved with the same woman named Chana. The first had been driven mad when she rejected him. The second was the man who succeeded in marrying her.

24

Nobelist

EACH YOM KIPPUR, along with Jews all over the world, Elie Wiesel spent virtually the entire day in synagogue, praying in his customary seat and observing the fast. But on Yom Kippur in 1986, Cantor Malovany noticed that Wiesel had slipped out before the conclusion of the morning prayers. This was most uncharacteristic, but he had spoken of a severe headache, another of the migraines that had afflicted him since childhood, and went home to rest.

Wiesel returned for *Neilah*, the service held just before the "Gates of Prayer" are closed, a service in which devout Jews believe they have a last chance to reverse any unfavorable verdicts from on high, often with tormented pleas. Yet Malovany noticed that Wiesel had "a little smile on his face." After the service they spoke and Wiesel whispered something about an odd encounter he'd had outside his apartment building. When he got to the front door, he told Malovany, a stranger stood waiting for him, a journalist from Norway's *Dagbladet*. Wiesel told the journalist that it was Yom Kippur and he could not deal with temporal matters like an interview, but the journalist insisted. He had something important to pass on. Could they talk in Wiesel's apartment? Wiesel relented, and once inside the apartment, the journalist produced a bouquet of flowers that he handed to Marion.

"You should know that tomorrow my newspaper's headline will be about you," the journalist said to Wiesel.

"You're mad, this is impossible," Wiesel replied, correctly surmising what the headline would say: that he had won the 1986 Nobel Prize for Peace.

There had been talk for several years that Wiesel might receive a Nobel, though the common expectation was that it would be for literature, given the scores of books he had written. Wiesel told Malovany that he had promised the journalist the interview, though in *And the Sea Is Never Full*, he chastised himself for breaching the sanctity of Yom Kippur. Wiesel concluded his tale, still skeptical that he would receive the prize, but Malovany beamed, signaling that he believed the reporter. "I said to him 'Gemacht—it's done!'" Malovany told me.

After sundown, Wiesel sat down for the "break-fast" and invited friends who were in New York—Sigmund Strochlitz, Per Ahlmark, the former deputy prime minister of Sweden, and Yossi Ciechanover, the dear friend who was a former top official in the Israeli Defense Department—to join him. While the news from Oslo was still uncertain, they hashed out what he might say at a possible press conference and how he might respond to likely questions, even working out how he might handle an almost certain one about the Palestinians. Wiesel, though, was not yet ready to give the news absolute credence. He needed to receive the official call from Oslo.

It came at 5 A.M. the next morning, October 14, after Wiesel had slept little more than an hour. He picked up the receiver in the living room to hear Jakub Sverdup, a professor of history who directs the Nobel Institute and had tracked down Wiesel's unlisted number, tell him: "I have the honor to inform you that you have won the Nobel Prize for Peace." The vote of the Nobel committee, Sverdup added, was unanimous.

Initially, Wiesel was elated, but, characteristically, he was soon overcome with feelings of melancholy. He found himself reflecting on the improbability of something like this happening to him given his roots in a forlorn place like Sighet. He remembered his parents and grandparents and the little sister whose deaths ironically turned him into the spokesman for the survivors that made this moment possible. Soon Strochlitz, Ahlmark, and Ciechanover were summoned back to the apartment and Malovany was asked to join them. Each friend embraced Wiesel in tears and drank a *L'Chaim* to him.[1]

In Oslo, meanwhile, Egil Aarvik, the Nobel Committee's chairman, read a statement to a roomful of international journalists: "Elie Wiesel has emerged as one of the most important spiritual leaders and guides in an age when violence, repression and racism continue to characterize the world," he said. "Wiesel is a messenger to mankind. His message is one of peace, atonement and human dignity. His belief that the forces fighting evil in the world can be victorious is a hard-won belief. His message is based on his own personal experience of total humiliation and of the utter contempt for humanity shown in Hitler's death camps. The message is in the form of a testimony, repeated and deepened through the works of a great author. Wiesel's commitment, which originated in the sufferings of the Jewish people, has been widened to embrace all oppressed peoples and races."[2] Wiesel, upon learning of the statement, was particularly stirred by the reference to his writing.

Within the hour, his doorman was on the apartment intercom asking Wiesel what he should do with a crush of journalists trying to enter the building, including ones from the networks, the *New York Times*, and Agence France-Presse. Wiesel let the doorman send them all up and he submitted to a string of interviews on the spot. The Oslo announcement was the lead story on the morning radio and television news, so the phone rang incessantly during the interviews. Henry Kissinger, François Mitterrand, Shimon Peres, Yitzchak Shamir, and the Lubavitcher Rebbe all called or sent telegrams as did countless friends. Wiesel interrupted the interviews to telephone his sister Hilda in Nice, where she had settled after years of struggle in Israel.

Nobel Prizes are more political than the public may realize, and lobbying by influential friends and associates is often intense even if a person overwhelmingly deserves it, as Wiesel surely did. What went into any particular Nobel decision is secret, but it could not have hurt that a Sighet native, Herman Kahan, a wealthy textile industrialist, was president of Oslo's Jewish community. Or that Olle Wästberg, a member of Sweden's parliament between 1976 and 1982, sent a letter to the committee just as he had done every year since 1980, praising Wiesel's writings about the Holocaust and his activities on behalf of other victims of genocide.

Strochlitz had campaigned around the world for his friend's consideration, soliciting letters from members of Congress, members of the German, French, and Norwegian parliaments, and previous prize winners—all those entitled by the Nobel rules to make nominations. Wiesel, by Strochlitz's count, was championed by no fewer than fifty American senators, 140 congressional representatives, seventy members of the West German Bundestag, French president Mitterrand, and the former Nobel Peace Prize winners Mother Teresa, Henry Kissinger, and Lech Walesa, the leader of Solidarity and later president of Poland. John Silber, the president of Boston University, helped Strochlitz gain access to the American legislators, and his own nominating letters kept reminding the Nobel committee that Wiesel had also championed the causes of the boat people in

Vietnam, the Miskito Indians in Honduras and Nicaragua, the disappeared in Argentina, and Soviet refuseniks. If nothing else, the lobbying kept Wiesel's name in the committee's sights; Nobel officials later acknowledged that Wiesel had been on the short list for the prize for several years before he received it. Strochlitz was "the real strategist and campaigner," Silber told the *New Republic*, and handled the effort with such discretion that Wiesel, while aware, never inquired about it. "We said, 'Stand still, Elie. Step aside. Do your work. Don't worry about our work, which is to make them aware of yours.' Nobody wins unless the Nobel Committee knows about them." But Silber refused any credit. "We may have fed the oats, and curried the flanks," he said, "but that horse could run."[3]

After the morning announcement, friends accompanied Wiesel, Marion, and Elisha to a press conference at the 92nd Street Y—home of Wiesel's lectures for twenty years at that point. While his doleful eyes reflected the horrific losses behind the triumph, he proclaimed the significance he saw in news of the Nobel arriving toward the end of Yom Kippur.

"In Jewish history there are no coincidences," he told the crowd of reporters and photographers. "If it happens after Yom Kippur here, then some of my friends and myself have prayed well."

He went on to explain why he had chosen the path that led to the prize. "I decided to devote my life to telling the story because I felt that, having survived, I owe something to the dead. That was their obsession, to be remembered, and anyone who does not remember betrays them again." He extended that mission to those threatened in Cambodia, South Africa, the Soviet Union, and elsewhere. Will the Nobel change you, he was asked, and he replied: "If the war did not change me, you think anything else will change me?"

I covered the press conference for the *Times* and managed to speak with Wiesel alone after the TV cameras and radio tape recorders had gone, for a "Man in the News" profile. While fourteen-year-old Elisha sat nearby wearing an emphatic symbol of his Americanness—a New York Yankees jacket—I asked Wiesel how he was able to bounce back from his losses. "I went from despair to despair," he replied. But "we have to go into the despair and go beyond it, by working and doing for somebody else, by using it for something else." I turned to the big theological enigma: "How could the God you believe in allow the slaughter of so many of His people?"

"I have not answered that question," he said, "but I have not lost faith in God. I have moments of anger and protest. Sometimes I've been closer to him for that reason."[4]

A year and a half after the Bitburg confrontation, the Nobel Peace Prize elevated Wiesel's stature yet again. New York mayor Ed Koch assigned two plainclothes security guards to protect him. Peter Ueberroth, the commissioner of baseball, invited him to throw out the first ball at the World Series, a game between the Mets and the Red Sox. Wiesel, who knew nothing about baseball, was relieved to discover the game fell on the first day of Succoth, when travel is forbidden. Elisha was beside himself and his father was pained to have disappointed his son, but Ueberroth resolved the situation by having him throw out the ball at the third game—on an intermediate day of the eight-day holiday when travel is allowed. Fortunately, Elisha had taught him enough about hurling a baseball that his performance was not, as Elisha feared, humiliating. A photograph of Wiesel throwing out the ball wound up on the front of the *Times* sports section.

In December, Wiesel and his family traveled to Oslo for the Nobel ceremony. His sister Hilda came from France. There was also a planeload of friends—Strochlitz; Yossi and Atara Ciechanover; lawyer and philanthropist Bernard Fishman; film producer John Heyman and his wife, Nizza; Arnold Thaler, a Chicago businessman; Norman Braman, the mega-auto dealer who at the time owned the Philadelphia Eagles and hosted the

Wiesels whenever they visited the French Riviera; his Summit Books publisher, James H. Silberman, and his young editor, Ileene Smith; and illustrator Mark Podwal. As is traditional, the Wiesels were given the Nobel suite at Oslo's palatial Grand Hotel situated between the Norwegian parliament and the Royal Palace. Kings and queens had slept there. Henrik Ibsen dined in its elegant café.

When they entered their room, the Wiesels were greeted with masses of flowers and chocolates, for which Wiesel had a special affection. He was soon whisked to a press conference where European reporters asked him questions about the chances for peace in the Middle East. Then Egil Aarvik escorted him to a private audience with King Olav V, the handsome, down-to-earth, and enormously popular monarch who had staunchly resisted the Nazis, first in Norway and then as head of a government-in-exile in Great Britain. Eighty-three years old and still full of zest and charm, he told Wiesel that if he had been allowed to nominate a peace prize winner he would have been his choice too.

On leaving the palace, however, he was disturbed to see a pack of Holocaust deniers distributing pamphlets to a crowd that had gathered to catch a glimpse of him.

The Wiesels traveled with Egil Aarvik to the Nobel presentation ceremony at the great *aula* or hall of Oslo University, its walls emblazoned with a vast series of expressionist murals by Edvard Munch. As he entered the hall for this crowning moment, took his seat, and listened to Aarvik's presentation of the peace prize in Norwegian, Wiesel's thoughts turned to "all those who are not present. The emotion that overcomes me is so powerful that . . . I feel choked, and there is a heavy weight on my chest. . . . Once again I see myself in my parents' house, I see my father and mother, and my two sisters who are gone, and all I can think of is how much I wish they could have known my son; I so long to tell them that I go on loving them, that I have remained faithful to them."[5]

Aarvik, as if intuiting what Wiesel was feeling, told him from the stage, "When your father was dying you were at his side. It was the darkest day of your life. This day, for you and for ourselves, is a glorious day. I would like your son to stand next to you as the greatest prize that mankind is able to grant is bestowed on you." Wiesel wrote that this unexpected link between his father and his son left him feeling "overwhelmed with sadness" as he headed toward the podium. He told Oprah Winfrey in a televised interview in 2012 that as he looked out at the audience he actually "saw my father in the hall . . . I couldn't speak. I couldn't open my mouth. It took me one, two or three endless minutes to start talking."[6]

"I don't hear the applause," he wrote in *And the Sea Is Never Full*. "I hear nothing, and then all I hear are the invisible tears flowing into my soul, I hear the prayers my dead parents are chanting on high, I hear the call of my little sister . . . whose suffering should have extinguished the sun for all eternity."

Wiesel also reminded himself that despite the accolades, Aarvik was mistaken. On the last day of his father's life, he heard him moaning in agony, but he could not comfort his father because to speak would have risked a fatal beating. Too afraid to help, he had not stood by his father's side, as Aarvik said. That was the guilt that shadowed Wiesel all his life.

Fighting back tears, Wiesel began his acceptance speech by openly wondering whether he had "the right to represent the multitudes who perished."

"No one may speak for the dead," he said, sounding a core belief of his. "No one may interpret their mutilated dreams and visions."

Yet he was pleased to receive the prize because the honor belonged to all the survivors, their children, and the Jewish people. The Jewish boy he was had endured cruelty that seemed to come out of the Middle Ages, not the civilized twentieth century. Later in the speech, Wiesel imagined that boy might still demand of his older self: "What have you done with your life?"

"I tell him that I have tried," he said in a weary voice. "That I have tried to keep memory alive, that I have tried to fight those who would forget. Because if we forget, we are guilty, we are accomplices. And then I explained to him how naive we were, that the world did know and remained silent. And that is why I swore never to be silent whenever and wherever human beings endure suffering and humiliation. We must always take sides. Neutrality helps the oppressor, never the victim. Silence encourages the tormentor, never the tormented. Sometimes we must interfere. When human lives are endangered, when human dignity is in jeopardy, national borders and sensitivities become irrelevant. Wherever men or women are persecuted because of their race, religion, or political views, that place must—at that moment—become the center of the universe."[7]

The sustained applause by the eight hundred guests in the hall was followed that evening by a spectacular torchlight parade. A river of light created by students and teachers, laborers and activists, young mothers pushing baby carriages, Jews and Gentiles, wound past the balcony outside the Wiesels' hotel suite, where Elie Wiesel and his beautiful wife Marion stood smiling. The words "Shalom! Shalom!" could be heard and at one point the marchers sang "We Shall Overcome." At another point, Mark Podwal dropped out of the parade to hand Wiesel a torch that he held aloft in honor of the crowd. In a life that had more than its share of tributes, there had never been anything like this.

A sumptuous dinner—rabbinically supervised—was followed by a gathering of friends in the Wiesels' suite that lasted until dawn. The next day, Wiesel delivered the traditional Nobel lecture. Magically, he opened with a song, the plaintive Hebrew prayer "Ani Ma'amin" that was sung quietly by Jews in the camps as they headed off to their doom. "I believe with utter faith in the coming of the Messiah," is what it says, but for Wiesel, who had used it as the theme of a cantata, it was his credo, and offered a profound and emotional introduction to the lecture he would give, "Hope, Despair and Memory."

In his Nobel lecture, he recalled how he emerged from Auschwitz and Buchenwald bereft of parents and a sister, an orphan alone in France, "on the verge of despair." Somehow he marshaled the resources to go on, learning a new language, making friends who, like him, needed to believe that the "memory of evil" would shield them from further evil. Yet what they had been through paradoxically turned them into skeptics. After all, these were people who felt God was covering His face "in order not to see," who had witnessed doctors of medicine and theology, lovers of art, poetry, Bach, and Goethe coldly order massacres of the elderly, the frail, and children. "Why bring children into a world in which God and man betrayed their trust in one another?" Wiesel said he asked himself. Many tried to repress memories that stirred so much pain. But for survivors "forgetting was never an option"; they bore the graves of their murdered relatives within themselves.

Survivors naively believed that if the world knew what had happened at Treblinka its distress would assure that such a horror would never be repeated. Yet when the survivors did speak up, too many people refused to listen; others could not comprehend. "Have we failed?" Wiesel asked. "I often think we have."

> If someone had told us in 1945 that in our lifetime religious wars would rage on virtually every continent, that thousands of children would once again be dying of starvation, we would not have believed it. Or that racism and fanaticism would flourish once again, we would not have believed it.

Nor would we have believed that there would be governments that would deprive a man like Lech Walesa of his freedom to travel merely because he dares to dissent. And he is not alone. Governments of the Right and of the Left go much further, subjecting those who dissent, writers, scientists, intellectuals, to torture and persecution. How to explain this defeat of memory?

How to explain any of it: the outrage of Apartheid which continues unabated. Racism itself is dreadful, but when it pretends to be legal, and therefore just, when a man like Nelson Mandela is imprisoned, it becomes even more repugnant. Without comparing Apartheid to Nazism and to its "final solution"—for that defies all comparison—one cannot help but assign the two systems, in their supposed legality, to the same camp.

He went on to speak about the "outrage of terrorism," mentioning the American hostages held by Iran and the massacre at an Istanbul synagogue, then pivoting to the Jews like Andrei Sakharov who were forbidden to leave the Soviet Union, and Israel's inability to achieve peace with its Arab neighbors after thirty-eight years of sovereignty.

"There may be times when we are powerless to prevent injustice, but there must never be a time when we fail to protest," he concluded. "Mankind needs peace more than ever, for our entire planet, threatened by nuclear war, is in danger of total destruction. A destruction only man can provoke, only man can prevent. Mankind must remember that peace is not God's gift to his creatures, it is our gift to each other."[8]

And so the glorious moment was over. But the power of the prize endured for the rest of Wiesel's life. He would go on to meet with princes and heads of state as an equal. His pronouncements were tracked by the press. A decade later, reflecting on the impact of the prize on his life, he told the reporter Clyde Haberman that the peace prize "creates situations which are very interesting. It's a kind of catalyst. Either people like me more or they like me less as a result of it." Characteristically, he found humbling humor in the experience, describing the strange correspondence he often received. He told the reporter: "I have letters from couples who can't get along saying, 'You try to make peace between countries. Big deal! Come to my home.'"[9]

25

·◆·◆·◆·

Catalyst for Change

IN THE WEEKS following the ceremony, with the almost $300,000 he received from the Norwegian Nobel Committee, Wiesel, along with Marion, conceived and established the Elie Wiesel Foundation for Humanity. He had long believed that the path to solving many of the world's overarching problems—"indifference, intolerance and injustice," as the foundation's mission statement names them—lay in dialogue and an exchange of ideas. So the foundation's first project was an international conference of Nobel laureates titled "Facing the 21st Century: Threats and Promises." Wiesel sought to mobilize the laureates' collective wisdom and moral authority to "propose fresh principles, policies and strategies" that might tackle the ethical and practical crises of the time and move the world closer to disarmament, peace, human rights, and economic and scientific development.

The conference drew seventy-five laureates and was held

over the course of four days in January 1988 in the Salle des Fêtes in the Élysée Palace, with gourmet meals, sumptuous accommodations, a tour of the new Musée d'Orsay, and recitals by such musicians as Mstislav Rostropovich and Anne-Sophie Mutter. Among the luminaries in attendance were Henry Kissinger, the former German chancellor Willy Brandt, novelist William Golding, playwright Wole Soyinka, and scientists Joshua Lederberg and Roslyn S. Yalow.

President Mitterrand opened the conference by urging humility in acclaiming the promise of science and technology. The twentieth century, he said, had brought penicillin, the green revolution, the conquest of space, and enhanced life expectancy, but it also introduced Auschwitz, brown shirts, and fanaticism of all kinds. When it was his turn, Wiesel, speaking in French, told the Nobel laureates that as a group they were more responsible for the state of the world than anyone else and therefore needed to affirm the principle that "we are all responsible for one another."[1]

"It is a question of saving humanity—or at least our humanity," he said. "We are all on a train that is running toward a precipice. We cannot change trains, so we have to slow it down.... When it is given to man to act upon events, how to make sure that he steers them toward the sun and not toward the abyss."[2]

In the break-out sessions, Kissinger distinguished between the political approaches of "the Prophet" and "the Statesman." Most great transformations, he said, have been achieved by prophets who believe in "the absoluteness of pure truth," while statesmen often "set their sights too low and bring on what they seek to avoid." But "it is possible that the prophets, in their quest for purity, have brought about even greater suffering." Dr. John Vane, a Nobel winner in 1982, delivered a paper on how the push for larger and larger profits was hamstringing pharmaceutical research and urged drug companies to cooperate in combating AIDS, a scourge then at its peak.

Beyond thought-provoking speeches, what that conference accomplished was fairly amorphous, something some of the laureates had anticipated. But after four days, many laureates said they were pleasantly surprised by the quality of the ideas exchanged and suggested the conference might yield some meaningful benefits in the future. "There are signs of a baby here aborning," said Sheldon L. Glashow, a 1979 Nobelist in physics who had been skeptical about the value of the conference when it opened.[3]

The foundation went on to sponsor a total of fourteen conferences through 2014 in venues that included Hiroshima, Haifa, Venice, Dublin, Oslo, Moscow, Boston, and New York. Six of the conferences were specifically for Nobel laureates, and many attracted some of the era's major figures, including South Africa's soon-to-be-president Nelson Mandela, Czech Republic president and playwright Vaclav Havel, the Dalai Lama, former U.S. presidents Jimmy Carter and Bill Clinton, Northern Irish political leader David Trimble, and former Israeli president and prime minister Shimon Peres. Four conferences, cosponsored by Jordan's King Abdullah II, were held annually between 2005 and 2008 in the ancient city of Petra amid the remarkable structures carved into rose-colored rock. The Petra conference in June 2006 featured the first meeting between Israeli prime minister Ehud Olmert and Palestinian Authority president Mahmoud Abbas, which was no mean feat. Afterward, the two men announced plans for a summit that led to extended though ultimately fruitless peace talks.

The stature of those who took part in the conferences was testimony to the respect, even reverence with which Elie Wiesel was held by so many political and religious leaders around the world, and he responded with some of his most eloquent messages. "We must harness our rich human potential in service of peace, progress and prosperity," he told the first Petra gathering. "To these ends, peoples must realize that no one is superior to another. No nation is worthier than another. No religion is holier than another. Racism, ethnic discrimination and religious fanaticism lead to antagonism, not salvation."

At a conference in New York in 1992 titled "Anatomy of Hate," Wiesel fashioned a message aimed at "saving our children," the conference's subtitle. "Hate knows no frontiers, neither racial nor ethnic," he said. "Hate is contagious. Wearing various masks, it can be found among all religious and social communities. Like cancer, if unchecked, it will destroy the body which nurtures and carries it. Ultimately hate is both destructive and self-destructive. Hate inevitably leads to self-hate," he said.

The foundation's conferences were conceived as "catalysts for change and action" in an effort to "create a world in which humanitarian atrocities are never forgotten or repeated." Wiesel's hope was that participants would take ideas generated in lectures, workshops or discussions and return home to shape plans for repairing their societies in both practical and moral ways. Menachem Rosensaft, who organized the last Petra conference for Wiesel, where a focus was world hunger, told me that while he could not point to a concrete accomplishment, "these things have unintended consequences, things that can't be predicted," that flow out of "sensitizing the Nobel laureates to wider global issues and providing opportunities for them to talk among themselves."[4]

With Marion taking the lead in raising funds, the foundation went on to create two thriving after-school centers in Ashkelon and Kiryat Malachi for Ethiopian Jewish children who had been airlifted to Israel in 1991 to escape the violence of a civil war. The remarkable covert rescue, known as Operation Solomon, deployed thirty-five El Al and Israeli Air Force planes to ferry 14,000 Ethiopian Jews to Israel in roughly thirty-six hours. Marion told me she was moved to help the Ethiopian children after a breakfast with her friend, Atara Ciechanover, in Tel Aviv.

"She impressed upon me that the situation was very bad, and we decided on the spot to get in a car and go to Akko [the city north of Haifa more commonly known as Acre]," Marion said. "They had trailers where young children lived, ate, studied. They had no books, no paper, no pencils, the rudiments you need, and I thought that was appalling. We decided this was a good place to help and I phoned Elie and he agreed, of course."[5]

The centers, each named Beit Tzipora after Elie's murdered sister, provide tutoring, computer labs, and hot meals and have helped the immigrants flourish in the Israeli school system. Elie and Marion made frequent trips to Israel to visit the centers and took deep pride in their success. In 2018, two years after her husband's death, Marion turned the project over to the Women's International Zionist Organization, an Israeli social welfare agency. Today the centers enroll roughly a thousand girls and boys.

Since 1989, the foundation has also run an annual essay contest for college juniors and seniors devoted to the theme of ethics. Students are asked to write about a moral issue they confronted and what it taught them about themselves. The winner receives $5,000, with smaller awards for four runners-up. Wiesel said he conceived of the contest because "we felt the theme of ethics must be predominant in whatever we do."

Over the course of thirty years, thousands of students from hundreds of colleges and universities have submitted essays, some very personal, others more philosophical, that reveal the rising generation's relationship to ethics. Jean Claude Vasquez, the 2014 winner, wrote about the ethical tensions inherent in America's immigration policy. Alexandra Stewart, the 2015 winner, described her struggle in deciding whether to tell the authorities about a close friend who had been sexually abused by her father.

A good example of the thoughtfulness and quality of the essays—with language that would do Wiesel proud—is one by the 2019 winner, David Olin, a student at the University of California, Berkeley. He wrote of his dismay at observing a march of neo-Nazis beneath his apartment window and how it forced him to ponder the ethics of using violence against such right-wing extremists.[6]

In 2010, Yale University Press published a twentieth-anniversary collection of the prizewinning essays called *An Ethical Compass: Coming of Age in the Twenty-first Century*, featuring a preface by Wiesel. And at a gathering of prizewinners in New York for the contest's thirtieth anniversary, many of the young participants spoke of the boost in self-confidence they felt as a result of the opportunity to articulate their views and have their thoughts affirmed by the foundation.

Siri Davenport, the 2006 winner, said writing the winning essay "helped me understand I have a voice, and I have hung on to that." And Dana Kiel, the 2016 winner, seconded that idea. "Receiving the prize has been a little like receiving a torch," she said. "I will continue to be a voice for the voiceless."

26

Reconciliations and Reprimands

BEFORE THE HIGH HOLIDAYS of 1997, an unusual op-ed appeared in the *Times*. It was called "A Prayer for the Days of Awe," and was written by Elie Wiesel. The compact format of the op-ed essay—eight hundred words or so—had become a crucial means for Wiesel to convey his thoughts to a wider public, and in this piece, he proclaimed that he no longer wished to be angry at God, that the time had come for reconciliation. The survivors had "learned to build on ruins," he wrote. By having children and creating new families, by finding new friends, the survivors, he continued, had "learned to have faith in their surroundings, even in their fellow men and women." So "gratitude has replaced bitterness in their hearts."

Admittedly, he would never understand where God was during Auschwitz "while your children were marked for humiliation, isolation and death only because they were Jewish." But he was nevertheless ready to "make up: for the child in me, it is unbearable to be divorced from you for so long," he wrote.[1]

When Ciechanover asked him how he could go to synagogue and recite morning prayers every day to a God who allowed Auschwitz, Wiesel suggested to him that he went to synagogue and prayed to resume the timeless rituals of his ancestors. He prayed, he said, because "that is what my father did all his life."[2]

In the days before Twitter and Facebook, Wiesel had been deploying op-ed essays to let the public know his views on issues he considered crucial. In 1986, he met with Soviet officials about granting visas for the remaining Jewish refuseniks, and the following year he wrote an op-ed piece in the *Los Angeles Times*, addressed to Mikhail Gorbachev's wife, Raisa. He was seeking her help in gaining emigration to Israel for Ida Nudel, a prominent activist in the refusenik movement. "Is it so wrong for a woman to wish to live with people she loves, and who love her?" Wiesel wrote. "Think of her loneliness and you will understand why her friends are so numerous. Won't you help her?"[3] With appeals from others as well, including the actresses Jane Fonda and Liv Ullmann, Nudel was finally allowed to emigrate in late October 1987. And before long, Wiesel succeeded in gaining emigration for the dissidents Vladimir and Masha Slepak as well.

An unauthorized leak by Vatican officials prompted him to cancel plans for what he had been promised would be a private meeting with Pope John Paul II at the Vatican. Instead, he publicly chided the pope for the Vatican's refusal to recognize Israel and the warmth it had displayed toward Kurt Waldheim. Waldheim, the former U.N. secretary general, had concealed the fact that he had served as an intelligence officer for the Wehrmacht in Greece and Yugoslavia during World War II.

Emboldened by the peace prize and with accolades pouring in from all over the world, he met with François Mitterrand seeking an explanation for the French leader's youthful allegiance to the Vichy regime. The two had begun an acquaintance just before Mitterrand's first electoral victory in 1980, after he heard Wiesel on the car radio giving a nuanced portrait of the biblical Jacob. Wiesel agreed to a meeting and the two men hit it off. After Mitterrand's election, they got together almost every time Wiesel was in Paris, lunching at the president's private quarters in the Elysée Palace. Over the next fifteen years, they shared a deep intellectual friendship. They discussed political, literary, and religious issues, with Wiesel explaining the subtleties of the laws of *Kashruth*, *kabbalah*, and the literary style of the Talmud to the French president. He enjoyed these exchanges with a leader whom he found uncommonly erudite. At the same time, Wiesel was aware that as a Jewish human rights activist, he would surely help boost the Socialist Mitterrand's appeal to French Jews and liberals.

But in 1994, a book, *Une jeunesse française* ("A French Youth") by Pierre Péan, was published detailing Mitterrand's collaboration with Vichy, which among other crimes had participated with the Nazis in the roundup and deportation of French Jews and Jewish refugees to the death camps. Though Mitterrand did join the Resistance in the last months of the war, it was disclosed that he had kept up a friendship with René Bousquet, the Vichy police chief who had organized the roundups and deportations to Auschwitz. And each year, without public knowledge, he had placed a wreath on the grave of Marshal Pétain, the Vichy leader.

Wiesel was in Paris promoting his memoir *All Rivers Run to the Sea* when news of the book about Mitterrand broke. Stunned, he promptly arranged a meeting with the French leader. The president, fatigued by the treatment he was undergoing for prostate cancer, expressed no remorse and made denials that simply did not square with the thoughtful and well-informed person Wiesel had come to know. Wiesel followed up on the conversation by faxing further questions to Mitterrand, to flesh out some of his answers, but Mitterrand never responded. Despite his considerable disappointment and anger, Wiesel went through with plans to publish a book of dialogues with Mitterrand on central questions of the day. That was an agonizing decision, but the friendship was over.[4]

In 2000, with a $1 million gift provided by Random House, Wiesel launched a project to publish memoirs by fellow Holocaust survivors. "What they have to say nobody else has to say," he told Dinitia Smith of the *New York Times*. Rosensaft, the project's director and editor, said the program received a thousand submissions. But mainstream publishers rejected almost all of the manuscripts, claiming the market was saturated. Although Wiesel spoke of publishing ten memoirs a year, that number proved overly optimistic. Three memoirs in English were published through the U.S. Holocaust Memorial Museum, another twenty-two through Yad Vashem, and there were four others published through other outlets. That came to thirty books between 2004 and 2012, when the project ran out of funds. (According to Rosensaft, the $1 million was spent on advertisements inviting survivors to contribute manuscripts, on editors to read the thousand manuscripts that were submitted, and on publishing the thirty manuscripts that were turned into books.)

In another endeavor on behalf of survivors, Wiesel used his considerable stature to call for reparations from Nazi accounts and gold stored in Swiss banks, to be used to sustain impoverished survivors. But he declined appeals that he chair organizations doling out such funds, saying he was a writer, not an administrator. Still some activist survivors felt he could have done more for organizations like the Claims Conference, which distributed the bulk of money that Germany set aside for reparations. Roman Kent, chairman of the American Gathering of Jewish Holocaust Survivors and treasurer of the Claims Conference, sounded a bitter note after Wiesel's death. "Sixty thousand Jewish survivors need home care," he told me. "But Elie didn't get involved in raising money. It was beneath his dignity."[5]

This once unassuming son of Sighet did, however, intrepidly take on presidents, prime ministers, and popes, discreetly and diplomatically, but with remarkable presence. For instance, he gently corrected John Cardinal O'Connor of New York when in 1987, during a visit to Yad Vashem, he referred to the Holocaust as "a gift" the Jewish people gave the world. "I told him why didn't you use the word lesson instead of gift. He agreed by the way. He said that as a Christian he spoke in Christian language."[6]

On a 1989 visit to the Soviet Union to open a cultural center named after Solomon Mykhoels, a famous Jewish actor and director who was a victim of a Stalinist purge, he was not afraid to urge Mikhail Gorbachev to establish diplomatic relations with Israel and to open the secret files on the death of Holocaust rescuer Raoul Wallenberg, whom Yad Vashem honored as one of the "Righteous Among the Nations."

When Wiesel testified at the French trial of Klaus Barbie, the Gestapo's "Butcher of Lyon," in June 1987, Barbie's lawyer, Jacques Verges, argued that there had been other atrocities where perpetrators went unpunished. He cited the My Lai massacre in Vietnam and a massacre of Arabs by Israelis in the village of Deir Yassin in 1948. Wiesel snapped back: "I am against brutality no matter where it comes from. But I find it regrettable, deplorable that the lawyer of the defense, who defends a man accused of crimes against humanity, dares to accuse the Jewish people." Later, not mincing words, he told the reporter Richard Bernstein that Verges "is full of hatred toward me personally, hatred for the Jewish people, and hatred for the victims."[7]

In early 1991, a newly independent Lithuania issued a blanket exoneration of all citizens who had been convicted by the previous Soviet rulers of collaborating in Nazi war crimes, arguing that the charges were trumped up or resulted from false confessions. When documentary evidence clearly showed that at least a dozen of those exonerated had collaborated in the killing of Jews, Wiesel wrote to president Vytautas Landsbergis to say that the disclosure had left him with "a sense of disappointment and deception and outrage." "Many of them have committed murder, assassinating men, women and children only because they were Jewish," he wrote. "To rehabilitate them today means to forgive them. That this would be among the first steps of an independent Lithuania is something no decent person can understand or accept."[8] With pressure from Secretary of State James Baker, the Lithuanian government agreed to review two and later three of the thirteen exonerations that had drawn Jewish complaints. By October, the government had suspended the exoneration program entirely and indicated it would seek legislation to reverse the exonerations of those whose war crimes had been documented. However, not one of the three convicted of collaboration was ever incarcerated, with the government citing a convict's ill health or that of a spouse as an explanation.[9]

In July 1991, Wiesel traveled to Bucharest for a ceremony to mark the deaths of half of Romania's 750,000 Jews at the hands of Germans aided by Romanians and Hungarians. The setting for the ceremony was particularly significant—the Choral Temple, the 125-year-old Moorish-style synagogue that had survived despite the insistent attempts of nineteenth-century anti-Semites, fascist vandals, and Communist bulldozers to destroy it. Yet, a half century after the slaughter, Romania was still treating the Jewish dead as the random casualties of war rather than the victims of a deliberate extermination. Wiesel was there to unveil a plaque on a wall in the synagogue's forecourt to commemorate the 130,000 Jews of his native northern Transylvania who were killed not only by Germans but by local military and police after Hitler declared the territory part of Hungary. But he specifically addressed Romanians because the chief rabbi, Moses Rosen, had informed him of an upsurge in anti-Semitism there.

"I hope you know," Wiesel told his audience, "that your representatives have great difficulties in the world to mobilize sympathy, political and economic support for your country. Your image is not the best. You must know that. You must know that unless these anti-Semites are shamed in society, you will suffer. You will be isolated. The world is following this with astonishment, dismay and outrage. . . . I plead with you. Allow me in the future, too, whenever I speak of the geography of my childhood, to speak of it with fondness. And that depends on you."[10]

The following day, he went to the city of Iasi, where the Romanian army had staged a wartime pogrom that left eight thousand Jews dead. But his speech warning about anti-Semitism was interrupted by a middle-aged woman. "It's a lie!" she shouted repeatedly. "The Jews didn't die. We won't allow Romanians to be insulted by foreigners in their own country." She was eventually out-shouted by others in the audience, including some of the nine hundred Jews left in Iasi, where before the war there had been more than forty thousand. The woman, a newspaper reported the next day, was the daughter of Colonel Dumitru Captaru, a key instigator of the pogrom and the officer believed responsible for the deportation of four thousand Jews.[11]

In July 2002, Wiesel returned to Romania, this time to Sighet, to open a Jewish museum in his boyhood home, an idea put forward by the Romanian president, Ion Iliescu. But the visit was different from earlier Sighet trips, which had been more personal. Wiesel spent the two days urging Romanians to face up to the role of their government and its people in murdering Jews. He told a crowd of five thousand people outside the town hall that had welcomed him with bread and Slivovitz that Sighet's Christians had stood by as the town was emptied of its Jewish citizens.

"Ask them if they shed a tear, if they cried, if they slept well," he said.

Sighet, he recalled, was part of Hungary during the deportations and was only returned to Romania after the war. But now that Sighet's people were Romanians they should know that it was the Romanian military under Marshal Ion Antonescu who carried out mass killings of Jews and incited the pogroms in Bucharest and Iasi, and in the regions of Bukovina and Bessarabia. Yet Antonescu was lionized by nationalistic Romanians as a great patriot because he had reclaimed territory from the Soviet Union.

"Antonescu is also the past," Wiesel said, in a soft but firm voice; "unfortunately those who glorify him are in the present." He closed his talk by addressing the young people in the audience. "And then you children, when you grow up, tell your children that you have seen a Jew in Sighet telling his story."[12]

Wiesel even took on Holocaust survivors who insisted that there should be no forbearance or understanding of any Germans, even those born after the war, or of German companies that were making efforts to compensate for work done in service of the Nazi war machine. The issue arose when the United Jewish Appeal honored Thomas Middelhoff, chief executive of Bertelsmann, the German company that owns Random House, with a dinner in New York on May 15, 2001. During the Third Reich, Bertelsmann had published Nazi propaganda. Not surprisingly, a number of survivors and their children protested the honor.

"Try me in five thousand years, and maybe we'll be ready to start talking" was an objection from Melvin Jules Bukiet, an English professor at Sarah Lawrence College and the son of a survivor. "They should be ashamed of themselves at UJA. Are we allowing ourselves to be purchased? Of course we are, and it's an outrage."

Chosen to give the keynote at the UJA dinner, Wiesel pushed back. He pointed out in a *Times* op-ed that Middelhoff was born eight years after the war's end, that he led efforts to fully unearth and publicly divulge Bertelsmann's work for the Nazis, and that Random House had contributed $1 million to the project that published memoirs by Holocaust survivors.

"Of course, Jews must never—and will never—forget the Jewish tragedy that marked the last century and will haunt all centuries to come. To forget would be a sin. To remember is essential. . . . But does it justify intolerance?"

"If, tragically, one chose to indict all Germans for the Holocaust, that would inevitably lead to exclusion and discrimination. Jewish academies could never invite German intellectuals and scholars to their conferences; Jewish music lovers would be expected to boycott concerts with German orchestras; and Jews could never, ever befriend Germans, no matter how long after the war they were born."

"Am I wrong to believe that to humiliate a German today just for having been born German and to boycott an evening for him is not what the Jewish ethos is about? I would like to remind some of my fellow Jews that Hitler's Germany condemned all of us not for what we did or did not do, but solely for having been born Jewish. . . . I know from my own experience with German students that their burden is, at times, difficult to carry, heavy as it is with painful memories and questions about their fathers' and grandfathers' roles in the most terrifying genocide in history."[13]

Yet Wiesel was not yet ready to wholly embrace the new Germany. While he was moved to see the exuberance of Germans celebrating the fall of the Berlin Wall, the strains of "Deutschland über Alles" triggered anxieties about the perils of a reunified, strengthened country while members of the Nazi generation were still alive. "I cannot hide the fact that the Jew in me is troubled, even worried," he wrote in an op-ed piece. "Whenever Germany was too powerful, it fell prey to perilous temptations of ultranationalism."[14]

Each country, it seemed, had its own perspective on how the Holocaust and the toll of the Second World War ought to be interpreted and memorialized, and those perspectives continued to be a source of bitterness and friction, demanding great delicacy on Wiesel's part. A good example was the Polish government's commemoration in January 1995 of the fiftieth anniversary of the liberation of Auschwitz. Jewish survivors anticipated that the Poles would not acknowledge that most of the camp's victims—1 million of the 1.1 million who perished there—were Jews and would turn the event into a more generic observance. "The organizers have no comprehension of the Jewish component," Wiesel told the reporter Jane Perlez. Particularly upsetting was the fact that *Kaddish* would be said only after the dignitaries had left. Should that remain the plan, Wiesel indicated, he would recite the prayer as part of his speech.

At the same time, Wiesel tried to smooth relations over with Lech Walesa, Poland's president and fellow Nobel laureate for his leadership of the Solidarity movement that eventually ended Communist rule. Wiesel had introduced him to Auschwitz a decade before and considered him a friend. Nevertheless, when Walesa lamented the Nazi effort to destroy Poland's "intellectual and spiritual strength," he did not single out Jewish victims.[15]

Ultimately, during a break, the Jewish delegates held a separate ceremony at the nearby killing fields of Birkenau—the location of the gas chambers, crematoria, and the "Pond of Ashes," where the ashes of tens of thousands of bodies burned in one of the crematoria were dumped. A cantor chanted the mournful *El Moleh Rachamim* and recited the names of other Nazi death camps—Treblinka, Majdanek, Sobibor—bringing tears to many eyes. Wiesel spoke as the sun shone faintly through bare poplars. "Although we know that God is merciful, please God, do not have mercy for those people who created this place," he said. "Remember the nocturnal procession of children, of more children, and more children, so frightened, so quiet, so beautiful. If we could simply look at one, our heart would break. But it did not break the hearts of the murderers."

Wiesel's stature on the world stage made him the go-to figure for securing the blessing of the Jewish community in all sorts of situations. For instance, when New York mayor David Dinkins needed to tamp down Jewish anger over the city's feeble response to the beating of Hasidim in Crown Heights after a car accident in 1991 that killed a black boy, Wiesel was called in to lead "a campaign against anti-Semitism." He joined civil rights leader Jesse Jackson to host a showing at the Apollo Theater of a documentary about black American soldiers who liberated Jewish prisoners like himself at Nazi death camps. Countering statements by other Jewish leaders, Wiesel told Joyce Purnick, a member of the *Times* editorial board, that the Crown Heights riots should not be considered a pogrom. "It shouldn't have happened, of course," he said. "But the pogrom was usually always with consent of authorities. Any pogrom was always with consent of police."[16]

Wiesel sometimes used his platform to venture into the unwieldy realm of politics. In 1998, for instance, he joined a rally at New York University of seven hundred artists and professors protesting the effort to impeach Bill Clinton. Calling the drive by Republicans, several of whom had been accused of similar dalliances, hypocritical, Wiesel challenged the audience: "Who shall judge the judges?"

Still, human rights and Jewish rights remained his focus. In 1999, at Clinton's request, he toured refugee camps in Macedonia teeming with people displaced by yet another Yugoslavian war, this time in Kosovo between ethnic Albanians seeking independence and a Serbian military trying to retain the territory. The reporter accompanying him was impressed by the hours he spent engaging refugees under a blistering sun. "When evil shows its face, you don't wait, you don't let it gain strength," Wiesel told the reporter David Rohde. "You must intervene."[17]

Intervene he did, and often indignantly, as happened in October 2000 with the news that two Israeli soldiers had been lynched by a Palestinian mob. "We have dreams of Israeli and Palestinian children playing together, studying together, laughing together," he told a rally outside the Israeli consulate in Manhattan. "It is with a heavy heart that we say that our dreams of peace have gone up into the smoke of ransacked synagogues with the lynching of Israeli prisoners and the bloodthirsty mobs. . . . I blame the supreme leader of the Palestinians, Yasser Arafat. . . . All of his promises were lies."[18]

In 2000, he traveled to Washington for a conference sponsored by the U.S. Holocaust Memorial Museum on life in the displaced persons camps after the war. Aware that the survivors were now deep into their seventies and eighties, he aimed his remarks mostly at their adult children, urging them to sustain the memory of what was done to the six million. He told me afterward that he believed the children, known as the Second Generation, or 2G's, would impress the memory of the Holocaust on the world's conscience since so many were already writing or producing books and films relating to the Holocaust, forming therapy or discussion groups, and immersing themselves in the Yiddish culture of prewar Europe.[19] "I believe a person who listens to a witness becomes a witness," he said.

Wiesel seemed to be turning up at one human rights event after another, offering his wisdom on this subject or that, and some critics like Walter Goodman of the *Times* found his ubiquity problematic. When Wiesel in 1991 appeared on a Bill Moyers television program analyzing the common elements of hate groups, Goodman filleted their conversation in several scathing sentences. With Moyers chasing Ahab-like after a big idea, Wiesel's sound bites—"Ultimately, whoever hates hates his brother, and whoever hates his brother always hates himself" was one—

had sounded like so much posturing. "Elie Wiesel seems to be playing Elie Wiesel as he sighs heavily and speaks portentously," Goodman wrote.[20]

As appeals flowed in for his help, Wiesel learned to be cautious—detractors might say, too cautious. One of the more curious chapters involved Jonathan Pollard, the Jewish naval intelligence analyst who pleaded guilty in 1987 to espionage for turning over important military secrets to Israel. Many Jewish American leaders thought his lifetime sentence too harsh. After all, Israel was an ally, and no one, these supporters argued, had ever received so long a sentence for spying for an ally. But other Jewish leaders, like former New York mayor Ed Koch, didn't want to touch the case because Pollard's actions raised the specter of divided loyalties among Jews.

In December 1988, Pollard sent Wiesel a handwritten, tightly spaced sixteen-page letter from the federal prison in Marion, Illinois, asking Wiesel to help his wife, Anne. She had been imprisoned for five years as an accomplice and now was suffering from a rare digestive ailment that without advanced medical attention would threaten her life, Pollard wrote. He also asked Wiesel to craft a public appeal for a reduction of his own life sentence. Wiesel responded with a note to Pollard's father that suggested the letter genuinely moved him.

"The punishment does seem too harsh for both your son and his wife," he wrote to Morris Pollard, a professor at Notre Dame. "I'll try to help—but for the moment I prefer it to be behind the scenes."[21]

Wiesel did as he promised. He wrote to Attorney General Edwin Meese, saying he was disturbed that Anne's physical condition was deteriorating, though he took pains to note: "Please understand that I do not condone the actions of either Mrs. Pollard or her husband Jonathan, but I do think she should not have to endure needless suffering." Over the next year, he wrote similar notes to Cardinal O'Connor and Senator Orrin Hatch.

But given the conflicting views about Pollard's sentence, he did not choose to risk his moral authority with a public plea for a reduction in Pollard's sentence in an op-ed or at a rally. His intervention would have drawn prominent coverage.

Anne was paroled in 1990 for health reasons, though there is no evidence that her release resulted from Wiesel's interventions. Soon after her parole Pollard filed for divorce, and in a prison ceremony in 1993, he married Esther Zeitz, a Canadian teacher who had vigorously campaigned for his release. Pollard's increasingly desperate pleas to Wiesel now focused only on himself. In April 1991, Wiesel wrote to reassure him that he had mentioned his plight during a visit to President George Bush's White House. "Do not give up hope," Wiesel advised. "Justice and compassion will prevail."

"The bottom line is that the best thing you can do for me is to write something—anything, that the whole world can see," Pollard replied. "I beg you to say something in the press on my behalf." Wiesel responded by reminding Pollard that he had signed petitions, called senators and congressmen, tried to enlist columnists. He also offered to visit Pollard, which he did the following year just before Passover, singing songs from the *Haggadah* to the prisoner.

"Your visit did so much for me, Dr. Wiesel, that I'm still basking in the afterglow," Pollard wrote afterward.

On the evening after the prison visit, Wiesel raised Pollard's case in a speech to six hundred people gathered in Washington to honor the ninetieth birthday of the Lubavitcher Rebbe, senators, ambassasdors and other federal officials among them. "Let's be honest: What he did wasn't right," Wiesel said. "But he was punished. And once he was punished, who am I to add to his punishment?"[22] He visited Pollard again in 1995 at the medium security prison in Butner, North Carolina, where Pollard had been transferred. But with top defense and intelligence officials vigorously opposed to mercy, Pollard was not paroled. Bill

Clinton declined to commute the sentence, as did George W. Bush and Barack Obama.

Pollard grew so desperate that in March 1996—nine years after he was jailed—he sent Wiesel a sarcastic letter that implied that Wiesel had been resisting writing an op-ed appeal because he would not be paid for the article. Pollard offered to pay him. "I have exactly $126 in my account," he wrote.

Wiesel replied with uncharacteristic irritation. "I am offended by your ridiculous and nasty note. If you know of people who have done more for you than I, just tell me who they are. If I chose not to write articles about you, it is simply because in my judgment I have better ways to communicate my views."

Afterward, the correspondence petered out, though the thick Pollard file in the Wiesel archives ends with Wiesel's note to a friend in 2004 mentioning that he is still trying to help Pollard.[23] Ultimately, Pollard was not released until 2015, his thirtieth year in prison, having served the minimum period before a federal prisoner sentenced to life is eligible for parole. Why wouldn't Wiesel have used his international clout to speak publicly on Pollard's behalf the way several prominent rabbis, politicians, and actors did? Clearly, Pollard's case was too ambiguous for Wiesel to take a bold public position. Officials quoted in articles by Seymour Hersh and other investigative reporters had accused Pollard of severely compromising American intelligence-gathering. Far from acting like a noble Zionist, they said, he had passed classified information to South Africa, Argentina, and Israel for substantial sums. For Wiesel, a more cautious approach seemed prudent.

Meanwhile, Wiesel's prominence as a novelist was overshadowed by his human rights activism, much as Vaclav Havel's writing was overshadowed by his political pursuits. *Twilight*, published in 1987, fared much better with critics than several of his earlier books. The novel is an unexpected weaving of Holocaust family history with strands of almost magical-realist narrative. The story centers on the wisdom imparted by residents of a mental institution who believe they are the biblical figures Adam, Abraham, Cain, and Joseph. As is true of other of Wiesel's characters, the protagonist, Raphael Lipkin, a Polish-born scholar of mysticism and his family's lone survivor, is obsessed with madmen—a compulsion the writer makes clear in the opening sentences: "As a boy, Raphael feared madness but was drawn to madmen. . . . Madmen can say anything, do or undo anything, without ever having to explain. Madmen are free, totally free."[24] In search of information about a friend who mysteriously vanished, once again named Pedro like a character in *The Town Beyond the Wall*, Lipkin visits a psychiatric hospital in upstate New York. The patients, adopting their biblical personae, articulate profound questions identified with Wiesel: Why would God create the Jewish people only to wipe out so many in the Nazi era? If we have objective standards for sanity, how sane was the God who permitted the Holocaust? Is it possible that it is God who is mad, not the patients? What if madness can be a path to truth? Or, as a reviewer for the *Los Angeles Times*, Janet Hadda, wrote: "Perhaps the madmen who believe that they are Adam, Cain, or even God are as sane as those who believe in the existence of their biblical originals."

Hadda demurred that the work tackled too many weighty issues in too few pages, but she added, in words that must have been a balm to Wiesel's pride as a literary craftsman: "The lover of poetry, however, will be well rewarded with the lyrical, elegiac, and epic qualities combined in one man's unique vision."[25] Stanley Moss, in the *Times Book Review*, found sections of the book too often "function more as meditation than fictional narrative." Still, he admired Wiesel's ability to let the reader experience "how good the family is, how good people are," despite war's atrocities. "Utterly without sentimentality he gives us a small but real measure of what the world's loss has been," wrote Moss, who sums up one of Wiesel's signal achievements as a writer.[26]

A *Times Book Review* essay on *The Judges* in 2002 illustrates the challenge Wiesel was facing with critics who thought of him as more of a political advocate than a fiction writer. The novel tells the improbable story of five passengers on a plane headed for Tel Aviv that during a blizzard is forced to make an emergency landing in Connecticut. The five passengers make their way to a house owned by a mysterious self-appointed "judge." This eccentric figure—perhaps he is a stand-in for a Jewish God often impugned for the arbitrariness of who lives and who dies—declares that one of them will die by the end of the night and requires the passengers to reveal certain truths about their lives. The reviewer Robert Leiter called Wiesel to task for cramming his novels with "philosophical notions and heavy theorizing."[27] But Wiesel did not write to please his critics. The philosophical threads in his novels were essential to his commitment to writing fiction.

As a result of his prominence, Wiesel found himself at many glamorous A-list events. In September 1990, the United Nations held a World Summit for Children; the Wiesels were invited to a party at the elegant Café des Artistes in Manhattan. There Wiesel introduced Jan P. Syse, the prime minister of Norway, to a legendary Hollywood couple, Paul Newman and Joanne Woodward. In 2002, he joined the global elite at the World Economic Forum in New York, conversed on stage with Bishop Desmond Tutu about the politics of apology, then at a party afterward at the Brasserie mingled with supermodel Heidi Klum, actress Kirsten Dunst, who was about to star in *Spiderman*, and jazz pianist Herbie Hancock.

So famous had Wiesel become that in 2002 PBS broadcast a documentary called *Elie Wiesel: First Person Singular*. His life story was interspersed with excerpts from his books read by the actor William Hurt. In January 2006, Oprah Winfrey transformed Wiesel into virtually a household name. She announced that her next book club selection would be the "classic" *Night*. *Night* was already doing well—selling roughly three hundred thousand copies a year in the United States alone, and it was available in thirty languages—but Winfrey's endorsement vaulted it into the stratosphere. Hill & Wang, now an imprint of Farrar, Straus and Giroux, promptly announced that it would print a million copies of a new translation by Marion. The book became an instant bestseller and sat on the national lists for eighteen months. Hundreds of schools began requiring *Night* for their history and social studies classes. The slim volume gradually became, like *Animal Farm* or *To Kill a Mockingbird*, one of the most popular books of all time. As Samantha Power said at a memorial service for Wiesel in Washington in 2016, "Alongside Atticus Finch and Scout, one of the narrators that will have an early shot at shaping our children's moral universe is 16-year-old Elie."

In the weeks following her endorsement, Winfrey and Wiesel visited Auschwitz-Birkenau together and the film of their excursion was riveting television. It showed the two of them walking in heavy winter clothes—Wiesel is wearing an astrakhan—through the frigid camps, their arms locked for warmth and emotional support.

"I think the souls are here—they listen, they cry, they warn," Wiesel tells Winfrey. "Look, this is the largest cemetery in recorded history. And what do you see? Nothing. The cemetery is in our hearts."

Winfrey recalled the scenes from *Night* of his family's arrival at Auschwitz and how he was separated from his mother, grandmother, and little sister. "I remember she had a red coat she got for the holiday," Wiesel told Winfrey, suppressing tears. "I saw them disappear. We went to the left. They went to the right, to the crematorium."

When he visited Winfrey in her studio in December 2012

for a retrospective interview and they again recounted the Auschwitz trip, Wiesel, now eighty-four, was just as emotional. "I have in my pocket a picture of my little sister. It's the only time I cry. Not when I speak about my parents, but when I speak about my little sister. She makes me cry. She was seven. . . . Why the children? A million and a half children were killed. They went straight from the train. Do you know what they could have done for humanity? How many of them could have grown up to become physicians, artists, poets, scholars, friends of humanity, saviors of the world?"[28]

27

Reversals

THE FIFTH AVENUE SYNAGOGUE is not one of the city's more spectacular houses of worship. Modest in scale and décor, it lacks the grandeur of Temple Emanu-El a few blocks to the north, and Central Synagogue, ten blocks to the south. But its membership may make it one of New York's wealthiest congregations. Among its billionaire congregants are Ira Rennert, the chairman and chief executive of Renco Group, a private holding company that invests in a wide range of industrial firms, including the largest magnesium producer in North America; financier Ron Perelman, chairman and biggest shareholder of Revlon; and Mortimer Zuckerman, real estate magnate and publisher.

Wiesel had been going to this Orthodox synagogue almost every Sabbath since he moved to the Upper East Side, first to Third Avenue in the East Sixties and then to a more elegant address across from Central Park. He would show up at 9 A.M., briefly socialize with other worshipers, then absorb himself in prayer.

Among the congregants he sometimes engaged with was J. Ezra Merkin, the synagogue's president. Money matters were not something Wiesel usually talked about, but friends and other synagogue members had told him that Merkin had a shrewd eye for investment and that one of Merkin's hedge funds was earning regular returns of ten percent. That alone might not have persuaded the Wiesels to invest their savings and their foundation's assets with Merkin, but Wiesel was impressed by Merkin's background. He was the son of a self-made refugee from Nazi Germany who became a major benefactor of Yeshiva University. Ezra Merkin had graduated from Harvard Law School, had worked for the white-shoe law firm of Millbank, Tweed, and was on the investment committee for the UJA-Federation of New York, as well as the boards of Yeshiva University and Carnegie Hall. Besides, he had a deep grasp of Torah and Talmud, something Wiesel prized.

"Everybody thought he was a genius," a magazine publisher familiar with Merkin's circle told me. "It was an unwritten rule at Fifth Avenue if you considered yourself part of the inner circle you invested with Merkin." After all, institutions like Yeshiva University were investing with him. But Merkin, despite collecting hefty management fees, was actually putting all of their money into funds run by someone who would become one of the most notorious figures in American financial history.

In December 2008, Bernard L. Madoff was arrested for running a Ponzi scheme that wiped out $64 billion in paper wealth of hundreds of investors and institutions—perhaps the largest fraud ever committed. Rennert reportedly lost $200 million, Zuckerman's charitable foundation lost $30 million, and Yeshiva University lost $110 million. Other nonprofit institutions and charities that suffered deep losses or whose major donors suffered big losses included the Gift of Life Bone Marrow

Foundation, Brandeis University, the Museum of Fine Arts in Boston, and the Beth Israel Deaconess Medical Center, also in Boston. The JEHT Foundation (an acronym for Justice, Equality, Human dignity, and Tolerance), which since 2000 had given away more than $62 million to support reform of criminal justice systems, was forced to dissolve.

Elisha, Wiesel's son, agreed with advisers cautioning his parents not to invest their money or that of the foundation in a single fund. But, he told me, "My father was not a man who took care of financial affairs."[1]

"For most of my adult life, I had made a conscious decision not to be involved with my parents' finances or with the Foundation," he said. "I had set out to create an identity for myself distinct from my father's work. But when the Madoff news broke, it became painfully clear to me that I had somehow let my parents down."

When the news broke, Elie and Marion had just returned from a dinner at the home of a friend. The phone rang, and it was Elisha. "Don't worry," he told them. "Everyone is good. Now sit down." He proceeded to tell them that Madoff had been jailed and that the Wiesel Foundation's $15.2 million was gone. Elie and Marion had also lost their personal savings, which had been invested with Madoff as well.

"We lost everything," Wiesel told Oprah Winfrey in their 2012 interview.

Yet Wiesel claimed that he and Marion quickly put what happened into perspective. "We looked at each other and our reaction was: we have seen worse," he told Winfrey.[2]

Wiesel was less measured in a panel discussion about the Madoff scandal held at the 21 Club two months after the world learned of the fraud. "This was a personal tragedy where we discovered all of a sudden what we had done in 40 years—my books, my lectures, everything—was gone. We checked the people who have business with him, and they were among the best minds on Wall Street, the geniuses of finance. I am not a genius of finance. I teach philosophy and literature, and so it happened."

"This man knew what he was doing," he said at another point. "I would simply call him a thief, scoundrel, criminal. . . . The imagination of the criminal exceeds that of the innocent."[3]

For a time, the losses undermined Wiesel's plan to cut back on his speaking engagements as he grew older. "I thought I'd be able to slow down and give fewer lectures and relax," he told Menachem Rosensaft. "I guess I won't be able to do that now."[4] Yet by the time he was interviewed by Oprah, his philosophical restraint had returned. This may have been the result of diminished economic worries about the fate of the foundation. Hundreds of people had sent in checks—some from wealthy patrons—to make the foundation whole. The Wiesels also received money recovered by Irving Picard, the bankruptcy court trustee overseeing the effort to compensate Madoff's victims. "Picard did an amazing job," Elisha told me.[5] There was also money from lawsuit settlements with Merkin, monetary gifts from friends, as well as Wiesel's salary from Boston University, lecture fees, and book royalties. But the mere fact that the Wiesels had invested with Madoff did complicate his image as an ascetic humanist.

Wiesel's fame had its pitfalls in other ways as well, as a frightening incident in 2007 revealed. On February 1, he was in San Francisco for an interfaith conference called "Facing Violence: Justice, Religion, and Conflict Resolution." Staying at the Argent Hotel, a luxury skyscraper, he was innocently taking an elevator up to his room when it stopped at the sixth floor and the car's other passenger—a young man—grabbed him and dragged him into the hallway. Only when Wiesel started screaming did the man run off and make his way out of the hotel. Afterward, Wiesel, then seventy-eight, told reporters that not since Auschwitz had he been so frightened for his life. "I was convinced that if he took me to his room, he would do me harm," Wiesel told a reporter for the *San Francisco Chronicle* website.

Police identified the assailant as Eric Hunt of Montgomery Township, New Jersey, the twenty-two-year-old son of a prison guard, when they found his wallet in a car parked in the hotel garage. Tracking his credit card purchases, they located him more than two weeks later at a psychiatric clinic in Belle Mead, New Jersey—sixty miles from his home—where his mother had arranged for his confinement. He was very different from those romanticized madmen that Wiesel had written about so affectionately. Since graduating from college, Hunt had been a devotee of websites that call the Holocaust a hoax. They often feature Elie Wiesel himself and question whether he really has an Auschwitz tattoo. (Even after his death, Wiesel remains targeted by such websites.)[6]

In court the following August, Hunt, who had been charged by then San Francisco district attorney Kamala Harris with stalking, attempted kidnapping, and hate crimes, pleaded not guilty by reason of insanity, and apologized. "Mr. Wiesel, I'm sorry for scaring you and I'm sorry you experienced the Holocaust," he said. "My grandfather fought the Nazis, and I'm sorry about what happened." Wiesel remained silent. Hunt was found guilty of false imprisonment during the commission of a hate crime and sentenced to two years in prison, but released immediately for displaying good behavior during his time in jail. Once free, he continued to deny the truths of the Holocaust with online pronouncements and created a website that he called a virtual "Holocaust hoax museum" that challenged the reality of death camps like Treblinka and Majdanek.

After the San Francisco attack, Wiesel was trailed by a bodyguard whenever he was out in public. Although Wiesel was a private man who would have preferred not to have resorted to such measures, friends insisted he get protection and helped pay for it. According to Elisha, his father "accepted it as a necessity" and "formed real friendships" with some of his guards.

By the time the Hunt attack occurred, Wiesel was in declining health. The migraines that had plagued him since childhood, except curiously while he was in Auschwitz and Buchenwald, continued to torment him into his eighties. But in 2005, he learned that he was suffering from a serious blood disorder, multiple myeloma. Patients can live with this condition for years, and chemotherapy and other treatments extended Wiesel's life. But they also brought about many debilitating side effects. He told Elisha of the diagnosis while they were together in Greenwich.

"He was worried," Elisha told me. "He hadn't done everything he wanted to do."

I interviewed Elie Wiesel in September 2008 when he was about to turn eighty, and at the time he did not mention his health. "It will sink in," he said of the milestone with a laugh. "I will think about those good years of being seventy." He was looking forward to a celebration right after Rosh Hashanah at the 92nd Street Y with tributes, songs, and interviews that would feature Theodore Bikel, Barbara Walters, and Arthur Gelb, the former managing editor of the *Times*. He told me that he counts every year a gift because "in truth when I entered Auschwitz I never thought I would leave it alive."

When I asked him whether he thought the Holocaust was fading in prominence as survivors die off, he firmly rejected that possibility. Every other day there seemed to be a Holocaust-related story in the news, he said. Moreover, the history of the Holocaust was being widely taught in high school and college, publishers released scores of memoirs by survivors and their children, and there were innumerable conferences.[7]

Even in his weakened state, Wiesel continued to produce novels, one published in the United States in 2009 and another in 2010. *A Mad Desire to Dance* is the story of a hidden war child, now an adult living in New York, who is seeing a psychotherapist for intense anxiety and survivor's guilt. The twist is that the psychotherapist is also a child of survivors, one whose parents had refused to speak about their experiences. *The Sonder-berg Case*, about a Jewish drama critic assigned to cover the trial of a German philosophy student accused of pushing his elderly uncle off a cliff, was his last work of fiction.

Leon Wieseltier summed up Wiesel's achievement as a novelist. "Elie was not a great [fiction] writer," he told me after his friend's death. "But the questions that preoccupied his writing were deep, genuine and urgent and his books had the integrity not of their style but of their subject."[8]

Thane Rosenbaum told me that Wiesel was deeply disappointed "that he wasn't taken more seriously as a novelist by the literary crowd, that he didn't crack the big three on anyone's list, of Bellow, Roth and Malamud. . . . Elie said to me many times 'I have written forty books. Most have nothing to do with the Holocaust and all people talk about is *Night*.'"

Though they had many conversations, Rosenbaum does not recall ever discussing contemporary fiction with Wiesel, and he doubts his friend read much fiction given the extraordinary demands on his time as a public figure and his deeper interest in theological questions. "If Elie ever had any free down time, he would more likely read Martin Buber or Emmanuel Levinas than Bellow or Roth," Rosenbaum said.

Still, Rosenbaum, a frequent book reviewer, esteemed him as a writer, describing *Gates of the Forest* and *The Fifth Son* as "just fabulous novels, European in style, original and emotionally complex. Why is it that Wiesel continues to be known only for his first book, a memoir?" When Imre Kertész, virtually unknown in America, received the Nobel for literature in 2002—the first Holocaust survivor to be so honored—Wiesel, Rosenbaum said, "no doubt wished and wondered why it had not gone to him."

Wiesel once wrote that every age produces a distinctive literary form. "If the Greeks invented tragedy, the Romans the epistle, and the Renaissance the sonnet, our generation invented a new literature, that of testimony."[9] Although they may not think of their work as testimony per se, contemporary novelists like Thane Rosenbaum, Jonathan Safran Foer, Nicole Krauss, and Allegra Goodman have all probed the meaning of the Holocaust, even if obliquely, and to that extent may be regarded as Wiesel's literary heirs.

In his waning years, Wiesel increasingly recognized how essential his friends had been to him. In an interview with Oprah Winfrey in 2012, this man who was left an orphan after the war spoke movingly about the importance of friendship to his life and well-being. "To me friendship is like a religion," he told Winfrey. "We can't live without it."[10] The value of friendship is a subtext of many of his novels and both later memoirs. The second volume, *And the Sea Is Never Full*, contains a chapter on the suicides of three distinguished survivor friends, all writers—Primo Levi, Jerzy Kosinski, and Piotr Rawicz—that haunted him. In one paragraph in which he tries to understand their despair he almost seems to be addressing himself. "Was it because as guardians of memory they felt misunderstood, unloved, exiles in the present, guilty of having failed in their task? Were they afraid of having spoken too much—or not enough? In light of the tragedies that continue to tear apart society, did they admit defeat?"[11]

Wiesel first met Primo Levi in Milan in the 1970s. At the age of twenty-four, Levi had spent a year in Auschwitz mostly working as a chemist in a factory that was supposed to—but never did—produce rubber. He went on to spend most of his working life as a chemist in a paint factory, writing all the while. His literary eminence derived from a handful of remarkable works, especially his own camp memoir, *Survival in Auschwitz*, and *The Periodic Table*. But Wiesel was sure that recognition did nothing to alleviate Levi's psychic wounds. The last time the two men spoke was in 1987 when Wiesel called Levi at his Turin apartment. Levi's spirits seemed low, his voice thick and heavy.

"Things are not good, not good at all. The world, the world's no good," he told Wiesel. Trying to cheer him up, Wiesel informed him how popular Levi's works were on American campuses, but Levi did not seem to react. Not too long after, Levi was found dead. He had allegedly leapt from a third-floor stairwell, although some friends contended that since he left no suicide note he must have become dizzy from the medications he was taking and fallen to his death.[12] "Primo Levi died at Auschwitz forty years later," Wiesel wrote. He found himself whispering, "You shouldn't have, Primo. . . . Death is never a solution." Yet, Wiesel added, "deep down I understand him."[13] Wiesel, as we've seen, mulled over such a solution several times—on his ocean voyages, for example. But he never succumbed, very likely because there was a driving purpose to his being and, as his cocoon of family and friends flourished and his esteem grew, he found his life too bountiful and meaningful to end it.

Wiesel was frequently surrounded by friends and family. He was extremely close to Bea's son, his nephew, Steve Jackson. The Wiesel archives at Boston University feature a sheaf of their correspondence, starting when Steve was a boy in Canada and later when he was living in Israel. Steve thanked Uncle Elie for a fishing rod, described the fun he was having at Camp Massad in Canada, and many years later revealed that he was engaged to a "very attractive girl," a letter Wiesel answered with a note of congratulations. When the engagement fell apart in 1985, Uncle Elie wrote back, "Whatever you do is all right with us. You used the term engaged so we congratulated you. Well, we will wait." Wiesel closely followed Jackson's progress at Tel Aviv University Sackler School of Medicine and throughout his specialized studies in neurosurgery. As a physician, Jackson became a recognized authority on the subject of brain death, yet his dedication to Jewish observance was such that he worked on the side as a *mohel*, circumcising boys eight days after birth, as prescribed by the Torah.

In January 2011, in St. Petersburg, Florida, where over many winters Wiesel taught a variety of one-month courses as a visiting professor at Eckerd College, he developed double pneumonia. He was so ill that Marion turned their hotel room into a makeshift hospital room and hired round-the-clock nurses.

That June, when he was eighty-two and back in New York, his primary care doctor, a cardiologist who had examined him and taken blood for testing a few days before, called to tell him to get to the Lenox Hill emergency room right away. Instead, he headed first to his office to take care of a few matters. When he finally reached the ER, further testing confirmed the elevated enzyme level that indicates damage to the heart. They performed an angiogram, which he hoped would require only the insertion of an artery-widening stent. But the surgeon said, "I don't have good news for you." He had five blocked arteries and would require immediate open-heart surgery.

Wiesel was as frightened as he had ever been. As he parted from Marion, who was holding back tears, and Elisha, who accompanied the gurney to the operating room, he wondered if he would ever see them again. In the O.R., he was told to count to ten but instead asked the doctors to wait. He needed to recite the *Shema Yisrael* (Hear O Israel), the daily prayer often murmured at moments of danger. When the anesthesia took hold, his heart functions were turned over to a mechanical pump, and the surgery was performed. In recovery, Wiesel heard a surgeon tell him: "It's over. Everything is fine. You'll live."[14]

Wiesel being Wiesel, he wrote a brief volume about his ordeal called *Open Heart*. In it he relived various scenes from his life. The most vivid involves his failure to save his father. He questioned his own accomplishments—as a champion of the Holocaust survivors, as a writer and teacher, as a human being. He once again thrashed out his quarrel with God, who, he notes, quoting Jeremiah, "assassinated his own people without compassion." But he wondered why, if God was at fault, did he ask Marion days after the operation to bring him his prayer shawl and *tefillin?*[15] A touching moment came at his bedside in the form of a question from his five-year-old grandson, Elijah: "If I love you more would you be in less pain?"

The bypass operation left him feeling very diminished. He walked, he said, like an old man, which of course he was, and fatigue clung to him. He no longer seemed able to write with confidence. In 2014, Menachem Rosensaft asked him to compose a prologue for a book-length collection of reflections by children and grandchildren of survivors, the kind of work Wiesel would regularly knock off gracefully in an hour or two. But this time the manuscript sat in his office for weeks. Finally, Rosensaft suggested that they use a condensed version of a speech Wiesel had delivered to a Second-Generation gathering. Wiesel seemed relieved. "If I waited for him to write it, it was not going to happen," Rosensaft told me.[16]

Because of his weakened health, Wiesel, according to friends like Wieseltier, may have made uncharacteristic judgments about the people he spent time with. Among the new companions and influencers was Sheldon Adelson, the Las Vegas casino-owning billionaire and publisher of a right-wing Israeli newspaper who became a leading financier of Trump's presidential campaign. He and a longtime acquaintance of Wiesel's, Shmuley Boteach, a self-promoting rabbi famous for his bestseller *Kosher Sex*, harbored views on Israel well to the right of Wiesel's own, yet he joined with them in publishing full-page newspaper ads that Adelson paid for, ones that seemed to lack Wiesel's voice and the empathy he usually displayed toward the Palestinians, irrespective of his emphatic scorn for their tactics.

"The bigger issue," said Elisha, who insisted his father was taking very little pain medication, "is that he didn't feel well; so we as a family kept most people away, and most visits short.

Only the most determined friends got through. In retrospect, I feel this was a mistake; my father cherished his friendships. We didn't have to keep the door as tightly closed as we did."

Wiesel had met Boteach around 1990 when the rabbi ran a Chabad House at Oxford University and founded a student organization there that invited Wiesel to deliver a lecture about the Holocaust and human rights. (The organization, the L'Chaim Society, also operated a charitable trust whose bank account was frozen in 1999 by the British Charity Commission over questions regarding excessive payments allegedly made to Boteach and his wife. The commission found that the payments were "difficult if not impossible to justify." Boteach reportedly repaid 150,000 pounds that had been spent on mortgage payments for his home. The issue was resolved, and Boteach claims he was cleared of wrongdoing.)[17]

In a telephone conversation, Boteach told me that he and Wiesel developed an "intimate and special bond." "He was my hero," Boteach said. "I saw in him the personification of the six million Jews of Europe."[18]

In time, however, Wiesel succumbed to requests from both Adelson and Boteach, who in Jewish matters seemed to serve as Adelson's right arm. Boston University sociologist Hillel Levine said that Wiesel was generally "conflict averse," and lately was "old and sick and didn't feel like having these fights" with friends seeking favors. Other friends said Wiesel's primary motivation in these associations was his overriding concern for the security and well-being of Israel. "I have never known Elie Wiesel to compromise his values for money," said Abe Foxman, national director of the Anti-Defamation League from 1987 to 2015. "Elie felt that Israel was in need of friends and even a tarnished friend is needed for support."

In 2012, Wiesel was the well-compensated keynote speaker at a Venetian Resort Hotel Casino gala to raise funds for the Dr. Miriam and Sheldon G. Adelson Campus, a Las Vegas-area

Jewish day school. Adelson made his private jets available to the Wiesels. Adelson had given $1 million to the Wiesel foundation before the investment's losses, and it is possible that in the aftermath of the Madoff debacle, and because of Adelson's beneficence toward Israel, Wiesel did not want to rebuff this connection. Moreover, Marion liked Adelson and his wife. "They are wonderful people, very generous, . . . and they care about Israel and their love for Israel is what connects us to them," she told me.[19] For the last few years of his life, Wiesel was also keynote speaker at the annual galas sponsored by Boteach's World Values Network, a non-profit that calls itself "the world's leading organization promoting Jewish values in culture, media and politics"; its chief mission, however, according to newspaper reports, seems to be to publicize Boteach and pay him a handsome salary.[20]

Wiesel had already gratified another benefactor with an uneven reputation. According to *Salon*, he accepted $500,000 for the foundation from pastor John Hagee for speaking to his congregation in Austin, Texas, in 2009, and made another appearance at the minister's Christians United for Israel before six thousand people in San Antonio. Although Hagee described himself as a Christian Zionist, he had made statements verging on anti-Semitism, calling Hitler a "half-breed Jew" and declaring that Hitler was sent by God to drive Jews to establish the state of Israel. John McCain, during his presidential bid in 2008, considered him so vile he rescinded a Hagee endorsement. Yet, in his speech, Wiesel praised Hagee for his support of Israel's Likud governments. "My father," Elisha explained, "was grateful for the tremendous support shown by Pastor Hagee and CUFI for the State of Israel. He wanted the chance to speak directly to the Christian Zionist movement to express that gratitude, which he saw as one of the most important Jewish values."

At the Adelson and Boteach functions, Wiesel found himself appearing with an assortment of celebrities whose association with him seemed incongruous, including the conservative politicians Newt Gingrich and Ted Cruz, and *Baywatch* star Pamela Anderson. Anderson appeared not to even know who Wiesel was, telling a TV reporter, "I'm overwhelmed and I can't wait to meet her." In return, Boteach could trumpet his association with a human-rights icon admired around the world.

As his father became increasingly infirm, Elisha seemed to grow close to Boteach. Boteach told me that Elisha calls him several times a week to discuss ethical issues. "He is obsessed with doing the right thing," Boteach said.

Wiesel did not back off the association with Adelson and Boteach, even when the rabbi found his way into the Donald Trump campaign and issued expressions of support for him in columns in the *New York Observer* (the newspaper then owned by Trump's son-in-law, Jared Kushner), the *Times of Israel*, and other outlets. (Adelson, who died on January 11, 2021, was the single largest donor to the 2016 Trump presidential campaign, having given him $25 million.) Friends say Wiesel met Trump only once and found him boorish; during Trump's presidential campaign he was "repulsed by his xenophobic rhetoric." Before his death, he was looking forward to a victory by Hillary Clinton, who as a New York senator had received his foundation's Humanitarian Award for her work on behalf of children.[21]

Another event that disturbed Wiesel's friends was his appearance in a full-page *Times* advertisement in 2014 during the Israeli incursion into the Gaza Strip, which was launched in response to missiles fired against Israeli villages. The ad, sponsored by Boteach's organization, accused Hamas of using Palestinian children as human shields to thwart bombings of military sites. Partisans of Hamas, the ad said, were "worshippers of death cults indistinguishable from that of the Molochites," adding: "Jews rejected child sacrifice 3,500 years ago." The ad featured a photograph of Wiesel and bore his signature. But the overheated language did not sound like him.

"Elie was a craftsman," Rosensaft said. "He wanted words to have an impact. Elie considered language, whether in Yiddish, French or English, an art."[22]

It was not surprising that Wiesel would articulate uncritical support for Israel, but the ad did not sufficiently display the compassion he had shown for the virtual quagmire Palestinians were in, even if it was largely of their own making. Nevertheless, the ad did have Marion and Elisha's approval. "My father asked for my help with this ad," Elisha said. "I asked my father several times if he was prepared to be criticized for the sharpness of the language in the ad, for the biblical framing of child sacrifice. He was crystal clear that we should move ahead. . . . The amazing thing about both my father's speech in 2000 and his advertisement in 2014 is his absolute insistence that the Palestinian people should be treated separately from their leadership. He believed in a possible peace with the Palestinians, if only their leadership would prioritize life over death."

"In general, we collectively felt Israel was being misportrayed in the media in significant ways," Elisha explained. "The UN report which came out in 2015 actually vindicates the ad and makes it very clear that Hamas was hiding weapons in schools and using them as a base for operations."[23]

At a Boteach organization gala on May 29, 2015, Wiesel, gaunt and pale, approached the rostrum with a wobbly gait, as Adelson called him "the king" of the Jewish people. In his remarks, Wiesel soon drifted off theme and contradicted himself; he said he woke up every morning to study Talmud after saying he woke up every morning to write. He rambled on in disjointed fashion about his teaching and his inability to say no to the persistent Boteach.[24] Boteach seemed to grow impatient, checked his watch, and took advantage of a burst of applause to nudge Wiesel off the stage.[25]

28

Memories

WHATEVER LATE-IN-LIFE MISSTEPS he made as a result of his infirmity, in his last decade or two Wiesel was largely treated as the towering world figure he had become. Tributes and honors for lifetime achievement continued to pour in, from sources as varied as the government of Hungary, the Tel Aviv Museum of Art, the International Campaign for Tibet, the Norman Mailer Center for writers, and the National Endowment for the Humanities. Ninety colleges worldwide conferred on him honorary degrees. And in 2011 the U.S. Holocaust Memorial Museum bestowed its first annual award on Wiesel, naming the award "for his singular role in establishing and advancing the cause of Holocaust remembrance."

He developed a close relationship with President Barack Obama. While a student at Columbia University, Obama had been deeply moved hearing Wiesel speak about his experiences in Auschwitz and Buchenwald. "Reading his books," Obama wrote in his 2020 memoir *A Promised Land,* "I'd found an impregnable moral core that both fortified me and challenged me to be better." They got to know each other after Obama was elected to the U.S. Senate, and they became friends; Obama called their friendship one of the great pleasures of his few years as a senator. When he told Wiesel that his great-uncle, Charles Payne, had been one of the liberators of a Buchenwald subcamp, Wiesel insisted that one day they would go to Buchenwald together.

In June 2009, during his first year as president, Obama was able to see that promise fulfilled when he decided to include a stop at Buchenwald on a diplomatic tour of Europe and the Middle East. Wiesel and German chancellor Angela Merkel joined him.

"If these trees could talk," Wiesel said softly as the three of them walked past the oaks leading to Buchenwald's entrance. They spent an hour among the guard towers and walls of barbed wire, "staring into the dark ovens of the crematorium." They came across a stone slab listing the names of victims, Elie's father among them, and gazed at photographs taken by American liberators, including the iconic one of sixteen-year-old Elie looking out from one of the bunks, with "the same handsome face and mournful eyes but jagged with hunger and illness and the enormity of all he had witnessed."[1]

Back in the States, Obama and Wiesel had two unreported lunches at the White House as well as other encounters. Wiesel tried to acquaint Obama with how Jews view the world and they talked about writing a book together, much as he had done with François Mitterrand. But the relationship began to fray over Wiesel's refusal to endorse Obama for reelection or appear at a campaign stop in Florida's Jewish precincts. (Wiesel had a wise policy of never endorsing any candidates, although he had done so when Bill Clinton sought reelection.) And it fractured for a time—Foxman spoke of "a rift"—when Wiesel publicly opposed the deal that suspended Iran's nuclear program in exchange for America's dropping punitive economic sanctions. Full-page ads that ran in the *Times* and the *Washington Post*, produced by Boteach, were appeals by Wiesel, complete with his photograph and signature, urging Americans to reject the deal because of the "catastrophic danger of a nuclear Iran." Wiesel even appeared in a VIP box in the House of Representatives as Prime Minister Benjamin Netanyahu brazenly urged Congress to turn the deal down.[2] Wiesel, friends told me, did not want to go to Washington, but Adelson had insisted.

Elisha disputes such interpretations. "My father built life-long friendships with both Democrats and Republicans," he told me. "Shmuley helped deepen my father's friendship with Miriam and Sheldon Adelson, but he also brought important Democratic party figures such as Samantha Power and Cory Booker to exchange ideas and perspectives with my father. I know some people want to invent a right-wing conspiracy for why my father would speak out against Hamas or the Iran Deal. But there was none. My father's position was that Prime Minister Netanyahu should be heard if he felt Israel was facing an existential threat, and he needed no convincing to take that position."[3]

In fact, Elisha said he asked his father to skip Netanyahu's speech because he was worried about his health. "But he was determined to go."

According to his memoir, Wiesel's thoughts in his later years often drifted to the past, to scenes from his childhood. He was haunted by the line at Sighet's train station, the wretched cattle car ride, the arrival at Auschwitz where his innocent sister, believing in her mother's assurances, walked off, never to be seen again.

And just as he had throughout his life, he turned his remaining powers of concentration to study. Every couple of Fridays, Abe Foxman would come to his home and they would read a sacred text together, usually the Torah portion that was going to be read that Sabbath, gleaning what lessons they could about themes essential to Wiesel. Foxman was also a survivor, having been hidden as a child during the war and baptized by a Polish nanny who futilely resisted his parents' efforts to reclaim him. After study, he and Wiesel would repair to Caviar Russe a few blocks from Wiesel's home to enjoy a lunch of smoked salmon, or to Harry Cipriani in the Sherry Netherland Hotel, also in the neighborhood.

"He struggled with faith," Foxman told me. "Every survivor does. But Elie's position was 'God left me but I didn't leave him. I'm angry at God, but does that mean I shouldn't observe *shabbos*?'"[4]

Leon Wieseltier also took pleasure in studying with Wiesel. The two would spend time on the phone analyzing, say, a poem by Hayim Nachman Bialik, or a rabbinical text or *midrash*. Wieseltier prized the "depth and intricacy of his Jewish cultivation." "His Hebrew was gorgeous, his Yiddish was gorgeous. He had studied Talmud with Saul Lieberman. He knew poetry. He knew Yiddish song, Jewish liturgy. Elie was one of the few Jews I have known who bothered to inherit the entirety of the civilization that was bequeathed to them."

But in Wiesel's last year or two it was painfully evident to his friends that age and poor health had taken their toll. Several mentioned how uncomfortable they were hearing Wiesel speak at a benefit in June 2015 at the Waldorf Astoria honoring Foxman for his service to the Anti-Defamation League. Wiesel, whose son was supposed to accompany him but arrived late, entered the ballroom in a confused state, seemed disoriented when he was called up to the stage, and after starting to speak lost his train of thought, scarcely mentioning Foxman. Many in the audience who had heard Wiesel in his heyday were stunned and saddened.

On the late afternoon of the first day of Rosh Hashanah that year, Wiesel and his close friend Cantor Malovany walked out of Wiesel's apartment building for the short stroll to the

Duck Pond in Central Park. Along with other observant neighborhood Jews, it had been their custom every year to symbolically hurl their sins into the pond, a service known as *Tashlich*. Malovany, a tall, sturdy man of seventy-six with a still-dark beard, was taken aback when Wiesel asked him, "Which direction are we going?" This was the same route they had taken many times before to a pond barely a block from Wiesel's home. Nevertheless, Malovany felt it important to qualify his observation. "Being confused about street directions does not mean Elie was confused about his views on Israel's war for survival with Iran and Hamas. As a friend of his who saw him often, I can tell you that Elie was clear on these issues until the very end." Similarly, Rosensaft and Ariel Burger, Wiesel's last teaching assistant, met with Wiesel in the weeks before he died and, according to Burger, he "was sharp as ever, canny in his analysis of current political trends, and clear-sighted about the complex issues we discussed."

"He made me laugh out loud with ironic references to Talmudic controversies, and made me think deeply about current events," Burger said. "He in no way seemed mentally impaired by old age or infirmity."

By summer, Wiesel was confined to a hospital bed in his apartment, with Marion and Elisha often by his side. "He was in terrible pain," Marion told me. On the last day of his life, Malovany visited Wiesel. He stood by the side of the bed and sang Elie's credo, "Ani Ma'amin"; Malovany had tears in his eyes as he described to me what happened after he finished the song.

"He held my hand and squeezed it. He couldn't talk anymore. His eyes were closed. I said to him 'Elie, what do you want me to do for you? You've got to get better.' I put my ears close to his mouth. Something tells me he may have said 'Pray!'"

Malovany choked up with emotion as he told me of that moment. "I'm sorry if I cry," he said. "I loved this man so much."[5]

In his last conversations with Marion, Elie indicated some

concerns about what would happen with his life's work. "He wanted Elisha and me to continue as much as we could," Marion told me. "I didn't go into specifics because I didn't want to acknowledge that he was near the end and I'm not sure he wanted to either."[6]

Wiesel told Elisha he did not want to die, and in his father's last days Elisha could hear his whispered negotiations with God to put off that event. Yet Wiesel also reflected on what a long, interesting life he had had. His mind returned often to Sighet and he would dream of walking in a park with his parents and sisters on a *shabbos*. A believer in an afterlife, he told his attentive caregiver, Margo, that seeing his parents and sisters again would be the consolation to his approaching death. As he took his last breaths, Elisha asked him to take a message to his parents and sisters "that he succeeded in his life's work, that we live, that he created life and created love and saved lives and most importantly that we remember them and love them and that there are Shlomos and Sarahs and Batyas and that the name Tzipora has returned with our daughter, his granddaughter."[7]

Elie Wiesel died at home on the morning of July 2, 2016. With him in his last hours were Marion, Elisha, and Marion's daughter, Jennifer Rose. His passing was major news around the world. Such was his stature and impact that the *Times* ran his obituary on the front page above the fold with a headline that proclaimed: "A Survivor Who Refused to Let the World Forget," and continued inside with a full broadsheet page featuring several photographs of Wiesel. There were also dozens of paid obituaries from a host of organizations he had helped. Heads of state issued tributes. President Obama tweeted: "Elie Wiesel was a great moral voice of our time and a conscience for our world. He was also a dear friend. We will miss him deeply." Israel's president, Reuven Rivlin, said he "embodied the determination of the human spirit to overcome the darkest of evils, and survive against all odds." Artists extolled him, with Lin-Manuel

Miranda, the creator of the musical *Hamilton*, tweeting: "The world is profoundly better because you were here."

In line with the Jewish custom that a body be buried soon after death, the funeral was held the next day at the Fifth Avenue Synagogue. Only family and close friends were invited, among them Rosensaft, Foxman, and Malovany. Marion, in a wheelchair, listened as Elisha spoke of his father's unconditional love, which he continued to feel even though he believed that death is final, "something becoming nothing, someone becoming no one."

"How is my father sending me that love, even now, stronger than ever, like a shock wave through my head and heart, when his body is lying there without life? Can someone tell me how is that possible?"[8]

The service captured Wiesel's whimsical side as mourners tried to humanize him beyond the sainted "messenger to mankind." His grandson Elijah remembered how he and his grandfather relished toasting English muffins then smothering them in blueberry jam. Ted Koppel recalled how Elie loved to laugh and how during their long friendship they would find ways of making each other laugh.[9]

Elie Wiesel's plain pine coffin was carried out of the synagogue by his nephew, Dr. Steve Jackson, and several of Elisha's friends—with Cantor Malovany mournfully chanting the Ninety-first Psalm, which in English begins:

> *Whoever dwells in the shelter of the Most High*
> *will rest in the shadow of the Almighty.*

The coffin was taken by hearse to Sharon Gardens in Valhalla, New York, to a grassy plot shaded by three young trees that has a sweeping view of the hills in the distance. The coffin was lowered into the grave, and relatives and friends took turns shoveling dirt atop the coffin, painfully alert to the thud of falling earth. They were following an old tradition of honoring the dead by having intimates rather than just paid gravediggers perform the mitzvah of burial while at the same time allowing mourners to participate in an act that underscores death's finality and opens the way to eventual acceptance of a loss. More than one mourner thought of all the Wiesel relatives who went up in smoke without receiving a proper burial.

The inscription on the modest stone that was placed atop the grave read:

ELIE WIESEL

Sept. 30, 1928–July 2, 2016

HUSBAND FATHER GRANDFATHER TEACHER

LIVED TO BEAR WITNESS

In January 2020 I spoke with Marion Wiesel in her husband's book-lined office overlooking the Duck Pond. The bookshelves are filled with photographs: of Elie, Marion, and Elisha on a rocky shore in Deal, New Jersey; of Elie and Marion at Kafka's grave; of Elie laughing with Obama and inscribed by the president with the words, "Thanks for your kindness, friendship and wisdom"; of Elie in an embrace with Colin Powell and bearing the inscription "Elie, my brother." As I got up to leave I asked her whether the dark wooden table in the middle of the room was Elie's desk. "This is where he worked," she said; "I've changed nothing." And then, staring at the desk, she added with a faint smile: "I miss him a lot. He was a big presence and now he is a big absence."

Several months after the funeral, a memorial service was held at the Holocaust Memorial Museum in Washington, which Wiesel, perhaps more than anyone, had helped found. The violinist Itzhak Perlman played the plaintive theme from *Schindler's List*. Cantor Malovany sang "Ani Ma'amin" in his resounding tenor. There were tributes by political leaders like Congresswoman Nancy Pelosi (two years before she became Speaker of the House) and Senator Orrin Hatch.

In his remarks, Elisha compared his father to the Patriarchs. "Like Jacob, he wrestled with God. Like Abraham he said after the war, 'Hineni!,' 'I am here,' and decided to marry, have a child."

"'Hineni!' my father cried loud and clear to us all," Elisha said, "'I am here. I survived. And I will not be silent.' He told the world what he saw and what he feared would come if it did not listen. And I stand before you today as the improbable evidence, a witness that, by my very existence, affirms my father's unrelenting optimism and hope for our species."

His father, Elisha suggested, was able to make the leap beyond family to call for social justice, not just for the Jewish survivors but for persecuted and endangered people everywhere, a message that resonated with particular power in the audience shortly after the election of an "America First," virulently anti-immigrant president.

"When Syrian refugees need our help, we must help them," Elisha said. "When Muslims in our midst are made to feel that they won't have the same rights as the rest of us, we must embrace them. When children of hard-working, law-abiding undocumented immigrants fear deportation, we must insist on compassion."

"He saw the best in this country. He saw it through the eyes of a survivor rescued by U.S. servicemen, through the eyes of an immigrant who had nothing, who was given a state when he was a stateless person. He loved this country."

Samantha Power, the U.N. representative, spoke of Wiesel as a joyful man. She wondered how, given the brutality he had witnessed, the losses he suffered, the frustrations he experienced fighting genocide, he could savor "the gifts of life with ferocious zeal" and remain "optimistic enough to keep going—and to feel the strength to shine his light" on all humanity.

"Amid all the pain and disappointment of Elie's remarkable life," she wondered, "how is it that the darkness did not envelop him or shield him from the sun? How is it that the twinkle in Elie Wiesel's eye was every bit as defining as his life's experiences? 'What is abnormal,' Elie once told Oprah Winfrey, 'is that I am normal. That I survived the Holocaust and went on to love beautiful girls, to talk, to write, to have toast and tea and live my life—that is what is abnormal.'"

Power guessed that "maybe it was because Elie has such a strong sense of purpose on his journey—to help those who could still be helped," that he felt "a duty to his neighbor, to the stranger, the stranger that he once was."[10]

That sense of purpose carried Wiesel to heights no other survivor achieved. He became the voice and face of the six million, and of those who escaped their fate. Irving Abrahamson, an English professor in Chicago who compiled a three-volume set of Wiesel's essays and lectures, put it simply: "He put the Holocaust on the map and kept it there."[11]

But he was wise enough to know that history's most horrific crime demanded that he call attention to other crimes against humanity, ones that have occurred in our time. He also knew he had to wrestle with eternal questions—about God, indifference, silence, forgiveness. Wiesel made sure such questions, which still hover over the post-Holocaust world, were explicitly articulated, even if they remained unanswered. His eloquence is why, long after his death, Wiesel proverbs are often summoned in situations that require moral or political courage.

His mentor Saul Lieberman had warned him that "a man must choose between inspiring pity or envy," and Elie Wiesel never wanted to be pitied for what he had been through.[12] Instead, he seared the Holocaust into the world's conscience, compelling everyone to confront the human capacity for brutality and evil. He sounded memorable warnings about the dangers of looking away and failing to speak out. Along the way, he elevated the image of the survivors, broken and pitiful as they seemed at war's end, to near sacredness.[13] And through his presence and singular achievements, he gave the world a shining example of the human potential for resilience and recovery, while reminding us of the enduring obligation to learn the lessons imparted by the abominable events of the past.

NOTES

Introduction

1. Elie Wiesel, "Will the World Ever Learn?" address to U.N. General Assembly, January 24, 2005; text available at www.beliefnet.com/faiths/judaism/2005/02/bearing-witness-60-years-on.aspx.

2. Michael Berenbaum, "Elie Wiesel, the Moral Force Who Made Sure We Will Never Forget Evil of Holocaust," *Forward*, July 2, 2016.

3. Joseph Berger, "Elie Wiesel, Holocaust Survivor Who Ensured World Would Never Forget," *New York Times*, July 3, 2016.

Chapter 1. Sighet, My Sighet

1. Elie Wiesel, *All Rivers Run to the Sea: Memoirs* (New York: Knopf, 1995), 31–32.

2. Elie Wiesel, "Floridiana," *New York Times*, October 9, 1983.

3. Elie Wiesel, *From the Kingdom of Memory* (New York: Summit, 1990), 41.

4. Elie Wiesel, "Pilgrimage to Sighet, a Haunted City," *New York Times*, October 14, 1984.

5. Elisha Wiesel, eulogy delivered at his father's funeral, July 3, 2016.

6. Wiesel, *All Rivers Run to the Sea*, 10.

7. "The Life and Work of Wiesel," *Elie Wiesel: First Person Singular*, PBS, 2002, www.pbs.org/eliewiesel/life/auschwitz.html.

8. Wiesel, *All Rivers Run to the Sea*, 3.

9. Elie Wiesel, *One Generation After* (New York: Bard/Anon, 1972), 23–24.

10. Elie Wiesel, "Dodye Feig, a Portrait," in *A Jew Today* (New York: Random House, 1978), 68.

11. Ibid., 66.

12. Ibid., 70.

13. Wiesel, *One Generation After*, 22–23.

14. Elie Wiesel, *Contemporary Authors, Autobiography Series*, vol. 4, ed. Adele Sarkissian (Gale Research, 1992).

15. Ibid., 13.

16. Wiesel, *All Rivers Run to the Sea*, 31.

17. Israel Shenker, "The Concerns of Elie Wiesel: Today and Yesterday," *New York Times*, February 10, 1979.

18. Wiesel, *All Rivers Run to the Sea*, 13.

19. Letter in the Elie Wiesel Archive, Howard Gotlieb Archival Research Center, Boston University, Box 92, Folder 8.

20. Wiesel, "Pilgrimage to Sighet, a Haunted City."

21. Wiesel, *All Rivers Run to the Sea*, 21.

22. Wiesel, *One Generation After*, 101.

Chapter 2. Deportation

1. Elie Wiesel, *The Night Trilogy: Night, Dawn, Day* (New York: Hill and Wang, 1972), 25.

2. United States Holocaust Memorial Museum, www.ushmm.org/wlc/en/article.php?ModuleId=10008204.

3. Wiesel, *All Rivers Run to the Sea*, 31.

4. Wiesel, *A Jew Today*, 70.

5. Ibid., 70.

6. Wiesel, *Kingdom of Memory*, 153–154.

7. Ibid., 60–61.

8. Ibid., 61.

9. Wiesel, *Night Trilogy*, 31.

10. Ibid., 35.

11. Ibid., 37.

12. Wiesel, *All Rivers Run to the Sea*, 70.

13. "ViHaolam Shatak" ("And the World Was Silent"), manuscript in Hebrew, the Elie Wiesel Archive, Howard Gotlieb Archival Research Center, Boston University, Box 237, F1.

14. Ofer Aderet, "Newly Unearthed Version of Elie Wiesel's Seminal Work Is a Scathing Indictment of God, Jewish World," *Haaretz*, May 1, 2016.

15. Joseph Wershba, "An Author Asks Why the World Let Hitler Do It," *New York Post*, October 2, 1961.

16. Aderet, "Newly Unearthed Version."

17. Wiesel, *Night Trilogy*, 40.

18. Wiesel, "Pilgrimage to Sighet."

19. Wiesel, *Night Trilogy*, 42–44.

20. Ruth Franklin, "A Thousand Darknesses," *New Republic*, March 20, 2006.

21. Aderet, "Newly Unearthed Version."

Chapter 3. Camps of Death

1. Aderet, "Newly Unearthed Version," 47.

2. Elie Wiesel, "Pilgrimage to the Country of Night," *New York Times*, November 4, 1979.

3. Wiesel, *Night Trilogy*, 52.

4. Ibid., 54–55.

5. Ibid., 63.

6. Ibid., 72.

7. Ibid., 82–83.

8. Ibid., 85.

9. Ibid., 87.

10. Aderet, "Newly Unearthed Version."

11. "Nobel Laureate Elie Wiesel Talks About His Friendship with Rabbi Menashe Klein," *Vos Iz Neias*, October 24, 2011; "Heart to Heart with Elie Wiesel," interview by Nadine Epstein, *Moment*, May–June 2013.

12. Wiesel, *All Rivers Run to the Sea*, 83–84.

13. Author's interview with Elisha Wiesel, 2016.

14. Berger, "Elie Wiesel, Holocaust Survivor Who Ensured World."

15. Robert McAfee Brown, Letter to the Editor, *New York Times*, April 2, 1989.

16. Wiesel, *All Rivers Run to the Sea*, 87–88.

17. Ibid., 74.

18. Ibid., 80–81.

19. Ibid., 80.

20. Wiesel, *Night Trilogy*, 109.

21. Alexander Cockburn, "Truth and Fiction in Elie Wiesel's 'Night,'" *CounterPunch*, www.counterpunch.org, October 21, 2014.

22. Ibid., 113.

23. Author's interview with Borchardt, January 2017.

24. Wiesel, *All Rivers Run to the Sea*, 79.

25. Wiesel, *Night Trilogy*, 117.

26. Ibid., 124–125.

27. Ibid., 130.

28. Author's correspondence with Kenneth Waltzer.

29. Wiesel, *From the Kingdom of Memory*, 155–156.

30. Wiesel, *Night Trilogy*, 133.

Chapter 4. Recovering

1. Elie Wiesel, "The Last Return," *Commentary*, March 1, 1965.

2. Cable, June 6, 1945, and convoy list, American Jewish Joint Distribution Committee archives.

3. Judith Hemmendinger and Robert Krell, *The Children of Buchenwald: Child Survivors of the Holocaust and Their Post-War Lives* (Jerusalem: Gefen, 2000), 27–28.

4. Wiesel, *All Rivers Run to the Sea*, 113.

5. Hemmendinger and Krell, *Children of Buchenwald*, 31.

6. Wiesel, *All Rivers Run to the Sea*, 113–114.

7. Many details of the Wiesel sisters' experience were taken from videotaped testimony Hilda (Wiesel) Kudler gave to the USC Shoah Foundation on December 11, 1995, in Nice, France; vha online.usc.edu/viewingPage?testimonyID=9443&returnIndex=0.

8. Hemmendinger and Krell, *Children of Buchenwald*, xiii.

9. Wiesel, *All Rivers Run to the Sea*, 117.

10. Hemmendinger and Krell, *Children of Buchenwald*, 142–143.

11. Wiesel, *All Rivers Run to the Sea*, 121–130.

12. Ibid., 115.

13. Author's interview with Ted Comet, January 12, 2017.

14. Wiesel, *All Rivers Run to the Sea*, 132–135.

15. Excellent studies of the American response to the displaced persons can be found in Leonard Dinnerstein, *America and the Survivors of the Holocaust* (New York: Columbia University Press, 1982) and in David Nasaw, *The Last Million: Europe's Displaced Persons from World War to Cold War* (New York: Penguin, 2020).

16. Wiesel, *All Rivers Run to the Sea*, 146.

17. Ibid., 140–142.

18. Ibid., 155.

19. Ibid., 156–157.

Chapter 5. Cub Reporter

1. Wiesel, *All Rivers Run to the Sea*, 164.

2. Author's interview with Marion Wiesel, March 9, 2017.

3. Wiesel, *All Rivers Run to the Sea*, 168.

4. Ibid., 179.

5. Ibid., 182.

6. Ibid., 183–184.

7. Author's interview with Yossi Ciechanover, February 6, 2018.

8. Steve Linde, "Why Elie Wiesel Never Moved to Israel," *Jerusalem Post*, December 7, 2016.

9. Wiesel, *A Jew Today*, 111–112.

Chapter 6. A Hungarian in Paris

1. Author's interview with Marion Wiesel, March 9, 2017.

2. Wiesel, *All Rivers Run to the Sea*, 188.

3. Author's interview with Joel Rappel, May 14, 2017.

4. Elie Wiesel, *The Town Beyond the Wall* (New York: Random House, 1962), 61.

5. Elie Wiesel, "An Open Letter to President Giscard D'Estaing of France," *New York Times*, January 20, 1977.

6. Wiesel, *All Rivers Run to the Sea*, 196.

7. Ibid., 194.

8. Ibid., 205–208.

9. Ibid., 210.

10. Ibid., 223–229.

11. Frederick L. Downing, *Elie Wiesel: A Religious Biography* (Macon, Georgia: Mercer University Press, 2008), 93.

Chapter 7. *Night* and Fog

1. Wiesel, *All Rivers Run to the Sea*, 238–239.

2. Ibid., 239.

3. Joel Rappel, "Shedding Light on *Night*," *Haaretz*, August 6, 2021.

4. Elie Wiesel, "Passover with Apostates: A Concert in Spain and a Seder in the Middle of the Ocean," *Forverts*, April 22, 1957 (translated into English by Shaul Seidler-Feller in 2018 for the *Seforim* blog), seforimblog.com/2018/03/passover-with-apostates -concert-in.

5. Wiesel, *All Rivers Run to the Sea*, 241.

6. Ibid., 242.

7. Wiesel, *One Generation After*, 126–138.

8. Wiesel, *All Rivers Run to the Sea*, 259–265.

9. Ibid., 265.

10. Shlomo Nakdimon, "How Elie Wiesel the Journalist Saw Israel," *Haaretz*, July 9, 2016.

11. Elie Wiesel, "An Interview Unlike Any Other," in *A Jew Today* (New York: Random House, 1978), 17.

12. Ibid., 19.

13. Wiesel, *All Rivers Run to the Sea*, 270–271.

14. Ruth R. Wisse, *The Modern Jewish Canon: A Journey Through Language and Culture* (Chicago: University of Chicago Press, 2003), 214.

15. Author's interview with Ruth R. Wisse, May 8, 2018.

16. Franklin, "A Thousand Darknesses."

17. Naomi Seidman, "Elie Wiesel and the Scandal of Jewish Rage," *Jewish Social Studies*, New Series, vol. 3, no. 1 (Autumn 1996), 1–19.

18. Elie Wiesel, "Art and Culture After the Holocaust," opening address, International Symposium on the Holocaust, June 3, 1974, as published in *Against Silence: The Words and Vision of Elie Wiesel*, ed. Irving Abrahamson (New York: Holocaust Library, 1985), vol. 2, 89.

19. Author's interview with Ruth Wisse, May 8, 2018.

20. Michael Berenbaum, "Elie Wiesel: French Writer, World Statesman, Cosmopolitan Jew," in *Europe in the Eyes of Survivors of the Holocaust*, ed. Zeev Mankowitz, David Weinberg, and Sharon Kangisser Cohen (Jerusalem: Yad Vashem, 2014), 217.

21. Franklin, "A Thousand Darknesses."

Chapter 8. Coming to America

1. Wiesel, *All Rivers Run to the Sea*, 293.

2. Internet Movie Data Base (IMDb), *The Brothers Karamazov*, www.imdb.com/title/tt0051435/releaseinfo?ref_=tt_dt_dt.

3. Wiesel, *All Rivers Run to the Sea*, 293–294.

4. Paul Braunstein, "Elie Wiesel: A Lasting Impression," in *Telling the Tale: A Tribute to Elie Wiesel*, ed. Harry James Cargas (St. Louis: Time Being Books, 1993), 117–118.

5. Wiesel, *Night Trilogy*, 230.

6. Ibid., 233.

7. Menachem Butler, "Elie Wiesel Visits Disneyland," *Tablet*, June 27, 2016.

8. Wiesel, *All Rivers Run to the Sea*, 301–303.

Chapter 9. Writer

1. Letter from Georges Borchardt to Arthur Wang, July 20, 1959.

2. Wiesel, *All Rivers Run to the Sea*, 322–323.

3. Author's interview with Georges Borchardt, February 7, 2017.

4. Rejection letters from various publishers shown me by Borchardt.

5. Author's interview with Borchardt.

6. Letter from Georges Borchardt to Jérôme Lindon, October 30, 1959.

7. Gertrude Samuels, "When Evil Closed In," *New York Times Book Review*, November 13, 1960.

8. Elie Wiesel, *And the Sea Is Never Full: Memoirs, 1969–* (New York: Schocken, 1999), 18.

9. William B. Helmreich, *The World of the Yeshiva: An Intimate Portrait of Orthodox Jewry* (New York: Free Press, 1982), 169.

10. Irving Spiegel, "Jews Urged to Teach Young About Nazi Crimes," *New York Times*, December 2, 1974.

11. Primo Levi's *Survival in Auschwitz* appeared in 1948 but was not published in English until 1959; until then its sales had been disappointing. Tadeusz Borowski's short stories, collected as *This Way for the Gas, Ladies and Gentlemen*, were written soon after the war but not published in English until 1967.

12. Hasia Diner, *We Remember with Reverence and Love: American Jews and the Myth of Silence After the Holocaust, 1945–1962* (New York: New York University Press, 2009).

13. Jerome Chanes, "Remembering, Not Remembering," *Forward*, August 26, 2009.

14. Dinitia Smith, "Arthur W. Wang, Founder of a Bold Publishing House, Is Dead at 87," *New York Times*, October 19, 2005.

15. Wiesel, *All Rivers Run to the Sea*, 320–321.

16. Ibid., 326–328.

17. Wiesel, *Night Trilogy*, 139–141.

18. Ibid., 221.

19. Herbert Mitgang, "An Eye for an Eye," *New York Times*, July 16, 1961.

20. Wiesel, *All Rivers Run to the Sea*, 348.

21. Adam Kirsch, "Beware of Pity: Hannah Arendt and the Power of the Impersonal," *New Yorker*, January 12, 2009.

22. Elie Wiesel, "A Plea for the Dead," in *The Judaic Tradition: Texts*, ed. Nahum Norbert Glatzer (Springfield, N.J.: Behrman House, 1982), 654–658.

23. Wershba, "An Author Asks Why."

24. Wiesel, "A Plea for the Dead," 654–658.

Chapter 10. Survivor

1. Author's interview with Menachem Rosensaft, May 23, 2017.

2. Elie Wiesel, "A Plea for Survivors," in *A Jew Today* (New York: Random House, 1978), 207.

3. Author's interview with Yitz Greenberg, January 6, 2017.

4. Author's interview with Joel Rappel, May 14, 2017.

5. Review: The Town Beyond the Wall, *Newsweek*, May 25, 1964.

6. Elie Wiesel, *The Town Beyond the Wall* (New York: Holt, Rinehart and Winston, 1964), 66.

7. Ibid., 153–164.

8. Ibid., 175–178.

9. Michael Berenbaum, *Elie Wiesel: God, the Holocaust, and the Children of Israel* (West Orange, N.J.: Behrman House, 1994), 31–37.

10. Wiesel, *All Rivers Run to the Sea*, 339.

11. Thane Rosenbaum, "The Survivor Who Survived," *New York Times*, October 12, 2002.

12. John Wain, "The Insulted and Injured," *New York Review of Books*, July 28, 1966.

13. Eliot Fremont-Smith, "Books of the Times: The Song and the Dagger," *New York Times*, May 23, 1966.

14. Wiesel, *All Rivers Run to the Sea*, 350.

15. Ibid., 350–351.

16. Author's interview with Dvorah M. Telushkin, May 4, 2017.

17. Dvorah M. Telushkin, *Master of Dreams: A Memoir of Isaac Bashevis Singer* (New York: Harper Perennial, 2004), 206.

18. Author's interview with close friend who chose to speak without attribution on this point.

Chapter 11. Return to Sighet

1. Wiesel, "The Last Return."

2. Elie Wiesel, "Sighet," manuscript in the Elie Wiesel Archive, Howard Gotlieb Archival Research Center, Boston University, Box 92, Folder 19.

3. Wiesel, "The Last Return."

4. Wiesel, *All Rivers Run to the Sea*, 360.

5. Steve Linde, "The Birthplace of a Legend," *Jerusalem Post*, May 30, 2014, magazine, 8.

6. Wiesel, "The Last Return."

Chapter 12. A Russian Revolution

1. Wiesel, *All Rivers Run to the Sea*, 366.

2. Elie Wiesel, *The Jews of Silence: A Personal Report on Soviet Jewry* (New York: Schocken, 2011), 25–26.

3. Ibid., 3.

4. Ibid., 23.

5. Ibid., 37.

6. Ibid., 45–51.

7. Ibid., 63.

8. Ibid., 87.

9. Ibid., 131–132.

10. Isaac Bashevis Singer, "A State of Fear," *New York Times*, January 8, 1967.

11. Clive Barnes, "'Zalmen,' Wiesel's Parable of Silence," *New York Times*, March 18, 1976.

Chapter 13. Love and War

1. Author's interview with Marion Wiesel, March 9, 2017.

2. Wiesel, *All Rivers Run to the Sea*, 338.

3. Author's interview with Marion Wiesel, January 29, 2020.

4. Elie Wiesel, *And the Sea Is Never Full: Memoirs, 1969–* (New York: Schocken, 1999), 13.

5. Author's interview with Elisha Wiesel, November 4, 2016.

6. Wiesel, *All Rivers Run to the Sea*, 402–403.

7. An English translation of the letter is available at "When the Lubavitcher Rebbe Told Elie Wiesel He Must Become a Father," *Jewish Mom: Inspiration from One Jewish Mother to Another,* blog, August 10, 2016, jewishmom.com/2016/08/10/when-the-lubavitcher -rebbe-told-elie-wiesel-he-must-become-a-father.

8. Wiesel, *All Rivers Run to the Sea*, 383.

9. Guy Laron, *The Six-Day War: The Breaking of the Middle East* (New Haven: Yale University Press, 2017), 106–117.

10. Ibid.

11. Wiesel, *All Rivers Run to the Sea*, 386–388.

12. Elie Wiesel, "Israel's Victory Is All of Ours," *Forward*, May 5, 2017, 19, translated by Chana Pollack.

13. Wiesel, *All Rivers Run to the Sea*, 392.

14. Ibid., 389–390.

15. Author's interview with Rabbi Irving Greenberg, January 6, 2017.

16. Henry Raymont, "French Literary Awards Given to Two Writers Who Live in U.S.," *New York Times*, November 27, 1968.

17. Manès Sperber, "A Beggar in Jerusalem," *New York Times Book Review*, January 25, 1970.

18. John Leonard, "History Has Bad Dreams," *New York Times*, January 27, 1970.

19. Telegram from Marion Wiesel to Elie Wiesel, March 3, 1969, Elie Wiesel Archive, Howard Gotlieb Archival Research Center, Boston University, Box 101, Folder 36.

20. Wiesel, *All Rivers Run to the Sea*, 416–418.

21. Author's interview with Georges Borchardt, February 7, 2017.

22. Wiesel, *And the Sea Is Never Full*, 10–11.

23. Author's interview with Hillel Levine, June 13, 2018.

24. Author's interview with Dr. Romana Strochlitz Primus, January 4, 2017.

25. Author's interview with Marion Wiesel, January 29, 2020.

26. Wiesel, *And the Sea Is Never Full*, 5, 11.

27. Author's interview with Menachem Rosensaft, May 23, 2017.

28. Wiesel, *And the Sea Is Never Full*, 5.

29. Ibid., 6.

Chapter 14. Transitions

1. Primo Levi, *The Voice of Memory: Interviews, 1961–1987*, ed. Marco Belpoliti and Robert Gordon (New York: New Press, 2002), 255.

2. Wiesel, *And the Sea Is Never Full*, 18.

3. Elie Wiesel, "In the Face of Barbarians a Victory of Spirit," review of *The Terezin Requiem* by Josef Bor, *New York Times Book Review*, October 27, 1963.

4. *English Language & Usage Stack Exchange*, english.stackex change.com/questions/106031/who-coined-the-term-holocaust -to-refer-to-the-nazi-final-solution-for-the-je.

5. Wiesel, *One Generation After*, 10–11.

6. Ibid., 16.

7. Ibid., 16–17.

8. Author's interview with Elliott Rosen, June 25, 2017.

9. Wiesel, *And the Sea Is Never Full*, 67.

10. Ibid., 68.

11. Ibid., 69–70.

12. Reuven Hammer, "Reminiscences of Elie Wiesel," *Jerusalem Post*, July 3, 2016.

13. Edward B. Fiske, "Archivist with a Mission," *New York Times*, January 31, 1973.

14. Author's interview with Rabbi Irving Greenberg, January 9, 2017.

15. Author's interview with Michael Berenbaum, January 5, 2017.

16. Author's interview with Ruth Wisse, May 8, 2018.

17. "To Life! A Celebration of Elie Wiesel's 180 Jewish Lec-

tures at 92Y," Elie Wiesel Living Archive at the 92nd Street Y, November 20, 2014, 92yondemand.org/elie-wiesel-life-celebration -180-jewish-lectures-92y.

18. Author's interview with Irving Greenberg, January 6, 2017.

19. M. A. Farber, ". . . but for City U.'s 'Distinguished Professors' Enthusiasm Prevails," *New York Times*, December 23, 1972.

20. Author's interview with Menachem Z. Rosensaft, July 2016.

21. Menachem Z. Rosensaft, "The Moral Imperative of Remembrance: The Enduring Legacy of Elie Wiesel," lecture at Case Western Reserve University, June 12, 2017.

22. Elie Wiesel, "Survivors' Children Relive the Holocaust," *New York Times*, November 16, 1975.

23. Ibid.

24. Ibid.

25. Ibid.

26. Author's interview with Irving Greenberg, January 6, 2017.

27. Author's interview with Greenberg, January 9, 2017.

28. Wiesel, *And the Sea Is Never Full*, 41–42.

Chapter 15. The Israel Conundrum

1. Abraham Rabinovitch, *The Yom Kippur War: The Epic Encounter That Transformed the Middle East* (New York: Schocken, 2005), 95–119.

2. Wiesel, *And the Sea Is Never Full*, 53–54.

3. Ibid., 56.

4. Ibid., 60–64.

5. Michael Berenbaum, "From Auschwitz to Oslo: The Journey of Elie Wiesel," *After Tragedy and Triumph* (Cambridge, England: Cambridge University Press, 1990), 123.

6. Author's interview with Ruth Wisse, May 8, 2018.

7. Author's interview with Leon Wieseltier, February 20, 2020.

Chapter 16. From Writer to Torchbearer

1. Alan Friedman, "Chronicle of a Pogrom," *New York Times Book Review*, November 18, 1973.

2. Leon Wieseltier, "'The Oath' by Elie Wiesel," *Commentary*, January 1, 1974.

3. Author's interview with Leon Wieseltier, March 23, 2017.

4. Wiesel, *And the Sea Is Never Full*, 52–53.

5. Elie Wiesel, "Ominous Signs and Unspeakable Thoughts," *New York Times*, December 28, 1974.

6. Henrietta Buckmaster, "From Wiesel, an Eloquent, Transfixing Parable," *Christian Science Monitor*, April 22, 1981.

7. Jeffrey Burke, "Jews Under Stalin," *New York Times*, April 12, 1981.

8. Frederic Morton, "Execution as an Act of Intimacy," *New York Times Book Review*, March 24, 1985.

9. Downing, *Elie Wiesel: A Religious Biography*, 193–195.

10. Hugh Nissenson, "Legends of Our Time," *New York Times*, January 12, 1969.

11. Charles E. Silberman, "How to Live Joyously When There Are No Answers," *New York Times Book Review*, March 5, 1972.

12. Martin Tolchin, "Hostility Toward Jews Decried at Emergency Conference Here," *New York Times*, May 16, 1972.

13. Elie Wiesel, "Letters to the Editor: Why Elie Wiesel Spoke Up," *New York Times*, May 27, 1972.

14. Edward B. Fiske, "Elie Wiesel: Archivist with a Mission," *New York Times*, January 31, 1973.

15. Wiesel, *All Rivers Run to the Sea*, 333–334.

16. Ibid., 70–71.

Chapter 17. A Boston Professor

1. Wiesel, *All Rivers Run to the Sea*, 106.

2. Author's interview with Greenberg, January 6, 2017.

3. Author's interview with Ariel Burger, May 15, 2018; author's interview with Martha Hauptman, July 3, 2018.

4. Author's interview with Ilene Semiatin, November 27, 2017.

5. Student notebook in Elie Wiesel's class on "The Jewish Response to Persecution," Fall 1976, the Elie Wiesel Archive, How-

ard Gotlieb Archival Research Center, Boston University, Box 93, Folder 1.

6. Author's interview with Rabbi Jeffrey Sirkman, April 16, 2018.

7. Ibid.

8. Author's interview with Ariel Burger, May 15, 2018.

Chapter 18. The Holocaust and the Arts

1. "NBC-TV Says *Holocaust* Drew 120 Million," *New York Times*, April 21, 1978.

2. Elie Wiesel, "Trivializing the Holocaust: Semi-Fact and Semi Fiction," *New York Times*, April 16, 1978.

3. Gerald Green, "TV View," *New York Times*, April 23, 1978.

4. As quoted in ibid.

5. Author's interview with Greenberg, January 6, 2017.

6. Author's interview with Thane Rosenbaum, January 12, 2017.

7. Wiesel, *And the Sea Is Never Full*, 122–123.

8. Elie Wiesel, "Art and the Holocaust: Trivializing Memory," *New York Times*, June 11, 1989.

9. Joshua Sobol, "Of Plays and Playwrights," Letter to the Editor, *New York Times*, July 2, 1989.

10. *The Algemeiner*, May 9, 2013.

Chapter 19. Museums and Memory

1. Rachel Bronson, *Thicker Than Oil: America's Uneasy Partnership with Saudi Arabia* (New York: Oxford University Press, 2006), 158–159.

2. Author's interview with Greenberg, January 6, 2017.

3. Author's interview with Berenbaum, January 5, 2017.

4. Wiesel, *And the Sea Is Never Full*, 181–182.

5. Author's interview with Berenbaum, January 5, 2017.

6. As quoted in *Kol Haneshamah: Prayerbook for the Days of Awe* (Elkins Park, Pa.: Reconstructionist Press, 1999), 649.

7. Author's interview with Romana Strochlitz, January 4, 2017.

8. Wiesel, *And the Sea Is Never Full*, 187–188.

9. Ibid., 189–190.

10. Elie Wiesel, "Pilgrimage to the Country of Night," *New York Times*, November 4, 1979.

11. Ibid.

12. Ibid.

13. Wiesel, *And the Sea Is Never Full*, 192.

14. Ibid., 193.

15. Wiesel, "Pilgrimage to the Country of Night."

16. Anthony Austin, "U.S. Unit, at Babi Yar, Stunned by Soviet Silence on Jews," *New York Times*, August 4, 1979.

17. Wiesel, "Pilgrimage to the Country of Night."

18. Wiesel, *And the Sea Is Never Full*, 200–202.

19. Author's interview with Menachem Rosensaft, June 8, 2017.

20. Wiesel, *And the Sea Is Never Full*, 204.

21. Author's interview with Elisha Wiesel, September 7, 2017.

22. "Report to the President: President's Commission on the Holocaust," September 27, 1979, Elie Wiesel, Chairman, www.ushmm.org/m/pdfs/20050707-presidents-commission-holocaust.pdf.

23. Judith Miller, "Holocaust Museum: A Troubled Start," *New York Times*, April 22, 1990.

24. Edward Tabor Linenthal, *Preserving Memory: The Struggle to Create America's Holocaust Museum* (New York: Columbia University Press, 1995), 72–75.

25. Peggy McClone, "For Rep. John Lewis, African American Museum Was a Recurring Dream," *Washington Post*, June 28, 2016.

26. Miller, "Holocaust Museum: A Troubled Start."

27. Author's interview with Berenbaum, January 5, 2017.

28. Miller, "Holocaust Museum: A Troubled Start."

29. Author's interview with Berenbaum, January 5, 2017.

30. Wiesel, *And the Sea Is Never Full*, 220.

31. Ibid., 221.

32. Douglas Martin, "Albert Abramson, Holocaust Museum Backer, Is Dead at 94," *New York Times*, March 13, 2012.

33. Wiesel, *And the Sea Is Never Full*, 243–247.

34. Ibid., 204.

35. Ibid., 249.

36. Martin, "Albert Abramson, Holocaust Museum Backer."

Chapter 20. World Stage

1. Murray Schumach, "Wiesel Urges Graduates to Have Faith," *New York Times*, May 28, 1972.

2. Wiesel, *And the Sea Is Never Full*, 79–81.

3. Kathleen Teltsch, "Private Relief Agencies to Lobby for 'Boat People,'" *New York Times*, June 25, 1979.

4. Henry Kamm, "Marchers with Food Aid Get No Cambodian Response," *New York Times*, February 7, 1980.

5. Wiesel, *And the Sea Is Never Full*, 90.

6. Aron Hirt-Manheimer, "Channeling Elie Wiesel: Words from the Past Bring Comfort to the Present," *ReformJudaism.org*, August 23, 2017, https://reformjudaism.org/blog/channeling-elie -wiesel-words-past-bring-comfort-present.

7. Wiesel, *And the Sea Is Never Full*, 95–96.

8. "Israelis Said to Oppose Parley After Threat to Turkish Jews," *New York Times*, June 3, 1982.

9. "Prominent U.S. Jews Support Israel, But Some Criticize Begin and Sharon," *New York Times*, September 22, 1982.

Chapter 21. "To Help the Dead Vanquish Death"

1. Wiesel, *And the Sea Is Never Full*, 81–82.

2. Author's interview with Elisha Wiesel, November 4, 2016.

3. Elie Wiesel, "Why I Write: Making No Become Yes," *New York Times Book Review*, August 14, 1985.

4. Elie Wiesel, *From the Kingdom of Memory* (New York: Summit, 1990), 13–21.

5. Edward Grossman, "Messengers of God," *New York Times*, June 20, 1976.

6. Wiesel, *A Jew Today*, 11–12.

7. Ron Rosenbaum, "Elie Wiesel's Secret," *Tablet*, September 29, 2017.

8. Author's interview with Menachem Rosensaft, June 8, 2017.

9. Irving Abrahamson, ed., *Against Silence: The Voice and Vision of Elie Wiesel* (New York: Holocaust Library, 1985), 215–216.

Chapter 22. The Bitburg Fiasco

1. Bernard Weinraub, "Aides Review Reagan's Plan to Visit German War Graves," *New York Times*, April 13, 1985.

2. Wiesel, *And the Sea Is Never Full*, 229.

3. Ibid.

4. Philip Shenon, "For Wiesel, the End of Two Long Days of a 'Nightmare' and 'Disbelief,'" *New York Times*, April 20, 1985.

5. "Reagan Remarks Bring New Outcry," *New York Times*, April 19, 1985.

6. Author's interview with Michael Berenbaum, October 2, 2017.

7. Shenon, "For Wiesel, the End of Two Long Days."

8. Wiesel, *And the Sea Is Never Full*, 236.

9. "Remarks on Presenting the Congressional Gold Medal to Elie Wiesel and on Signing the Jewish Heritage Week Proclamation," April 19, 1985, Ronald Reagan Presidential Library and Museum, National Archives, www.reaganlibrary.gov/archives/speech/remarks-presenting-congressional-gold-medal-elie-wiesel-and-signing-jewish-heritage.

10. Wiesel, *And the Sea Is Never Full*, 239.

11. Shenon, "For Wiesel the End of Two Long Days."

12. Wiesel, *And the Sea Is Never Full*, 240.

13. Gil Troy, "When Elie Wiesel Confronted Ronald Reagan," *Daily Beast*, July 3, 2016.

14. Author's interview with Marion Wiesel, March 9, 2017.

15. Author's interview with Marion Wiesel, January 29, 2020.

16. Elisha Wiesel interview with Nadine Epstein of *Moment Magazine*, emailed to subscribers July 7, 2020.

17. John Tagliabue, "Elie Wiesel Back in Germany After 41 Years," *New York Times*, January 23, 1986.

18. Elie Wiesel, "Reflections of a Survivor," a speech delivered in the Reichstag in November 1987; its contents can be found at

historymuse.net/readings/WieselREFLECTIONSOFASURVI
VOR.htm.

19. Ibid.

20. Michael Berenbaum, "Elie Wiesel: French Writer, World Statesman, Cosmopolitan Jew," in *Europe in the Eyes of Survivors of the Holocaust*, ed. Zeev Mankowitz, David Weinberg, and Sharon Kangisser Cohen (Jerusalem: Yad Vashem, 2014).

Chapter 23. Family Time

1. Author's interview with Elisha Wiesel, September 7, 2017.

2. Rick Lyman, "Elie Wiesel's Only Son Steps Up to His Father's Legacy," *New York Times*, May 12, 2017.

3. "Elisha Wiesel Remembers His Father," *Moment*, September–October 2016.

4. Author's interview with Elisha Wiesel, November 4, 2016.

5. Author's interview with Romana Strochlitz, January 4, 2017.

6. Author's interview with Joseph Malovany, December 12, 2016.

7. Author's interview with Mark Podwal, November 6, 2019.

8. Author's interview with Thane Rosenbaum, January 12, 2017.

9. "Elisha Wiesel Remembers His Father," interview published in *Moment*, September 14, 2016.

10. Author's interview with Mark Podwal, December 5, 2016.

11. Author's interview with Joseph Malovany, December 12, 2016.

12. Ibid.

13. Richard L. Rubenstein, *After Auschwitz: Radical Theology and Contemporary Judaism* (Indianapolis: Bobbs-Merrill, 1966), 153.

14. Michael Berenbaum, *Elie Wiesel: God, the Holocaust, and the Children of Israel* (West Orange, N.J.: Behrman House, 1994), 31–37.

15. Wiesel, *One Generation After*, 15.

16. Rubenstein, *After Auschwitz*, 246.

17. Elie Wiesel, Address, National Conference of Anti-Defamation League of B'nai B'rith and the National Council for the

Social Studies, New York, October 9, 1977, as published in *Against Silence: The Words and Vision of Elie Wiesel*, ed. Irving Abrahamson (New York: Holocaust Library, 1985), vol. 1, 147.

18. Morton Landowne, "Wiesel Sings at 92Y," *Tablet*, December 20, 2010.

19. Author's interview with Leon Wieseltier, March 23, 2017.

20. Author's interview with Gabriel Erem, March 21, 2017.

Chapter 24. Nobelist

1. Author's interview with Joseph Malovany, December 12, 2016.

2. James Markham, "Elie Wiesel Gets Nobel for Peace as 'Messenger,'" *New York Times*, October 15, 1986.

3. Jacob Weisberg, "Pop Goes Elie Wiesel: How to Get a Nobel Prize," *New Republic*, November 10, 1986.

4. Joseph Berger, "Man in the News: Witness to Evil, Eliezer Wiesel," *New York Times*, October 15, 1986.

5. Wiesel, *And the Sea Is Never Full*, 268–270.

6. Oprah Winfrey interview with Elie Wiesel, published on YouTube, December 9, 2012, www.youtube.com/watch?v=cgWJr Ln2SGk.

7. "Elie Wiesel: Acceptance Speech," on the occasion of the award of the Nobel Peace Prize in Oslo, December 10, 1986, *The Nobel Prize*, www.nobelprize.org/nobel_prizes/peace/laureates/1986 /wiesel-acceptance_en.html.

8. Elie Wiesel, "Hope, Despair, and Memory," Nobel Lecture, December 11, 1986, *The Nobel Prize*, www.nobelprize.org/nobel _prizes/peace/laureates/1986/wiesel-lecture.html.

9. Clyde Haberman, "An Unofficial but Very Public Bearer of Pain, Peace and Human Dignity," *New York Times*, March 5, 1997.

Chapter 25. Catalyst for Change

1. Elie Wiesel Foundation for Humanity, brochure summarizing the 1988 conference, "Facing the 21st Century: Threats and Promises."

2. James Markham, "76 Laureates Consider the Century's Legacy," *New York Times*, January 19, 1988.

3. James Markham, "Nobel Laureates Agree to Meet Again in 1990," *New York Times*, January 22, 1988.

4. Author's interview with Menachem Rosensaft, January 9, 2018.

5. Author's interview with Marion Wiesel, January 29, 2020.

6. David Olin, "The View from My Window: The Ethics of Using Violence to Fight Fascism," winner of First Prize in Ethics Essay Contest, 2019, the Elie Wiesel Foundation for Humanity, eliewieselfoundation.org/prize-ethics/winners.

Chapter 26. Reconciliations and Reprimands

1. Elie Wiesel, "A Prayer for the Days of Awe," *New York Times*, October 2, 1997.

2. Author's interview with Yossi Ciechanover, February 6, 2018.

3. Elie Wiesel, "Before New Beginnings, Free Ida Nudel," *Los Angeles Times*, October 2, 1987.

4. Wiesel, *And the Sea Is Never Full*, 313–342.

5. Author's interview with Roman Kent, February 28, 2018.

6. Ari Goldman, "Religion Notes: For Cardinal, Wiesel Visit Proved a Calm in Storm, Over Trip," February 15, 1987.

7. Richard Bernstein, "Wiesel Testifies at Barbie's Trial," *New York Times*, June 3, 1987.

8. David Binder, "U.S. Expects Lithuania Not to Erase War Crimes," *New York Times*, September 6, 1991.

9. Daniel Brook, "Double Genocide," *Slate*, July 25, 2015, slate.com/news-and-politics/2015/07/lithuania-and-nazis-the -country-wants-to-forget-its-collaborationist-past-by-accusing -jewish-partisans-of-war-crimes.html.

10. Henry Kamm, "Romanians Are Told of Nation's Role in Mass Killing of Jews," *New York Times*, July 2, 1991.

11. Henry Kamm, "Anti-Semitic Taunt at Wiesel Talk in Romania," *New York Times*, July 3, 1991.

12. Daniel Simpson, "Sighet Journal: Elie Wiesel Asks a Haunted Hometown to Face Up," *New York Times*, July 31, 2002.

13. Elie Wiesel, "Opinion: Only the Guilty Are Guilty, Not Their Sons," *New York Times*, May 5, 2001.

14. Elie Wiesel, "I Fear What Lies Beyond the Wall," *New York Times*, November 18, 1988.

15. Jane Perlez, "Survivors Pray at the Crematories of Auschwitz," *New York Times*, January 27, 1995.

16. Joyce Purnick, "Editorial Notebook: Crown Heights Was Not Iasi," *New York Times*, June 3, 1993.

17. David Rohde, "Wiesel, a Man of Peace, Cites Need to Act," *New York Times*, June 2, 1999.

18. Eric Lipton, "Midtown Throng Gathers, Rallying Support for Israel," *New York Times*, October 13, 2000.

19. Joseph Berger, "The 'Second Generation' Reflects on the Holocaust," *New York Times*, January 17, 2000.

20. Walter Goodman, "Review: Behind the Hate with Bill Moyers," *New York Times*, May 13, 1991.

21. The Elie Wiesel Archive, Howard Gotlieb Archival Research Center, Boston University, Box 99, Folders 5–8, 61.

22. "Wiesel Visits Pollard in Prison, Becoming Latest to Take Up Cause," *Jewish Telegraphic Agency*, April 14, 1992, www.jta.org /1992/04/14/archive/wiesel-visits-pollard-in-prison-becoming -latest-to-take-up-cause.

23. Wiesel Archive, Box 99, Folders 5–8, 61.

24. Elie Wiesel, *Twilight* (New York: Summit, 1988), 11–12.

25. Janet Hadda, "Buried in the Starry Sky: TWILIGHT, A Novel by Elie Wiesel," *Los Angeles Times*, June 19, 1988.

26. Stanley Moss, "Adam and Cain in the Madhouse," *New York Times Book Review*, July 10, 1988.

27. Robert Leiter, "Perhaps You Wonder Why I Called You Here," *New York Times Book Review*, August 25, 2002.

28. Oprah Winfrey interview with Elie Wiesel, shown on YouTube, December 9, 2012, www.youtube.com/watch?v=ofMiFlqcnsA.

Chapter 27. Reversals

1. Author's interview with Elisha Wiesel, September 7, 2017.

2. Oprah Winfrey interview with Elie Wiesel, shown on

YouTube, December 9, 2012, www.youtube.com/watch?v=oXo-ga_hhYM.

3. Stephanie Strom, "Elie Wiesel Levels Scorn at Madoff," *New York Times*, February 26, 2009.

4. Author's interview with Menachem Rosensaft, January 9, 2018.

5. Author's interview with Elisha Wiesel, September 7, 2017.

6. Jaxon von Derbeken, "Man, 22, Arrested in Wiesel Attack," *SFGate* (website of the *San Francisco Chronicle*), February 17, 2007.

7. Joseph Berger, "City Room: Elie Wiesel Reflects on Turning Eighty," *New York Times*, September 29, 2008.

8. Author's interview with Leon Wieseltier, March 23, 2017.

9. Elie Wiesel, "The Holocaust as Literary Inspiration," in *Dimensions of the Holocaust* (Evanston: Northwestern University Press, 1977), 9.

10. Oprah Winfrey interview with Elie Wiesel, shown on YouTube, December 9, 2012, www.youtube.com/watch?v=1OF9_p7dYoY.

11. Wiesel, *And the Sea Is Never Full*, 345.

12. Adam Kirsch, "Primo Levi's Unlikely Suicide Haunts His Lasting Work," *Tablet*, September 21, 2015.

13. Wiesel, *And the Sea Is Never Full*, 345–347.

14. Elie Wiesel, *Open Heart* (New York: Knopf, 2012), 3–25.

15. Ibid., 69.

16. Author's interview with Rosensaft, March 15, 2018.

17. "Sex Guru Rabbi Gets Passed Over," *The Guardian*, September 4, 1999. Batya Ungar-Sargon, "Celebrity Rabbi, Heal Thyself," *Tablet Magazine*, July 23, 2014, www.tabletmag.com/sections/news/articles/shmuley-boteach.

18. Author's interview with Shmuley Boteach, April 2018.

19. Author's interview with Marion Wiesel, January 29, 2020.

20. Josh Nathan-Kazis, "Mulling Run for Congress, Boteach May Face Questions About His Charity," *The Forward*, February 23, 2012.

21. Menachem Z. Rosensaft, "The Moral Imperative of Remembrance," lecture delivered at Case Western Reserve Univer-

sity, June 12, 2017, www.youtube.com/watch?v=UT03ObKnb_Q &feature=youtu.be.

22. Author's interview with Rosensaft, March 15, 2018.

23. Author's interview with Elisha Wiesel, October 26, 2018.

24. Professor Elie Wiesel's speech at the World Values Gala, www.youtube.com/watch?v=5uS8c-k3zzA.

25. Ibid.

Chapter 28. Memories

1. Barack Obama, *A Promised Land* (New York: Crown, 2020), 368–369.

2. Author's interview with Abe Foxman, January 24, 2018.

3. Author's interview with Elisha Wiesel, March 22, 2021.

4. Author's interview with Abe Foxman, July 25, 2016.

5. Author's interview with Joseph Malovany, November 30, 2016.

6. Author's interview with Marion Wiesel, January 29, 2020.

7. Elisha Wiesel, text of his eulogy for his father, July 3, 2016.

8. Ibid.

9. Sarah Maslin Nir and Annie Correal, "Elie Wiesel Is Recalled at Funeral for a Legacy Beyond His Moral Voice," *New York Times*, July 4, 2016.

10. Samantha Power, text of speech at memorial service for Eli Wiesel, December 1, 2016.

11. Author's interview with Irving Abrahamson, February 2018.

12. Wiesel, *And the Sea Is Never Full*, 273.

13. This is a thought that Holocaust scholar Michael Berenbaum first articulated and shared with me in one of our interviews.

CREDITS

Excerpts from *All Rivers Run to the Sea: Memoirs*, by Elie Wiesel, copyright © 1995 by Alfred A. Knopf, a division of Random House LLC, used by permission of Alfred A. Knopf, a division of Penguin Random House, LLC, all rights reserved; copyright © 1994 by Elie Wiesel, used by permission of Georges Borchardt, Inc.

Excerpts from *And the Sea Is Never Full: Memoirs, 1969–*, by Elie Wiesel, translated from the French by Marion Wiesel, copyright © 1999 by Penguin Random House LLC, used by permission of Alfred A. Knopf, an imprint of the Knopf Doubleday Publishing Group, a division of Penguin Random House LLC, all rights reserved; copyright © 1999 by Elie Wiesel, used by permission of Georges Borchardt, Inc.

Excerpts from *Night*, by Elie Wiesel, translated by Marion Wiesel, translation copyright © 2006 by Marion Wiesel, reprinted by permission of Hill and Wang, a division of Farrar, Straus and Gi-

ACKNOWLEDGMENTS

ELIE WIESEL WAS so admired for his intellect, eloquence, resilience, and devotion to preserving the memory of the Holocaust that he risked, for better or worse, becoming something of a static icon. In writing his biography I am most grateful to those who offered me the earthly details that turned the improbable outlines of his epic life—a Hasidic boy from Hungary survives Auschwitz and becomes the Nobel Prize–winning torchbearer for human rights, sturdy enough to confront an American president in the White House—into a very imaginable story and Wiesel into a fallible person of flesh and blood. They illuminated the virtues for which he was deservedly revered but were honest enough to let me see how his towering achievements were sometimes tempered by mistakes and misjudgments. The Elie Wiesel they knew was a real person, not a myth, someone they could love, not just revere.

Wiesel, I believe, would have wanted it no other way, having written memoirs striking in their honesty as if he sought to brush off the aura of saintliness that was accumulating around him.

The friends, colleagues, and students of Wiesel who spoke openly to me about a man for whom they had deep affection included: Michael Berenbaum, Menachem Rosensaft, Yitz Greenberg, Joseph Malovany, Joel Rappel, Thane Rosenbaum, Leon Wieseltier, Mark Podwal, Georges Borchardt, Abe Foxman, Ruth Wisse, and Ariel Burger. Also helpful with insights and vignettes were Martha Hauptman, Rabbi Jeffrey Sirkman, George Schwab, Yossi Ciechanover, Hillel Levine, Matthew Lazar, Ted Comet, Sam Norich, Gabriel Erem, Kenneth Waltzer, Nadine Epstein, William Helmreich, Roman Kent, Romana Strochlitz, Dvorah Telushkin, Elliott Rosen, Ilene Semiatin, Irving Abrahamson, and Menachem Butler.

I was fortunate to get to know Wiesel after reporting on his Nobel Peace Prize honor, and he eased my research by laying out most of his own story in *Night*, two memoirs completed in the 1990s, and dozens of introspective essays. These works certainly provided a detailed blueprint for this biography. The Elie Wiesel Archive at Boston University was an invaluable source of letters, documents, photographs, and articles. I'm particularly appreciative of Ryan Hendrickson for graciously guiding me through the labyrinth of more than three hundred boxes of files. Jeff Roth, guardian of the *New York Times* morgue, was essential for clippings and photographs, not to mention passing on intriguing tidbits through family connections to Wiesel and his hometown. Special thanks go to two *Times* editors, Marv Siegel, for assigning me the advance obituary of Wiesel that became the catalyst for this biography, and William McDonald, for his consistently wise and literate shepherding of the advance after Wiesel had died.

It isn't easy for family members to offer an intimate portrait of a venerated relative, but Wiesel's son, Elisha, and his widow, Marion, separately talked with me for several hours each. Marion, still visibly mourning the loss of her husband, took me around their sunny, elegant apartment on Fifth Avenue, filled with Elie's books and photographs and the desk where he worked.

Among the professionals at Yale University Press I'm most grateful to Ileene Smith, for her meticulous, sensitive editing of the manuscript. As someone who had edited Wiesel's books and regarded him as a friend, she made sure the biography lived up to the truths of Wiesel's character and his accomplishments. A big thank you also to Heather Gold and Eva Skewes, who midwifed the manuscript after its revisions, and took pains to safeguard the narrators of Wiesel's haunting and compelling tale, and to Phillip King, who took exceptional care in making sure the manuscript was accurate, grammatical, and free of unwelcome flaws. The ever attentive Jane Dystel, my literary agent, after homing in on Yale as the publisher, saw to it that the book received appropriate handling and a fitting launch.

The book might not have happened without two consequential women. My daughter Annie, a senior editor of young adult books, patiently explained the vagaries of publishing and reminded me that whatever anxieties I was feeling were not much different than those most authors tangle with. My wife, Brenda, helped me understand the forces driving Wiesel and gave me the loving support I needed to see this project through to completion. Finally, I need to give prominent mention to my parents, Marcus and Rachel Berger, Holocaust refugees like Wiesel who too had to forge a new life in America with little more than their raw talents and a good deal of moxie. Their rage and sorrow at what had been done to their families and communities, combined with their refusal to let such emotions overwhelm their chance for a decent life, helped make Wiesel a familiar, understandable figure. And they imbued me with a love for and deep interest in the Jewish culture of Europe that the Nazis sought to destroy. Elie Wiesel worked tenaciously to keep that culture flickering, and he succeeded because of compatriots like my parents who, by their tender examples, also taught their children how indispensable a strong sense of that culture was to their passage through life.

INDEX

Bugsy Siegel: The Dark Side of the American Dream,
    by Michael Shnayerson
Solomon: The Lure of Wisdom, by Steven Weitzman
Steven Spielberg: A Life in Films, by Molly Haskell
Alfred Stieglitz: Taking Pictures, Making Painters, by Phyllis Rose
Barbra Streisand: Redefining Beauty, Femininity, and Power,
    by Neal Gabler
Leon Trotsky: A Revolutionary's Life, by Joshua Rubenstein
Warner Bros: The Making of an American Movie Studio,
    by David Thomson

FORTHCOMING TITLES INCLUDE:

Abraham, by Anthony Julius
Hannah Arendt, by Masha Gessen
Walter Benjamin, by Peter Gordon
Franz Boas, by Noga Arikha
Alfred Dreyfus, by Maurice Samuels
Anne Frank, by Ruth Franklin
Betty Friedan, by Rachel Shteir
George Gershwin, by Gary Giddins
Allen Ginsberg, by Ed Hirsch
Herod, by Martin Goodman
Jesus, by Jack Miles
Josephus, by Daniel Boyarin
Louis Kahn, by Gini Alhadeff
Mordecai Kaplan, by Jenna Weissman Joselit
Carole King, by Jane Eisner
Fiorello La Guardia, by Brenda Wineapple
Hedy Lamarr, by Sarah Wildman
Mahler, by Leon Botstein
Norman Mailer, by David Bromwich